BEAUTY
in the
STREET

SCOTT J. TURNER

Beauty in the Street.
Copyright © 2021
Scott J. Turner.
Produced and printed
by Stillwater River Publications.
All rights reserved. Written and produced in the
United States of America. This book may not be reproduced
or sold in any form without the expressed, written
permission of the author and publisher.
Visit our website at
www.StillwaterPress.com
for more information.
First Stillwater River Publications Edition.
Library of Congress Control Number: 2021912719
ISBN-13: 978-1-955123-27-3
1 2 3 4 5 6 7 8 9 10
Written by Scott J. Turner.
Cover image by Rachel Turner.
Illustrations by Jim Bush.
Published by Stillwater River Publications,
Pawtucket, RI, USA.
Publisher's Cataloging-In-Publication Data
(Prepared by The Donohue Group, Inc.)
Names: Turner, Scott J., 1958- author.
Title: Beauty in the street / Scott J. Turner.
Description: First Stillwater River Publications edition. |
Pawtucket, RI, USA : Stillwater River Publications,
[2021] | Summary: "A collection of previously pub-
lished newspaper columns that discuss the natural
world"--Provided by publisher.
Identifiers: ISBN 9781955123273
Subjects: LCSH: Natural history--New York (State)--New
York. | Natural history--Rhode Island. | Natural his-
tory--New Hampshire. | Natural history--Ohio.
Classification: LCC QH104.5.N58 T87 2021 | DDC
508.74--dc23

To my adventure buddies, Karen, Rachel and Noah.

TABLE OF CONTENTS

RHODE ISLAND

NEW HAMPSHIRE

OHIO

ELSEWHERE

ACKNOWLEDGEMENTS

For a dozen years, Karen, my wife, read each commentary draft and offered invaluable guidance. Karen, and our kids, Rachel and Noah, steadfastly encouraged me to tell my tales and provided me with the space to do it. Thanks to my Mom, Renee Turner, for her love and strong support through thick and thin, and to my siblings, Lee, Harriet, Paul and Willie for their companionship on life's journey. My inlaws, Jan and John, are always excited by my stories, and their interest in my writing is inspirational. Kurt Knebusch kindly and thoroughly reviewed and edited the commentaries in this book. His friendship these past 35 years is priceless. Speaking of friends, Rob Ledig has provided solid, balanced fellowship for more than 50 years. Tom Ryther is a loyal companion, whether we're together in person or a thousand miles apart. Bob Whitcomb and Ed Achorn gave me a chance at The Providence Journal. GoLocal picked me up when I was down. Rick Reamer at The Public's Radio is an excellent editor and airwaves guide. I am grateful for the feedback and loyalty of Bronx buddy Steve Mirsky, and lucky to have the members of the Paragraph Club, Jim Bush (who graciously provided art for this book), Peter Case, Bill Collins and Paul Mahoney, in my life. Lastly, a shout out to the late Norman Boucher. He was the best editor I ever worked with and an excellent motivator.

THE BRONX

Trees Remind Us of Good and Bad
November 14, 2009

Amid the maze of apartment buildings that composed my childhood neighborhood, you could walk one block south of where I lived, cross the street and head about 100 feet east to spend time with one of the community's most colorful and unusual residents—a tree.

There was no better sun blocker than that Norway maple. Under its somewhat spreading canopy I sought relief, particularly when the sun sizzled at its highest point in the sky during the midday of summer.

But the shade from that maple was illusory. In a flat four stories above lived a family composed of two teenage children and their parents. Lucy, the mom, stayed indoors most of the time, because, as her son, Frankie, put it, she was "crazy."

Among Lucy's greatest obsessions was protecting her daughter's purity. Frankie's sister, Sandra, was a wildly striking young woman, with long black hair and black eyes. None of us awkward teens knew how to speak to Sandra, who made matters worse by flirting with or teasing us.

If Sandra passed by us, or one of us crossed paths with her, we would divert our eyes, as if to avoid looking directly into the sun.

When some of us congregated on the street corner, Lucy leaned out the window, waved an assortment of kitchen knives, and cursed at us. I can still see the sun glinting off the metal blades.

Lucy possessed a one-of-a-kind sense that allowed her to detect the presence of a testosterone-producing teen.

Besides displaying cutlery, Lucy tossed objects out the window. Often it was fruit. Once she dropped a salad on the head of a friend of mine.

Lucy also collected foot-tall religious statues of stone that her timorous husband lugged home for her. If Lucy believed or detected that a teenage boy was beneath the tree, she might drop an effigy on him.

I will never forget the violently frightening sound of a religious figure crashing through the foliage and striking the sidewalk, splintering into hundreds of chips.

To avoid the flying figurines, I would press up against the rough red brick and mortar of the aging apartment building or wedge myself into the well of a ground floor window to seek some of the maple's shade.

Very rarely did I get extended relief before Lucy sensed my presence. The stone shrapnel from the smashed statues hurt appreciably. Soon, I spent more time observing the tree than chilling beneath it.

Speaking of fast-falling objects, Frankie developed a heroin hunger back then. One day, he jumped out of the shadows, grabbed my younger brother and held a knife to his Adam's apple. I had to talk glaze-eyed Frankie out of cutting the throat of my sibling, who had done nothing to bring on the attack.

In addition to learning to stay away from dangerous people, as a teenager I found that you could feel at peace and safe under a single tree, as well as develop a personal attachment to it.

Over the years, I also discovered that trees conserved water, cooled us off, improved the air and harbored wildlife. They provided privacy, screened out unwanted sights and softened the landscape.

Every November, trees re-dominate the landscape. With their foliage gone, trees stand out in backyards, forests, fields and along our streets, which is why I remember Frankie, Lucy and the maple.

Trees often produce a religious or spiritual response in us, feelings that go beyond the fact that they are beautiful and make our lives more pleasant.

It seems apt that a tree I considered a shrine in the midst of the concrete of my upbringing ended up surrounded by a supply of shattered statuary.

Fragrance, Friendship and Fast Living
June 20, 2008

My best friend Jaime, with the long eyelashes and thick brown hair, led me on a 20-block walk along teeming, tree-less, four-lane Fordham Road in the Bronx. He wouldn't tell me where we were going, but I trusted Jaime enough to let him surprise me. "You gotta see what I found," he said.

That late June morning in 1968 was bright and sunny as we slipped our bony, soon-to-be-10-year-old bodies through two bent wrought-iron bars on Southern Boulevard, sneaking into The New York Botanical Garden (NYBG).

During the summer of 1968, my parents split their time between two hospitals. One of my brothers had shattered his leg, requiring a body cast, while the other was recovering from being hit by a car. Neighbors watched my little brother and sister. Maybe the neighbors were supposed to keep an eye on me, but I found a lot of time to roam.

In the NYBG, we walked through woods, which scared me. I had never been in a forest before, and it seemed dark. We passed the Bronx River, where I encountered my first waterfall.

Then Jaime showed me his find—a garden of roses. There were flowers of lavender, peach, pink, purple, orange, red, white and yellow. One scarlet bloom, nestled in dark green leaves, felt like silk. It suggested why we celebrated love with rose petals, sprinkling them on bridal paths and across boudoirs.

Some roses smelled like candy, others like spice. A few blossoms sported light, fruity scents. We stuffed our faces into flowers like dogs sniffing hydrants or deer browsing broadleaf weeds. We praised the most pungent blooms and disparaged those free of fragrance, despite their beauty. I don't remember encountering roses before that day, but I never forgot them.

I've learned since that June is remarkable for ambient fragrance. Lilac aroma fills the air first, as does the heavenly-sweet smell of black locust. A dreamy scent emanates from the wisteria-like flowers of yellow-wood. Then come the pleasant fragrance of mock orange, the rich scent of Japanese honeysuckle and the fresh perfume of peonies.

As we strolled the rose garden in the Bronx 40 years ago, Jaime said "the best thing about this place is that we can bring flowers home to our mothers." With that he pulled out a pocket knife and sliced off enough for two bouquets. (We also learned about thorns that day.)

Having never been in a garden before, public or private, I lacked the etiquette to know that "do not pick the flowers" was the rule. Still no one stopped us, as we retraced our steps out.

That summer, Jaime's parents split. His mom became involved with a heroin pusher, and she took up the habit. Just short of six feet tall, she withered to 100 pounds, perishing two years later in an apartment fire.

Jaime's father, meanwhile, developed a "Wild Bunch" reputation for driving down populated sidewalks on a Harley Davidson.

The last time I saw Jaime he was a glue-sniffing, pill-popping 13-year-old addict—eyes droopy and hair matted.

This summer, do take time to smell the roses, as the saying goes. But unless they belong to you, let the flowers be. Others may need to smell them, too.

Some Rambles Worth Skipping
February 21, 2009

Friends headed to ski Hunter Mountain during the February school break reminded me of my first visit to the Catskills.

I was a freshman in college, and my girlfriend had just moved with her mom from our neighborhood in the bowels of the Bronx to a rural mountainside south and west of Cairo (pronounced Kay-row), New York, about 30 miles from Hunter.

"Sara," as I will call her, promised that if I visited her during the upcoming school break, we would consummate our pairing.

Previously, my parents had warned me that getting involved with Sara meant getting involved with her family. But my brain was as bewildering a mix of hormones and immaturity as the wild confusion of boulders and trees, called the Catskills, that Sara and her mom had fled to.

Just a few weeks earlier, we'd watched two of Sara's brothers pulverize each other into bloody flesh. One sibling repeatedly slammed the head of the other into the sidewalk. A policewoman, who tried to break up the fight, was thrown into a brick wall. This beating came on the heels of Sara's sister springing her boyfriend out of jail. The duo had led a string of police cars on a chase down the New York State Thruway.

When school vacation came around, I told my parents that I was headed by bus to visit an old friend in Pennsylvania. Instead I took a bus north. I watched the mighty Hudson River contract in width significantly north of Haverstraw Bay, and caught glimpses of the irregular peaks of the Ramapo Mountains, the Hudson Highlands and the Shawangunk Mountains. The trip ended in the deep forests, plateaus and panoramas of the Catskills.

Sara's mom, who had recently left her fourth husband, had settled into a shack, with a boyfriend I will call "Jay." They shared the small, slanting, crumbling abode with a young woman and her two tow-headed twins.

At noon, Jay and Sara greeted me at the bus stop. I could smell alcohol on his breath. Jay, who lacked most of his upper-front teeth, was a sweet talker, who came across as someone either on the road to prison, or an early grave.

Sara had also promised me a walk through hemlock woods, past jagged, jumbled rock outcrops to a waterfall and up to an overlook. The Catskills, she said, were full of superb views.

But Jay insisted that I spend the day with him and two friends, firing a 22-caliber rifle at cans, bottles and other targets. By late afternoon, Sara and I had barely time for a short stroll in a rocky forest.

Folks at the shack were poor, but generous. We ate Spam for lunch and dinner. I swigged whiskey when the bottle came my way, and I got drunk.

That night Sara said there would be no consummation. She wasn't ready. I said that I hoped to take the first bus back to New York in the morning.

Twelve hours later I sat on the couch, eyes closed, waiting for Jay, my ride. He walked in drunk, with the same two guys as the day before, carrying the rifle. Jay loaded the weapon with a handful of click-clacking bullets, took off the safety and placed the muzzle against my right temple.

"You better treat my daughter right," he warned. Sara stepped into the room and told Jay to remove the gun, shouting, "I AM NOT YOUR DAUGHTER!"

With the rifle pressed against my head, I whispered, "I hope this is just a dream." The three men laughed and Jay pointed down the gun.

The sages said, "To everything there is a season, a time for every purpose under the sun." I was not ready for a walk on the wild side.

On the bus ride home, it occurred to me that if Jay had pulled the trigger, my parents might never have known what happened to me. Until

6

now, I've never told them this story. I will not mind if they express their anger and shock, and even a belated, "We told you so."

FIGHTING POPPA NATURE
June 16, 2012

Close it, my father ordered.

We stood on the mudflat of Orchard Beach in the Bronx circa 1965. I was 7, and monarch butterflies danced south over the surf on their annual migration.

Flopped between the opened pages of a hardcover book, a monarch twitched its body and antennae. Using a cobbled-together stick and net, we'd knocked down the insect. Next, dad said, we would entomb it.

When I told him that I didn't want to kill the butterfly, he called me weak, and a whiner.

So, I shut the book.

In the Bible, God said, let man "have dominion over the fish of the sea, and over the birds of the air, and over the cattle, and over all the earth..."

Dominion, in my opinion, is open to interpretation. I've long considered it to mean "responsibility." Dad was mega old school. He saw creation as something to control. If he could not contain a creature, he discarded it.

For years (there were four kids, then five, and finally, six), we were commanded to bring home crabs, fish and other sea life, imprisoned in pails. I remember one bucket of pink-shelled moon snails in saltwater. The organisms died slowly in stink and slime before we flushed them down the toilet.

When the wildlife perished, we got the blame in an expansion of the English language that only a Brooklyn-born man, such as my father, could assemble. Sometimes a punch, slap or painful squeeze on the arm accompanied his words.

Beach business wasn't always so salty. I recall sweetly how when the song "Wooly Bully" came on the radio, dad sped up the '55 Chevy Bel Air around the Pelham Bay Park traffic circle, and us kids, sitting side by side in the back, tumbled forward in giggles.

Dad would tell us to get up. Then somewhere down Pelham Parkway, before the elevated train above White Plains Road, he would hit the brakes, once, twice, three times until we all flopped back onto the floorboards.

It was also around 1965 that dad told me I would become a doctor. I was an early and hungry reader, and he bought me the book, *Microbe Hunters*, an account of the work of the first scientists to observe microscopic life. It was a tome more suitable for adults.

Months later, when he asked about *Microbe Hunters*, I told him the truth: I found it slow going and boring. He called me an idiot.

Somewhere on a shelf in my parent's attic, *Microbe Hunters* sits beside books that contain dead, desiccated monarchs.

When I was 13, dad cut off further financial support, except for a bed, doctor care and food.

So, through junior high and high school, I held up to three jobs at a time. When I graduated just short of my 17th birthday, I left for college, which I paid for myself, never moving back home.

My father's name was Edward. Most folks called him Ed, or Eddie. He scorned most of my adult discussions and decisions. And, unless you were following Eddie's commands, or one of his schemes, he was uninterested in what you were up to, or had to say.

Educational achievement did bring dad some delight. He and my mom visited me when I graduated from college in Indiana, and when I received a master's degree in Ohio.

Over the last few years, my nature commentaries have linked us. About a decade ago, dad became blind, and he enjoyed it when my mother read him my stories, particularly if they included his grand-children.

Eddie also suffered from emphysema; heart disease; esophageal, bladder and skin cancers; and lastly liver disease, which topped the cause-of-death list, when he passed away May 29, 2012, at age 84.

Pondering his passing, I have thought about how scientists learned a few years ago that it was the antennae of monarch butterflies that governed their migration, via sun-related directional sensing. Without antennae, monarchs were lost.

In an oft-miserable manner, dad provided me with direction. Through him, I discovered the natural world. When he was done with me, I learned how to control my own life.

Over the next few months, I will seek closure on Eddie's life and my relationship to him. Love, I've learned, is the opposite of possession, suffocation and desertion. Moreover, no one likes to be forgotten.

Every creature needs a mechanism to direct it. Don't let anyone take away your maneuvering apparatus. And please, don't allow anybody to seal the book on you, especially when you're still alive.

Civil Service in the Urban Jungle
April 13, 2013

Acalloused, meaty and formidable hand covered my mouth while a second one dragged me across the office foyer.

Pound for pound I was a powerful 25-year-old but no match for my larger co-worker. Another colleague used sections of climbing rope to tie me to a support column in the foyer of our office of climbers and pruners and gardeners in the Bronx headquarters of the New York City Department of Parks and Recreation.

The two men then gagged me with a cloth used to clean chainsaws.

On that spring morning in 1984, I would get what I deserved, they said.

The first attacker, and I can still see his 30-ish, blond-haired, pock-marked face, released my belt and pulled down my jeans. They were the tough fabric that I needed to tangle with brambles, as a City gardener.

The other man was a dark-haired veteran of the department. Maybe in his late 40s, this fellow possessed a cruel streak. I remember how he sneered, when a family of gray squirrels met their end after their tree-limbed home was fed through a chipper.

According to my accusers, I was an outsider, unable to adapt to the rules of the office.

Rule one was that I participate in its schemes. One dusty, sweaty early afternoon, for example, we'd received a call on the truck radio to come back in.

11

Upon our return, we found that the office had brought in a prostitute, who was stationed on a cot in the attic, reached via a pull-down staircase from the ceiling.

As we were informed of the costs of her services, foresters formed a line. I declined.

Then there was the particularly vicious storm that felled branches and trees along city streets and in the parks. As we prepared to clear the debris, my colleagues invited me to snort cocaine with them. I politely refused.

I will never forget one of those euphoric coworkers, leaning from a truck's bucket to clear live electrical wires of foliage. Through the transmission lines, he extended a chainsaw one-handed, whooping with each branch buzzed away.

As the climber and pruner worked, I stepped back from the truck. If he hit a line, I didn't want to go up in smoke with him.

The second rule was to keep my mouth shut. Without thinking that summer, I'd mentioned to a colleague in Queens that when supplies—wood, wire and more—were delivered, some of the men filled their personal vehicles with materials meant for City parks.

Without telling me, she informed a Parks official, who let my colleagues know that they had a snitch.

In front of my peers the two men yanked my legs apart. Get on line, they told the others. I would get what the prostitute received, they said, employing more colorful language.

Suddenly, and with a big round of laughs, they untied and ungagged me. I was warned, they said.

A few days later I was called into the office of the borough Parks Commissioner, where I was told that I would be reassigned to driving a truck.

My education and experience was read aloud like a list of accusations. I had a four-year degree in forest management, plus I was a former horticulturist, naturalist and park ranger. "We don't need those skills," I was told.

Natural selection suggests that we either adapt or die. I perished in the Parks Department, quitting two months later.

Back then, outer-borough dudes like me succumbed by the hundreds in our attempts to perform civil service on behalf of the city.

Was I a rodent fed to a chipper? Or, maybe I was a squirrel dashing across a great snow-covered lawn under the eyes of a predator. I was a creature in the wrong place at the wrong time, plucked, carried to a perch, and eviscerated.

One might never understand that such a death even occurred unless you recognized the signs—bits of blood, guts and flesh scattered across the landscape—you know, signs of the wild you find on a walk through the park with a naturalist.

Flesh And Blood Under a Bright Moon
June 6, 2015

High tide patted sand and mud in the dark, as Karen and I worked our way north along the shoreline of upper Narragansett Bay.

We looked for horseshoe crabs, which spawn on beaches under full moons of May and June, as they have for 450 million years.

At several stops, we trained flashlight beams on bouncing waters without a sign of a single crab. But the experience remained profound.

In April, my brother, Jeff, died from the complications of a stroke. He was 58. One of the last times I saw Jeff was on a June evening a few years ago, when we strolled along mudflats, witnessing dozens of horseshoe crabs mating.

During our childhood, the public beach was our summer home. It was there that at least once a year a greaser would come out of the water holding a horseshoe crab by its tail. The guy would act as if he had just saved all of us from a killer creature emerging from the swamp.

Beachgoers would gather around the man and the crab, which hung helplessly, kicking its tangle of legs. Then, before the excited crowd, the fellow would crush the crab to bits.

This infuriated Jeff. The crabs were innocent, and the greasers were idiots, he said.

Just so you know, it's a myth that the long and pointed tail of a horseshoe crab is poisonous and that the crab uses its tail to sting people.

The tail, known scientifically as a telson, is harmless. The crab uses it to navigate, feel around, and to flip over if pushed on its back.

With hard shells and ten legs, you might guess that a horseshoe crab is a real crab. But it is actually a cousin of scorpions and spiders.

Born with rare skeletal abnormalities, such as a tiny frame and brittle bones, Jeff underwent corrective or reparative surgeries almost every year during childhood.

Jeff lived in pain, and walked with a profound limp, but neither kept him from participating in street games such as stickball, skelly and Johnny on the pony. In the latter, Jeff was positioned at the front of the "pony," meaning he was the first to be jumped *over* and the last to be jumped *on*.

Because Jeff was small, he was a target for other kids; prey for human predators. I remember one incident, in junior high school, when I found Jeff on the corridor floor, as another student kicked him.

Often, my father was mean to Jeff. Dad would call Jeff "gimp," "shrimp" or words I can't repeat here.

As a kid, Jeff smiled a lot. He was both funny and charming. Jeff used all of those traits as a shield against bullies.

Unfortunately, a significant stretch of Jeff's adult life was like a mix of the crime dramas, Breaking Bad, The Wire and CSI.

At times, Jeff perpetrated grotesque behavior, resulting in bad blood among Jeff, family members and others. Jeff was clean the last few years, but in emotional and physical pain.

One of my other brothers said of Jeff, "He was cursed at conception, cursed in the womb, cursed at birth, and cursed in life."

Although I was estranged from Jeff, I've worked to remember the fun we had as kids, and how we stuck together in the face of brutality.

All of this was on my mind as Karen and I searched the bay's murky and salty waters in vain.

Horseshoe crab numbers are in a rapid decline. Not only do some people still label them as dangerous, the crabs are exceptionally popular bait for conch and eel commercial fisheries.

Moreover, horseshoe crab blood contains cells that rapidly trap invaders and keep infections from spreading. People use the blood to test vaccines and medical equipment. The blood goes for about $15,000 per liter.

More than 600,000 horseshoe crabs are harvested for bloodletting annually. Each creature is tapped for up to 30 percent of its blood.

Although the crabs are returned to the water, up to one-third die shortly after the blood harvest. Research also shows that "bled" female crabs show lower rates of reproduction than un-harvested crabs.

People associate blood with the soul. Indeed the scriptural, "The soul of every sort of flesh is its blood," is said to establish fundamental ethics for human behavior. Blood can be bad. Blood can be good. Either way, it is sacred.

Privet Fragrance
Carries 50 Years of History
June 15, 2018

Any day now, privet will bloom. Privet is a shrub, usually planted as a hedge. Its flowers are creamy white and syrupy scented. Typically, privet flowers extend from deep green foliage—lots of little leaves on many bunched branches.

Privet hedges are often used as vegetative screens. They grow thick and tall. It is difficult to peer through a privet hedge.

On my childhood block in the Bronx, a few privet shrubs grew alongside one of the apartment buildings. Compared to the dense privet hedges separating stately homes of Newport and Narragansett, this Bronx shrubbery was short and scraggly. Moreover, it lacked full sun, so it bloomed haphazardly.

Privet was the lone shrub and produced the only flowers on the street. And it was among the sweet smell of those scattered blooms on the sweltering afternoon of June 8, 1968, that I played hide and seek with my mates.

Upstairs in our third-floor flat was my mom, and three of my siblings. They were in front of the TV, watching the funeral for former U.S. Senator Robert Kennedy, whose assassination followed that of Martin Luther King Jr. two months earlier.

One sibling was my brother Jeff, just home from the hospital after hip surgery. Jeff, who was a year older than me (I turned 10 in 1968), was born with rare skeletal abnormalities that required regular surgeries.

That June, Jeff wore a cast, with two pins sticking outside the plaster, which went fully up one leg, and halfway up the other. The middle was open, and my mother would attach a towel or diaper to provide Jeff with some privacy.

Sudden commotions outside the privet interrupted the hide and seek. Peering out, I saw a neighborhood fellow, Mike, carrying another of my brothers, Stu, who was covered in blood. Stu was a year younger than me.

Stu and other kids had been cooling off in the spray of a fire hydrant. As I learned later, a woman drove through the group—a hit and run. A car-door handle ripped open Stu's mouth, removed some of his teeth and sliced up his gums.

I raced upstairs ahead of Mike and Stu, who arrived just as my mom opened the door. One minute she was crying at a TV funeral, and the next she was toweling blood off Stu's slumping head.

Days later, Stu came home from the hospital, deeply medicated, and with a cement-like guard over his mouth.

That summer, and over many years, my brothers would end up back in hospitals, enduring physical pain, medication hitches, and multiple other difficulties.

During the summer of 1968, my parents, who fought incessantly, split time between two hospitals. Some evenings my dad did not come home, entrenching himself on a bar stool. A babysitter took care of my little sister and brother. I watched a lot of TV, including coverage of riots across the nation and violence at the Democratic Convention. Otherwise, I wandered the streets, witnessing such wild things as a shooting right in front of the privet shrubs.

A remarkable trait of privet is that it blooms from most any garden soil, even Bronx dust. Every June when privet flowers, I don't just sniff the scent, I absorb it. I think of shrubs from long ago, for privet knows the troubles that I've seen.

APPOINTMENT WITH SAMARAS
May 2, 2003

I am a sucker for survivors. But I draw the line in the poor soil of my flowerbeds.

Thousands of Norway maple sprouts have sprung up in the wood chips and leaf litter around our small home.

It is a ritual, like Passover, Easter and Opening Day. Those seedlings will emerge from winged seeds, called samaras. How curious that samara is similar to the word samsara, or Buddhist reincarnation based on past actions.

Years ago, a master horticulturist told me that to maintain a garden you had to feel comfortable killing flora that you didn't want or couldn't share.

Removing the tiny Norway maples is something I do thoughtfully, because the species and I have history.

I grew up in the '60s and '70s amidst a sea of apartment buildings in a gritty part of the Fordham Road section of the Bronx. Across the street in a tree pit that was more broken glass than earth was my connection to Mother Nature. There grew a wide-crowned, thick-leaved Norway maple that produced cool summer shade.

As kids, we used to catch the spinning winged seeds, peeling open and sticking their little arms on our noses. I remember waiting for the tree to leaf out in April and turn golden yellow in October.

If some errant robin or blue jay happened by, that maple was its way station. Common across Europe, the Norway maple has an uncanny ability to thrive in lousy, polluted growing conditions. In these urban parts, it takes just a few years for Norway-maple seedlings to turn bare soil into a forest. When we bought our home, six years ago, we inherited dusty, abandoned flowerbeds, thick with rotting shrubs.

Now finally accessible to tilling and replanting, the thin, poor, sandy soil is nirvana for Norway-maple seeds. Overplanted throughout New England, Norway maples account for almost every street tree in some Providence neighborhoods. Each September those leafy citizens send a cascade of seeds twirling into our garden.

It is impossible to remove them from mulch and leaves. So they stay, and I keep in the back of my mind that when those winged woodlots sprout, in about eight months, I will tug them out. In the past I have plucked up to 1,500 in an hour. Each is different. Some germinate in the early seasonal cold. Others wait until the ground has warmed.

Weeding them takes at least a month. It must be done before the first leaves unfurl. Otherwise, a deep root makes yanking the tiny trees troublesome. I am mindful of the aesthetic and the other valuable traits of the Norway maple. Also I am thankful for gifts from past trees.

That said, this home represents our first chance to create gardens as a family. We envision tending flowers, herbs and vegetables in our soil, not a monoculture of maples. However, if we ever change our minds, I'll know where to get my hands on a few trees.

LIFE ON THE EDGE
November 24, 2012

Foam-fronted green waves slammed the darkened granite base of Fort Wetherill's bluffs.

I peered over the cliff. On the left side of the chasm, a lone male harlequin bobbed atop crashing surf, while on the right, a single male common eider did the same.

The dramatic sea locale of Fort Wetherill served as a central setting for the movie, "Moonrise Kingdom," which explored a 1960s pre-adolescent summer.

One reviewer said the film presented a "texture of childhood," with "the sense of having a limited amount of time in which to do unlimited things." Another critic wrote that the movie took, "as its primary subject matter odd, precocious children, rather than the damaged and dissatisfied adults they will one day become."

The glacial outcrop beneath my feet resembled the bedrock of my childhood—the gneiss, marble and schist of the Bronx and Northern Manhattan upon which I experienced earth-shattering events.

In the late 1960s and early 1970s, Tommy was a peer who weathered unevenly into adolescence. Tommy lived with his mother and two brothers in a cellar apartment, where I remember we listened to the rock music of the Doors, led by the iconic Jim Morrison.

Besides enjoying music, what Tommy and I had in common was climbing the boulders and outcrops over the nearby Harlem River. But it was there that we took different routes.

Tommy and other kids would cross blind curves of the commuter train line on the Bronx side, step over the electrified third rails and climb

21

a 50-foot wall of gneiss painted with a huge C in Columbia blue—massive, Ivy League graffiti.

From the top of the rock, they would plunge into the filthy black, whirlpool-rich waters, often timing their leaps to the passing of a Circle Line Sightseeing boat.

Standing on the other side of the waterway I'd watch the boys jump. I was in love with the stony terrain of Inwood Hill Park and its trails of tall trees at the northern tip of Manhattan that wound to the great open Hudson River. Inwood was my escape.

Tommy embraced every drug out there, from pot to pills, speed to heroin. He seemed to spend his waking hours on the streets. Gripped by darkness and despair, Tommy once said through wild eyes that we'd all die before our time.

By ninth grade, Tommy was possessed with an erratic idea: Lugging a bicycle up Columbia Rock and riding off into the river.

One night, he did. Hooting and hollering, according to others there, an acid-fueled Tommy rode a tricycle off the ridge. He was never seen again.

Then, there was kerchief-wearing Kippy, who led a small swarm of boys during the gang-war days.

One afternoon, I ambled along a bedrock ridge above the Major Deegan Expressway just north of Fordham Road. There, I crossed paths with Kippy, whose posse used to gather at the outfield wall of a softball field nearby.

"Hey," I said. He responded in kind. He didn't shake me down, knock my teeth in or toss me from the rocks.

That could be why when I looked out from the substratum of Fort Wetherill, I thought of the day 40 years ago when a youngster stuck a gun out the window of a mass transit bus and fired at a group of kids, standing on a corner.

The bullet passed through Kippy's kerchief, scalp and skull, and he dropped dead.

From the crest and breathtaking expanse of Wetherill, I shoved mitted hands into my coat pockets. A wisp-of-winter wind squeezed skinny tears from the outer corners of my eyes. I scanned graffiti painted on the rocks. The words memorialized two cliff jumpers who fell to their deaths there.

I thought of the opening line of Roadhouse Blues, by the Doors: "Yeah, keep your eyes on the road, your hands upon the wheel," and the pre-chorus closing line, "The future's uncertain, and the end is always near."

Five things occurred to me. First, it was OK to seek space, especially when your head was a mess. Second, there was always hope in the murkiness. Third, don't believe all that you hear. Fourth, don't believe everything that you think. And fifth, if there are loved ones at home, and you are standing alone in the cold, go home.

An Acky Tale
March 3, 2019

Way back in 1963, I was five years old and feral. Our eight-member family lived in a three-bedroom, third-floor apartment in a west Bronx walk-up.

My mother was busy having and tending to kids, while also caring for her mom, who was dying of cancer. My dad spoke through fists and insults. I didn't like being his prey, plus I was curious. So, I often simply left the apartment to roam.

We lived at 2305 Grand Avenue, with Evelyn Place to the south and North Street to the north. I was a wanderer, but one thing my mother told me was not to go around the corner onto Evelyn Place.

"Stay on the front stoop," was her mantra. Indeed, it was a great spot—the cool marble of those steps—to watch the comings and goings. Yet one warm afternoon, I motored off to Evelyn Place.

Each block in our neighborhood possessed a personality. My mother was raised in the same apartment in which I grew up. For decades, Evelyn Place was a stronghold of families that wanted nothing to do with people who were different from them, even if you lived just around the corner.

I got about 50 feet down Evelyn Place before one of its denizens, a kid about my age, pedaled his tricycle over me.

I can still recall smacking the pavement face first, entangling my arms in the tire spokes and getting dragged, my face, arms and legs bloodied.

Moreover, I recall looking up, as a now-gathered gaggle of kids laughed at me, while a trio of their parents watched. None helped. Two of those parents had grown up with my mom.

Two weeks ago, for the first time since I moved from what was left of the neighborhood, following the 1977 blackout, I strolled from 2305 Grand Avenue onto Evelyn Place, walking hand-in-hand with my wife, Karen.

We headed west one block to Aqueduct Avenue, which we crossed, and then climbed a wide staircase set into the hillside of Aqueduct Walk, a linear park built atop the path of the Old Croton Aqueduct, which provided clean water to a booming New York between 1842 and 1958.

When I was a little boy, we called the Aqueduct Walk, "the Acky." In those days, I usually reached the Acky via North Street, which was a relatively safe side street compared to Evelyn Place.

As a child, the Acky was where I first discovered nature—from the acorns that descended in fall from the pin oaks to the "itchy" balls, which dropped every winter from the London plane trees. Given the Acky stretched for several blocks north and south, you could stroll off into new neighborhoods and conjure up all sorts of explorer adventures in the process.

Of course, danger was always near. Once, for example, five boys jumped me, dragged me down the park slope, stopping at a point where my head hung over a stonewall terminus. The boys held me down, peering at me like doctors examining a patient.

In shame and frustration, I spit up at them, but the laws of physics were in my attackers' favor. They spit back, splattering my mug, their warm spew rolling off my brow and cheeks.

Caught like a rodent and defiled, the boys suddenly let me go. I slid off the wall, landing on my head on the overgrown cobblestone three-feet below.

Now, with Karen, I saw that the oak and plane trees were still there. They were bigger in trunk and crown, impressive sentinels of the old path. I said hello to the trees, as we strolled the lane.

Interestingly, we found the backyards of the apartment buildings that bordered the park's ridge rich in feral cats. A feline seemed to step out from behind each battered and rusted gas grill, washing machine or other large item scattered about these spaces.

We walked north two blocks to 184th Street, exiting down the slope via another set of stairs. When I told my mother about the visit, she asked me if the shrubs were still beside the steps. Yes, I responded, and we recalled how the city planted those bushes in the early 1970s, and they immediately became hiding places for muggers and worse.

That afternoon, Evelyn Place was quiet. Only a couple of people ambled by on the Aqueduct Walk. There was a calm and tranquility to the sojourn.

My childhood was like a long-running game of kick the can, and I was the can. In some way during that February stroll in the west Bronx, I felt that a few of my broken pieces were put back together—that somehow that day I turned a corner, feeling much more at home within myself and in the old neighborhood.

Blooming in the Bronx
February 24, 2019

As kids growing up in the Bronx of the 1960s and 70s, we would occasionally tromp east along Fordham Road to the New York Botanical Garden (NYBG), avoiding any number of street gangs and other dangers to enter the greenery through a bent rail in the property's wrought iron fence.

Back then, relatively few folks visited the NYBG to stroll the grounds and greenhouses, as much as they did to find mugging targets or items to steal.

In my 20s, during the 1980s, I lived just three blocks from the NYBG, which I typically accessed via a tunnel under the commuter rail line. That passageway was dark, damp and dangerous. When news spread of an assault within that tunnel, I walked the extra block or two to reach the flowers and plants, during a decade when a deserted NYBG looked like hardly anyone knew it was there.

The tunnel is no longer open, and as far as I can tell, no deathtraps exist to reach one of the most bucolic landscapes of New York City. So, when Karen and I looked to escape to somewhere warm, humid and colorful in mid-February, we drove the 170 miles to visit the NYBG.

When you haven't been to a place in 35 years, you tend to think of it as you last saw it: empty and somewhat sinister. But that's not what we found.

In the bright sun on a chilly, cloudless day, we encountered a revitalized and lively National Historic Landmark full of other visitors, and rich with spiffy facilities that I didn't recall such as the Levy Visitor Center, Pine Tree Café and Discovery Center.

27

We headed straight for the spot to revive our winter-weary souls (and skins)—the Enid A. Haupt Conservatory, which the NYBG calls "a stunning example of Victorian-style glasshouse artistry." The conservatory contains room after room of "lush tropical rain forests, cactus-filled deserts, curated displays of palms from around the world, aquatic and carnivorous plants, and much more."

The houses were moist, green and fragrant with a smell of spring and summer. Orchids provided bursts of color. Fruits, such as cacao, offered bounty at which to marvel.

The textures, shapes, sizes, light and spaces, led me to want to touch everything. However, there was no touching the cycads, ferns and other plants, according to the rules.

Just as stunning as the clammy tropical houses were those of bright sun and dry sand that accommodated desert plants. Here, you didn't want to handle the vegetation. Much of it, such as the sharp teeth of agave or the needle-like spines of saguaro, were better off observed than touched.

Even in winter, the NYBG grounds looked picture-postcard perfect, such as the conifer arboretum and its evergreens of unusual trunks, branching patterns and foliage, which we strolled through on our way to the Steere Herbarium on the second floor of the Mertz Library and Art Gallery.

Lexico.com defines a herbarium as a "systematically arranged collection of dried plants." The NYBG's Steere Herbarium contains some 7.8 million specimens, making it the second-largest herbarium in the world, according to the Garden's website. Steere Herbarium was open on the day we visited, as part of "#plantlove" weekend at the NYBG.

On display for us to touch and learn about were dozens of "pressed" plants from around the world. One exhibition featured seaweed and ferns collected by women, during the Victorian era. Among the items, my favorite was a book, published by someone named Jennie Knox in 1888. Her name in the front of the volume was spelled out in delicate algae lifted deftly and dried from the Pacific Ocean.

The world of plants that we found inside and outside at the NYBG immersed us in nature's beauty and diversity.

Were we transported elsewhere by the experience? You bet, and it wasn't to the bad old '70s and '80s. It was to the present, and "now" felt much better than "then."

This week, the first blossoms of snowdrops are likely out on the NYBG grounds, but I can tell you firsthand that my old stomping grounds are already in full bloom.

GIVING NATURE AND NURTURE A SECOND CHANCE

January 2, 2009

When my mother's water broke, we gained more than a baby sister.

My father trekked us to the hospital 6 blocks away. Yet somehow the three of us kids ended up on the sidewalk. I was three, one brother was five and the other two.

Alone, we toddled into the evening outdoors. Standing together, we watched the sun set over the woods behind the hospital.

At age 10, I entered those woods for the first time after word had reached our street that kids had broken into an abandoned home within the property.

A quartet of youngsters set out for that house.

Inside the dark interior we found a surge of savagery. Kids used stones from the fireplace to smash windows. They pulled shells off walls and tore down fixtures and wiring from the ceilings.

We left.

As an adolescent, I shared my first bottle of cheap beer with a brother and buddies in the forest. I wandered there, too, trying to shake off drunkenness, before heading home for dinner.

In time, I noticed and learned to appreciate the flowering trees in spring and colorful foliage in fall of 3.3-acre University Woods Park.

The site sits atop a ridge overlooking the Harlem River. The hard rock that formed the steep slope sparkled with bits of the minerals gneiss, mica and schist.

University Woods was also where British Fort #8 sat intact through the American Revolution. In fact some of the original stonewalls used by British troops still remained.

By the 1970s a soil-layers-worth of broken glass covered the forest floor, plus condoms, animal-sacrifice carcasses and glassine envelopes that earlier held heroin.

No matter how troubling one's childhood, we often long for where we were born.

So at age 30, when the woman I loved dumped me before New Year's Eve in Columbus, Ohio, I got into my aging Honda Civic 1200 and drove 565 miles to University Woods.

Once again, I stood amidst discarded hypodermic needles, looking west at the setting sun over the Fort Tryon, Inwood Hill and Marble Hill neighborhoods of Northern Manhattan, and at glimpses of the Hudson River and New Jersey Palisades beyond.

Same as it ever was, University Woods Park was a mess. But it was my mess.

Between 2003 and 2005, the civic group, New Yorkers for Parks, ranked University Woods the worst small park in New York City.

A year later community members formed a conservancy. They partnered with the parks department to begin cleaning the forest, fixing the walls, removing invasive plants and replanting the park.

The group, Friends of the Woods, even had a slogan: "The natural escape you never knew existed in your own backyard."

This transformation filled me with hope. In particular, I enjoyed reading about young people who filled the park with new life.

Next May my sister will turn 48. In that span I learned to surround myself with loving family and friends. That understanding, plus the evolution of University Park Woods from urban hell to community-embraced gateway, suggests to me that if we give people and nature half a chance they rebound.

Whether you long for a faraway location and time, or your place is here and now, I wish you a lighter and sweeter load in the New Year.

Redemption in a Snippet of Soil
March 27, 2010

One glimpse through the weathered gray slats of a picket fence carried me back to Jan. 27, 1963.

I saw a mini-me, telling my father that I had counted through the calendar and that "Today I turned four and a half."

My dad looked like a long-striding giant of a man (actually he was about 5' 8"). He glanced down at me and replied, "Shut up, that's stupid."

We walked up a hill on Grand Avenue in the Bronx along the red brick wall of an apartment building.

By the age of four and a half, I had already developed an inner voice that warned me before speaking, "Don't do it!"

That morning I ignored my own advice, as I often did through childhood, and shared my thoughts in a tentative, lip-biting blurt.

Outside of four-letter-word name-calling, "shut up" was the most common verb and "stupid" the most frequent adjective directed at me during my youth. My dad was as involuntarily swift with these words, as he was with his fists.

When I was demeaned, I would lapse into counting, which kept me occupied and quiet. So as soon as my father responded to me, I began tallying bricks in the wall, switching to sidewalk squares, when we passed the building.

My comment about the calendar was a test. I was excited about sharing my work to determine my half birthday but equally as thrilled because I wanted to show my dad a secret garden behind a fence between the buildings.

I skipped that tale.

Forty-seven years later, here it is.

As a small child I often wandered the neighborhood unsupervised, with my two brothers, one a year older and the other a year younger.

One of us had black bangs, the other brown hair that stood straight out and the third a round face. We liked to call ourselves the Three Stooges.

On a ramble in late summer of 1962, we looked through the planks of a fence that separated the back of two buildings about one and one-half city blocks from where we lived. A set of stairs on the other side of the fence led down to a plot of soil about eight by 10 feet.

In that ground grew blossoms, arranged in a display of pink and red, white and yellow. Two wrought-iron lawn chairs framed the vegetation in what I believe was the first tended plot we had ever seen in the neighborhood.

The flowers were fueled by sun streaming through a lane that ran straight through the spine of the city block. In retrospect, with its criss-crossing lines of laundry overhead, it looked like one of those alleys you saw in city cop-and-criminal chase scenes.

What unleashed this memory was the sight of a garden on the other side of a worn fence here in Providence that the dog tugged me over to on one of our wider rambles of the spring last week.

The Providence patch included a rose bush, and what I guessed were withered remains of the perennials, coreopsis and black-eyed Susan, and the annual, cosmos. At our feet, daylily shoots sprouted green, lance-shaped leaves.

It took a split second for this experience to take me back to 1963. I not only saw that Bronx garden again, but also felt sadness unearthed by the memory.

To this day, I am in awe of whoever tended that Bronx patch, given our neighborhood was the kind that folks sped through in their cars, doors locked and windows raised, on their way somewhere else.

The garden suggested an order and tranquility that contrasted piercingly with the hostility of life on the other side of the fence.

It also reinforced something I learned later than most folks: No matter what you are told, you can always make something out of nothing.

THE TRUTH ABOUT STREET TREES
January 17, 2009

A tall, snow-draped, vase-shaped American elm on a Providence roadway activated a childhood memory.

I thought of tall elms that once lined both sides of my block in the west Bronx. Their high-arching limbs formed a canopy that protected us from the searing sun of summer and gave shape to the thoroughfare in winter.

Then the trucks came along with men with ravenous saws and chippers. Dutch elm disease, the fungus that had arrived via European logs, was spreading across New York. Bark beetles carried the disease, and the borers hit the weakest trees, typically found on the streets.

In little more than a day, the elms were gone. We went from leafy to empty.

I shared a bedroom with two brothers in our third-floor apartment.

With the trees not there, the three of us began a post-bedtime ritual of nestling together on a windowsill to follow events on the block. It was like sitting in the upper deck of a sports stadium.

One night, we watched a man wobble, stagger and fall. The fellow lay motionless.

"He's dead," said my brother Jeff, who was blunt, smart and usually right. My other brother, Stuart, was four. I was five and couldn't or wouldn't believe that someone had died in front of us.

"The man is sick," I said. Stuart, silent and wide-eyed, just nodded.

No cars came. No pedestrians passed.

"Someone should tell mom," said Jeff.

I trekked through the living room, past the kitchen and down the short hallway to my parent's bedroom.

"A man fell in the street," I said.

My parents stared at me. "Why were you looking out the window?" asked my mother. I tried to explain that street gazing was a new activity and that we didn't stay up late, but the words came out garbled, and I grew flustered at the grilling and growing fear that a man was dead outside.

My mother followed me back. A cab had stopped, and the driver had placed a balled-up jacket under the fellow's head. Mom looked out the window, turned around, and headed for the phone.

The detective in my bedroom looked as lofty and wide as a tree. Ours was a tough neighborhood on the decline. He implored me to tell the truth.

"Yes, the man just fell over," and "No, we saw no one else," I said.

We never learned anything about the fellow outside, but knew we were the last people to see him alive.

Twice this winter I have come across a large American elm on a Providence street—once on the East Side and again on the West Side—their crowns spreading impressively over concrete and asphalt.

Somehow these specimens survived and thrived, despite Dutch elm disease, and the salt, slams and other shames of subsisting in a strip of soil by the gutter.

In my mind's eye I see similar-shaped, long-gone elms of my early days.

I hear their leaves swishing in the first cool breezes of fall, or watch snow settling on their branches. I also see an empty street, where a man's life ended.

Trees provide communities with a sense of place. Anyone who says differently is not telling the truth.

STEER CLEAR OF THE POISON IVY
June 4, 2011

The vine's rich green foliage swathed the furrowed willow trunk like a silky shawl.

One of the vine's climbing shoots reached out toward where I stood.

When I inspected its newest growth of red-tinged and green-veined leaves, I was seized by a long-bottled-up memory, as if the young branch had morphed into the bony finger of a skeleton.

Among my duties as a park ranger 30 years ago was to patrol a rarely used railway bed in Van Cortlandt Park in the Bronx.

On one of those rounds, I encountered two boys about 10 years old, chasing each other through a thicket of sun-dappled poison ivy. The June day was hot and each boy was dressed in shorts and shirtsleeves.

When I was about their age, I had crawled through a tangle of poison ivy. The result was a painful, oozing, head-to-toe inflammation, which only abated after I received a steroid injection.

I stepped up to the two boys, urging them to leave the shrubbery.

Their response was to mock me.

In shrill voices, each youngster chanted, "This is poison ivy. This is poison ivy."

Calmly, I told the boys, "You're going to get sick."

The duo scrambled into the heart of the noxious plant, turned, faced me, and insisted that I come in and get them.

"I'm not going in there, and I'm telling you that you're going to get sick," I said. "You're going to regret what you're doing."

My words equaled a flick of their noses. The two youngsters exploded into obscenity in both word and gesture.

Native to a bad neighborhood in the Bronx, I had worked three summers, plus two full years in the borough's parks. I thought I had seen everything.

As I watched, each boy tore off handfuls of the three-leaved foliage and began rubbing it on their bare arms, necks and faces.

The kids looked like they were showering with poison ivy soap.

Then, the boys took off their shirts and stripped away fists of younger leaves, shiny and red, with prominent green veins, and stuffed the foliage into their mouths.

As each kid munched and swallowed, they again intoned, "This is poison ivy."

Shaking my head, I walked away. To that point in my life (I was 21), the encounter felt like one of the most chilling incidents I had ever witnessed.

How did these young men get so twisted, I wondered? When I got sick with poison ivy, my mom whisked me to a hospital. Who would take them to a doctor?

In subsequent days, I checked the newspaper for some blaring headline about poison ivy-eating boys.

Today, poison ivy may be the most widespread plant in the landscape.

It is a groundcover, a border plant, a shrub and a hairy-stemmed snake that winds to the tops of trees.

I am clueless as to why the vine on the willow activated the memory of two unexpected and misery-inviting boys.

Whatever our route, it is always our choice to step into, out of or away from poison ivy. We decide how to act, what to think, and who we will become.

The memory has since flowed from the forefront of my brain to its bowels, because that is where it ultimately belongs.

NOW IS WHEN ORDINARY DAYS IN THE PARK CAN TURN UGLY
March 15, 2014

For me, the thrill of new growth budding in spring contains a dark side.

My first lesson in foliage malevolence occurred during the summer after first grade.

I was alone two blocks from home, visiting what local kids dubbed, "the clubhouse." It was a ring of dense privet shrubs just north of 183rd Street in what is now called Aqueduct Walk in The Bronx.

Just before ducking inside, out sprang Jaime, a kid whom I thought was my best friend.

Jaime, and four other youngsters, who I vaguely recognized, tackled me. Then they dragged me down the dusty park incline. At its stonewall terminus, they hung my head over the edge.

Surprised and humiliated, I spit into Jaime's face. Bad idea.

Repeatedly, Jaime spit back. Warm spew rolled off my mug. Suddenly, the boys let go, and I slid off the wall to the ground three feet below.

To this day, who is your friend, and who isn't, during childhood, and the sudden shifting of youthful affiliations, remain enigmatic to me.

In the summer of my 10th year, a stray mutt—small, brown, dirty, and shorthaired—began following me around. For the first time I thought about owning a puppy.

One morning, some friends called me over to the ring of privet shrubbery. While no longer "the clubhouse," I still visited it from time to time. For my buddies and me it was the only enclosed public spot around, a sort of womb for ragamuffins.

Something smelled awful as I slid inside the privet. There, my friends stared at the dog, which was on its back, opened, bloated and filled with tan, squirming maggots. Dead.

Although feeling revolted, shocked and sad, I stood riveted. I can still hear the mushy squirming sound of the larvae devouring the canine.

Rapidly, a kid stepped forward, sprayed the corpse with cigarette lighter fluid, dropped a match, and the carcass went up in a funeral pyre. Everyone took off running.

When I became a park ranger, I learned that emerging from foliage could turn life threatening.

On solo patrol in Van Cortlandt Park, I stepped from a wooded path into an open stretch to find four men, two on either side of an abandoned car. Each set of men pointed guns at the other. It was a scene right out of The French Connection.

Nodding to them, I kept walking. Shortly, the path curved back into the woods. There, I called-in "code zero" on my walkie-talkie, which meant that someone in the main office must call 911 immediately.

What I learned in the following days was that two men on one side of the car were drug dealers. The other two men were plainclothes detectives. Both sets had come to retrieve drugs, supposedly stashed in the car. No shots were ever fired.

What are my takeaways from these experiences? I believe that the arrival of greenery provides both beauty and wonder. But it also creates hiding places six months a year for folks bent on illicit activity.

Of course, I will revel in the splendor of spring, once again, just as long as it feels safe. And, don't be surprised if I look around first before smelling the roses.

TALES OF WINTER ON THE ROOF
February 3, 2017

The 1962 song, "Up on the Roof," contains this bit of enchanting lyrics, "On the roof, it's peaceful as can be."

To me, that sentence is more fantasy than glimpse of urban bliss. As someone who grew up in a five-floor walk up in the Bronx, the roof door was a gateway to the apocalypse.

Up on the roof, illicit lovers coupled and users shot up. One young man in my building, who grew up to become a rodeo star, once hung off the brick lip of the roof by his fingertips, while his compatriots screamed "don't do it." He wasn't going to. The young man craved both peril and attention. He and his buds scrammed when police showed up on the street below.

Another time, those same young men dressed up and stuffed a full-sized scarecrow, dangled it from the roof, pleading with "it" not to jump. Thinking that the shape was real, folks on the sidewalk screamed, "don't do it." Then the boys dropped the human figure to its demise, while on-lookers shrieked.

Over the years, I noticed that the roof was empty in winter. That's when I visited.

The wintertime roof was a place to enjoy "alone time," and to see the wider sky. Both were invigorating, even if I froze.

"Up on the Roof" also notes, "I go up where the air is fresh and sweet." Again, that is charming make-believe. Air on the rooftop was no different than it was five floors below, except that sometimes it smelled of tar. But in winter, it was definitely breezier and colder up there, with fewer ways to shelter from the wind.

One winter morning while I was alone on the roof, someone locked the door behind me.

Previously, a man who lived on the top floor had warned us kids to stay off the roof or he'd bolt the door if he heard footsteps overhead.

The fire escape was my only route of exodus. I climbed down the outdoor staircase only to find that the ladder was raised and tucked into the first-floor landing. I would have to jump the final 10-12 feet.

So, I peeked into an apartment window. There was a four-member family at the kitchen table. Embarrassed, but out of options, I tapped the glass.

The dad (I knew the family and they knew me) walked over and unlocked the window. I climbed inside. It was warm in there, and the kitchen smelled of bacon. Shaking her head, the mom said, "I'm not even going to ask," as she led me out of the apartment.

Winter up on a Bronx roof meant a little bit of solitude and a lot of chill. A sense of escape, however, implied more than one meaning.

A Tree Grows in the Bronx
November 3, 2017

B ack in the early 1960s, in the west-central Bronx, many of my neighbors personified the shtetl life of their Eastern European upbringings.

One of them, Molly, mostly spoke Yiddish. She wore high, dark shoes; long skirts; a shawl, blanket or lengthy coat, depending on the season; and a headscarf.

A relatively short, elderly woman, Molly oversaw a rooming house on North Street between Grand and Davidson avenues. Like a U.S. Navy master chief, she kept the little private home, tucked between much-larger apartment buildings, in good order.

Except for us kids. You see, a handful of us sidewalk hedgehogs had found that a missing section of wood lattice below the home's front porch led to a dark quiet space that became our clubhouse.

Our little gang was also Jewish. We acted, dressed and played like other kids of the day, but being known as Jews made us targets for disdain and body blows from our peers. So, like schools of fish, or flocks of birds, we traveled tightly together to try to ward off predation.

We did not play in the silty clubhouse, but sat and chatted, learning to speak in soft tones, or sit silently at the sound of footsteps on the porch or steps, or when someone walked by on the sidewalk.

Still, Molly found us. And it was in the fall, because as she ordered us out, Molly used the curved stem of a fallen leaf of an Ailanthus tree to whack each of our tushies, as we backed out of the hole.

A native of China, the Ailanthus was introduced into the North American landscape more than 250 years ago. Each "leaf" on an Ailanthus tree is one- to four-feet long and holds between 11 and 41 leaflets.

One of the most invasive trees in the United States, Ailanthus is also the species at the core of the classic novel, *A Tree Grows in Brooklyn*.

Molly's whippings didn't hurt much, especially compared with the beatings we took at the hands of our parents, and from other kids in the neighborhood.

Although we returned to the clubhouse, Molly was wise to us now, ushering us out with a leaf-stem smack.

We were slow to learn to respect private property but fairly quick to understand that leaves fell in fall and that some of them persisted on the ground as "whips," or what I came to learn were called "switches."

Indeed, our gang began collecting Ailanthus leaf stems for use as swords in imaginary pirate adventures.

Meanwhile, Molly had the lattice hole closed, and just a year or so later she passed away.

Fifty years later, who would think that an autumnal whack from a wiry stem would deliver such a warm memory?

COMINGS AND GOINGS OF BIRDS AND PEOPLE IN MAY
May 27, 2016

Some birdwatchers use the phrase, "second-week warbler" to refer to species of little songbird that typically arrive in migration around the middle of May. Blackburnian warbler and chestnut-sided warbler are among such species.

Thirty-nine years ago I arrived in The Bronx in mid-May, home to work for the summer between my sophomore and junior years of college.

At the time I was also a budding birdwatcher, who padded around local parks post dawn, $10 binoculars in hand, to watch tiny songbirds migrate through the big city.

St. James Park was my local greenery. Nearly a dozen acres in size, the park was full of recreational facilities that were in disrepair back in 1977.

The park was also rich with tall oaks. Their flowers attracted insects, which drew in migrating birds. There were some scattered shrubs in the park, as well.

The soil was a dusty, somewhat sandy and eroded earth that was filthy with broken glass, tossed-away tubes of model glue (used for sniffing), and discarded glassine envelopes that once held heroin.

Warbler watching works best post dawn, when the birds feed, call and sing before quieting in the heat of day.

Early morning, it was peaceful within St. James Park, except for the birds, and an occasional barking dog. The park exterior was noisy, though, with the rumblings of the adjacent Jerome Avenue Line elevated train and the clinks, clanks and screeches of passing motor vehicles.

This was not the place to loiter long. Back then, St. James Park was an anarchic and violent daytime and evening gathering spot for addicts, dealers and gangs. Gone were the days when stroller-pushing mothers gathered on park benches to chitchat.

Warblers in the morning were the gentler contrast, calling or singing amidst the greenery, and flashing through on their travels north.

Maybe because no one else was around, some warblers dropped into the shrubbery, and we literally came face-to-face.

One of those birds was a male black-throated green warbler. The bird featured a stunning contrast between yellow face and black throat. And it repeatedly sang its diagnostic, "zoo-zee, zoo-zoo-zee."

Another visitor was a male magnolia warbler. It displayed a yellow throat and chest marked by a black band across the upper breast and black streaks on the side. The bird's head was blue with a white eyebrow stripe and a black mask over the bill and around the eyes.

The magnolia warbler sang a non-stop, "weta, weta, WETA." And I can still see it pulling a slight caterpillar off a leaf and devouring the insect.

Black-throated green warblers winter from Mexico through Central America into northern South America. Magnolia warblers spend the winter in the Caribbean. Both birds breed in forests of Canada and the upper reaches of the Northeast. All of this bird background astounded me, as I'd never visited any of those places.

Somehow these little creatures, each weighing less than half an ounce, survived thousands of miles of travel, while I had to worry for my life each time I walked to and from the park.

Over the years, I came to realize that the wild nature of these tiny creatures and the untidy humanity and make-up of St. James Park were like light and dark, or fire and water. They were complementary and interconnected, a yin and yang in an unsettled urban setting.

GREAT HORNED OWLS:
JANUARY LOVE BIRDS
January 5, 2008

If he were alive today, my former birding buddy, Kenny Rubin would enjoy the role of owls as carriers of mail, packages and new brooms between the everyday and supernatural worlds in the Harry Potter series.

Kenny adored owls for any number of reasons. He associated the birds with strength, wisdom and clairvoyance. Owls, he said, were mystical in the ability to swivel their heads 180 degrees and to hunt silently by sound in the pitch dark.

Over the three-year period of our friendship, Kenny and I owl-prowled regularly. We found and observed barn, barred, great gray, great horned, long-eared, saw-whet, screech, short-eared and snowy owls.

Kenny's favorite owl was the great horned. As the largest and most powerful predatory local bird, it could kill, carry and digest an adult skunk. So mighty was a great horned owl, he said, the bird had been known to drive bald eagles from their nests.

In his baritone voice, Kenny liked to call me "Bubo," which is the genus name for the great horned owl.

January was our favorite time for "owling." We knew where to find overwintering birds. More importantly, great horned owls were in the throes of courtship, hooting up a storm in territories defined during the fall.

Both male and female great horned owls hoot. Unlike the owls in Harry Potter that carry all sorts of envelopes, local owls convey that it is time to build intimate relationships. Because great horned owls are the first birds to nest in the New Year, their behavior indicates that no matter how bleak the winter, springtime is not far away.

The other day I visited a stretch of riparian woods to search for a male great horned owl that I had heard recently. I did not find the bird. From the sounds of the forest, dozens of crows, crying in a deafening, desperate roar had mobbed and driven the raptor deeper into the woods.

The word "mob" reminds me of a day in early January 1983 when Kenny and I visited a great horned owl. I suggested that the bird was hidden high in a tall white pine given the whitewash (droppings) and pellets (regurgitated balls of fur, bones and feathers) at the tree's base. My finding was confirmed when fresh whitewash splattered down through the feathery pine needles. We laughed until our sides ached.

But the trip turned serious when we left the woods. Two men approached, one holding a bulky item under a zippered jacket. "Youse seen da great horny owl?" he asked. "No" we both said. "You sure?" he questioned us, offering a peek at what appeared to be a sawed-off shotgun under his coat. "No," we repeated. We left and so did they.

Given the teen-age-like ferocity of the great horned owl courtship, the hoods' name for the bird may not have been that far from the truth.

I met Kenny in Sept. 1981. This was 10 years after he had received a diagnosis of stage 3 melanoma. Doctors loved him, because he was a walking miracle. Kenny never complained, even as the cancer eventually spread into his brain over the next three years.

Four days before he died on May 19, 1984 at age 34 (I was 26), I called upon Kenny at the hospital. About a week earlier he had fallen into a coma. I showed up daily to share birding and other news.

I told Kenny that I had visited a local great horned owl nest. The young looked like oblong balls of gray fluffy lint. But they were now capable of flying, I said. To the wonder of all of us in the room, Kenny pronounced a single "Hoo."

You don't have to follow Harry Potter to understand that owls link the mundane and the miraculous. Owls are magical.

SEARCHING FOR SOOTHING SOUNDS IN FALL
September 8, 2017

Fifty years ago, acorns dripped off pin oaks on Aqueduct Avenue just north of 183rd Street in the Bronx.

I was nine years old, and those falling nuts were the projectiles for my homemade slingshot.

On a quiet weekend morning in mid-September, I filled a little bag with the small, round acorns. Abruptly, a group of neighborhood boys came running around the corner, shouting "fight."

I joined the gang to find two men fighting in front of the apartment building where I lived with my parents and four siblings.

One of the fighters was Mike, my neighbor on the third-floor. A wiry Puerto Rican fellow about age 25, Mike was battling some pudgy, red-faced chap.

Mike lived in an apartment with Mary, a fair-skinned blonde from the West Coast, and her daughter, Theresa. Mary's sister, Ellen, and her one-year-old daughter, Cindy, resided with them.

The flushed guy, I learned from the other kids, was named Donald. He claimed to be Cindy's father. Donald was there, as he shouted, to take her away.

Later, I found out that Donald had previously expressed near-zero interest in Cindy. To me, Donald appeared off, as if fueled by alcohol or drugs.

The two men battled in what looked like a staged TV-show fight, such as the ones on "Batman" or "Star Trek," both popular programs at the time. But the action grew acutely real, when Donald pulled a knife and raised it over Mike's head.

Mike twisted Donald's wrist, and the knife fell away. When Mike lunged for the weapon, Donald took off up the courtyard steps and into the apartment building. Mike and us kids followed.

When Donald reached the third-floor landing, he didn't bang on Mike and Mary's door. Instead he pounded on my family's apartment door.

"Give me Cindy," he shouted.

My mother opened the still-chained door a crack. She was a small and wispy 30-year-old, maxing out at four feet ten inches in height and maybe 100 pounds.

"Your child is not here," she said.

"I want Cindy," Donald replied.

"I don't have her," my mother said, and closed the door.

Mike suggested that they go outside to work out the dispute.

As the rest of the kids followed the men downstairs, I knocked on our apartment door.

My mother let me in. As I walked through the narrow foyer into the living room, there sat Ellen with Cindy on her lap.

My mother had hid them! Her acting was spectacular.

Sworn to secrecy, I sprinted outside to witness Mike handing Donald a roll of bills. In short, Mike had bought-off Donald, who left.

As the other kids melted away, I went back to the oaks.

Except for the sound of a passing car, all I heard was the "plik" of falling acorns hitting the Belgian blocks of stone set into the ground below the trees.

This was what autumn sounded like in my neighborhood. I much preferred that tone to the one of fists striking flesh.

Developing a Taste for Life
July 26, 2008

As a boy he walked the tide line nibbling on seaweed, shells and twine.

Those early years his mother would rush down from her beach chair to pull the detritus from her son's mouth. But every once in a while, before she could reach him, he would bite into something painful and howl.

Over the years, into adolescence and adulthood, he grew taller and stronger, and continued to sample the buffet line of clamshells, crab legs and jellyfish. Meanwhile his mother grew older, slower and more tired looking.

Eventually, he was a man walking the mile-long crescent of beach, placing bits of driftwood and straw in his mouth, his mom no longer rising from her chair.

For 15 or so years, with two of my brothers, I walked that tide line, too. The three of us often walked past the fellow who tasted what the saltwater left behind, all of us, part of the "mixed bag," as my own mother called it, of creatures and people found at Orchard Beach on Long Island Sound in the Bronx.

Orchard Beach was where I first cut my teeth, learning about nature. Its open sand, sky and waters suggested salvation from stifling apartments and treeless streets.

I can remember all the way back to the early 1960s, when the water was clean enough to sustain soft-shell clams. As toddlers, the three of us boys, born between 1957-59, would stomp the tidal flats until the clams squirted around our feet.

Our father introduced us to hermit crabs, killifish and moon snails, and under his direction, we chased tiny fish over netting set down in the shallows, capturing the animals.

We were one of the only families on the block with a car, albeit a beat-up 1955 Chevy Bel Air. When we returned home from the beach to the West Bronx—an ocean of apartment buildings—folks on the corners and stoops watched as we carried buckets of fish, crabs and snails upstairs, poor, trapped creatures that would die sooner than later.

Orchard Beach was where we watched the weekend ritual of a group of German Jews, gathering in a corner of the sand to folk dance early in the morning, then swimming for both enjoyment and exercise.

As pre-adolescents on the boardwalk at Orchard Beach, we noticed our first bikini. This was enough to launch us into a fidgety, nerdy nervousness, distracted only by a steady swim or another walk down the mud flats.

When we strolled, smelling of Coppertone and squinting against the sun, we discussed stickball swings and exciting lives ahead as rock drummers or ballplayers, all against the din of 100,000 other beachgoers.

Like different species of shorebirds that mingled on a mudflat, we often ambled into the presence of the tide-line taster. As he grew older, so did we. One of my brothers, saddled with significant birth defects and great heartache, turned his life over to drugs and crime. Several years ago, he vanished into the bowels of the city, and none of us went looking for him.

Also carrying his share of pain, my other brother, after a military career, told the rest of us to cease contact. He disappeared, too.

Today I have a family of my own. Here in the Ocean State, we prefer a nature-laden stretch of sand early in the day, where the children surf the waves. Sometimes the four of us walk leisurely, collecting small rocks and shells.

I've never been back to Orchard Beach in the summer. That would hurt, I think. It would be akin, maybe, to what another boy felt 40 years ago, biting down on a sharp object.

ONE BIRD CHANGES TWO LIVES
September 27, 2008

Sometime during the night of Sept. 6, the ghost of tropical storm Hanna snapped off a thick, dead limb from the street tree out front.

The branch, which had previously reached toward our bedroom window, hit the ground with a vibrating crack, scattering both rotted wood and carpenter ants.

The dawn before the storm, a northern flicker visited the limb to feed on the ants. At one point, the bird unleashed its loud "peah" call, which resonated in our bedroom like a fire alarm.

Lying in bed in that first light of day, I thought of how the flicker had once represented a ray of hope for me, and how the bird had also changed the life of the late, great naturalist, artist, ornithologist and educator, Roger Tory Peterson.

Said Peterson, "Very often a single bird will get a person started bird watching. In my case it was a flicker that I saw when I was eleven, which I thought was dead—it was just a bundle of brown feathers. All of a sudden it exploded into life. That was the crucial moment of my life. I was overwhelmed by the contrast between something that was so vital and something I had taken for dead. Ever since that day I've felt that birds are the most vivid expression of life. Birds symbolize freedom, and I think that is why bird watching is so important to so many people."

Peterson grew up in Jamestown, New York, about 500 miles north and west of where I was raised in the Bronx. As a young man, Peterson moved to New York City, where he worked his way through art school.

In New York, Peterson associated with an assemblage of local fellows also spellbound by birds. That group was called the Bronx County Bird Club.

Besides Peterson, many of the young men in that Club, such as Ludlow Griscom and Alan Cruickshank, went on to distinguished bird-centered careers as ornithologists, conservationists, activists and photographers. For the rest of their lives, these "boys" influenced and supported one another in their endeavors.

At age 19, I discovered the flicker. This was during the late spring of 1977, when I shared an apartment with two of my brothers. We lived in the same apartment in which we'd grown up, in which my mother was raised, in what had degraded into a decayed stretch of the Bronx.

Starting in May, I worked the 5 a.m. to 1:30 p.m. shift at a local golf course, returning to college in mid-August. Each morning, my arrival at work would coincide with the departure of "the ghost," as we called him, a fellow who climbed the front gate before dawn to sprint the fairways, whacking a golf ball along the way, and disappearing into the pre-dawn mists.

I'd survived my upbringing partly through crackerjack observation skills. Often I was the first to see a gun tucked into a waistband or a gang coming along to bust heads. In the summer of 1977, I used those observation skills to expand my place in the world. The trigger was a lone bird that flashed golden wings on a golf course fairway.

With borrowed binoculars and field guide I determined that the bird was a yellow-shafted flicker, now called northern flicker. It was a male, with a black mustache, gray crown and red chevron on the back of the head. The yellow shafts of the primary flight feathers produced the "golden wings."

Out of nowhere my space now included glittering creatures, not just struggling or desperate people, with whom I believed I shared a common destiny.

During the blackout in July 1977, the apartment building across the street burned. Rioters looted and torched the supermarket, Laundromat and candy store.

For the rest of the summer the narrow tree-lined fairways and rolling terrain of the golf course became a sanctuary from the reek of wet embers.

That August, my younger brother lost his girlfriend to a gang leader, and in revenge, stole the guy's red Pontiac Firebird.

The day after I left for college (my older brother had departed for school, as well), the gang battered down the front door and obliterated the apartment. My younger brother fled up the fire escape and across the roof. My family gave up the lease after 40 years.

Among gang members, "Ghost Town" is slang for the Bronx. In the summer of 1977, I could have become another Bronx specter, but I didn't, thanks, in part, to a flicker.

LESSONS LEARNED AT CAMP
July 17, 2010

Forty years ago this month, I attended weekday summer camp at Henry Kaufmann Campgrounds about 45 minutes north of our West Bronx neighborhood.

There were ball fields and open shelters, a couple of ponds, swimming pools, and a forest.

Soon after camp started, I contracted the flu. After a few days back at home, I returned to camp thinner and weaker, with a doctor's note, indicating a hiatus from swimming.

Somehow I also got out of arts and crafts, the substitute activity for non-swimmers. That's when I met the year-younger Eddie, who simply refused to participate in anything scheduled.

Each day, during swim/craft hour, we headed for nature, turning over moist logs for salamanders or searching ponds for tadpoles.

Like many other kids at camp, Eddie came from a single-parent home. His mother did not work, having been abandoned by her husband. Eddie and his mom lived on welfare and philanthropy, on a street off the lower Grand Concourse, a once glorious neighborhood, freefalling into chaos and want.

Eddie liked to share his enthusiasm for amphibians and reptiles, birds, flowers, and trees. But most campers could care less. Maybe that was why Eddie spoke in a loud voice—he wanted someone to take notice.

I can still hear Eddie in his powerful New York accent, shouting "dese, dem and dose" on the bus, as he described a red-spotted newt.

With each adventure, I regained stamina and strength. The escapades fed my imagination and presented new feelings of freedom and wonder to me.

Our favorite nature place was a rocky stream, where we turned over rocks, searching for crayfish.

When we found one, we would examine it and then return the creature to the water. Every crayfish seemed miraculous.

One midsummer swim hour, Eddie showed another side. That day, as we stood on a stone ledge over the stream, we spotted a plump two-foot-long garter snake swimming across the water.

The snake wriggled past us, its pattern of yellow stripes on brown clearly visible.

We had never seen a wild snake before. It was a creature of our loftiest outdoor dreams, the king of our untamed natural fantasies.

As I watched the reptile, I did not notice that Eddie was hoisting a large rock over his head. Just as Eddie lobbed the stone, I turned toward him. His eyes blazed with a rapturous look.

Eddie, the eccentric, sensitive kid, who also happened to steer clear of all sports, so much so that he would not have known how to put on a baseball glove, hit the snake directly. The animal went under, came up oozing yellow liquid, turned over on its back and floated downstream.

"Why did you do that?" I shouted, as I hopped off the outcrop and chased after the snake. I caught up with it quickly, but the animal was dead. Eddie just stared at me and said, "I don't know."

My doctor's note had said that I could return to the pool, only no one at camp but me had seemed to remember. That afternoon, I decided to go back to swimming.

Eddie did not revisit the pool with me. I am not sure how he spent swim/craft hour the rest of the summer.

I felt guilty about abandoning Eddie. He was 10 years old, and what kid his age did not want to crush something?

Maybe I was overly sensitive. But at the time, Eddie's moment of aggression was too close to the spontaneous and unpredictable violence that I lived with on the streets and within my family circle.

Swimming suddenly seemed stable, sensible, structured and safe.

That summer I discovered that spending time outdoors imparted health-giving properties. Simultaneously, a seed of awareness also sprouted inside me, suggesting that staying away from unhealthy behaviors was equally as important to my long-term vitality and survival.

PEACE OUT, NIGHTHAWKS
August 15, 2003

At some stage in grade school, most city boys develop an overwhelming urge to find what is left of Mother Earth amid the brick and concrete of their daily lives.

For me, that meant seeking out small strips of weedy terrain that were too rocky to build on, or the occasional patch of neglected parkland. My greatest find, however, would not be on the ground.

During that stage, 40 years ago, I spent summer evenings nestled on a windowsill of our third-floor apartment. One young night, amid the comings and goings below, I heard a nasal *peenting* overhead—a rough toot coming from the milky sky. No one took me seriously when I told them something was up there.

It was not until I was a teenager, sitting on a stoop one evening, that I glimpsed a silhouette banking past a street lamp. I waited, and my reward was the first clear view of a robin-sized brown bird with long-tapered wings, each marked by a white patch. Suddenly, my cityscape had expanded to the heavens.

Within days, I went to the public library, thumbed through my first field guide, and found that this mysterious creature was a bug-eating, rooftop-breeding common nighthawk.

Later, as a young adult, I discovered that nighthawks picked off insects around the lights in Fenway and other ballparks. I also learned that they gathered in large flocks in late summer, migrating south until dispersing mysteriously into South America.

But like so much of what was once common in nature, nighthawks have become a rarity.

From St. Louis to Bangor, it is now quite unusual to spot the bird during breeding season. Like the peculiar night creatures they are, their evaporation confounds ornithologists. Scientists and bird watchers are asking if the birds are affected by a loss of greenspace, particularly wetlands. Is it the widespread use of pesticides? Global warming? Has development disrupted nighthawk wintering grounds?

I want my youngsters, ages 6 and 3, to see and hear a nighthawk. But the once common common nighthawk is yet another species of flora and fauna—from frogs to ferns to fowl—that is vanishing in my lifetime. I pray these species are not "canaries in a coal mine," their decline suggesting that we are poisoning our place in the name of progress.

This summer, I learned through the birders' grapevine that a territorial nighthawk was being heard nightly near Wayland Square, in the East Side of Providence. We live a few miles away. One late evening, after the kids were asleep, I heard faint *peents* in the distance. I stepped into the backyard and within five minutes a nighthawk had appeared—twisting and turning as it snatched insects from midair. The children missed it.

In late August across North America, nighthawks will draw together and head south. Just one or two birds will originate from Rhode Island. For many birdwatchers, this migration ritual is now the only chance to glimpse a nighthawk. Look up, if you get the chance. Life in the night sky is precious and fleeting.

Season's Signs Seep
into the Soul
March 25, 2011

I rediscovered the brilliance, color and passion of spring after nibbling on one of the garlic chives that provide fresh greenery to the garden this time of year.

The mild, scallion-like flavor and smell transported me back to March 1983, when a widowed, dark-eyed, dark-haired Italian immigrant mother of two cooed over me as lividly as an adolescent.

Rosetta reminded me of Sophia Loren, but in an apron, dusted in flour, and scented with fresh garlic.

I was 24 and Rosetta was about 35. She owned and operated a bakery that produced buttery, flaky, chocolate- and cream-filled pastries.

That year, I worked as a New York City gardener in greenhouses roughly five blocks from her shop.

Rosetta spied me the first time I entered. She stepped out from the back of the store to take my order for cannoli and sfogliatella (a clam-shaped flaky pastry with a lemon-ricotta filling).

As spring blossomed in extravagance, Rosetta came to the counter each time I arrived. Some might consider it a reversal of roles, but I felt like an unfurling flower, and Rosetta the bee eager to crawl inside.

"You know, she's got a thing for you," said a fellow gardener, as the young girls behind the pastry cases giggled.

At one point, Rosetta asked me as loudly as a teen-ager, if I would date her. Beautiful, sensual and hardworking, Rosetta was a great catch. But I just wanted her biscotti.

61

I left the garden to find more signs of the new season.

My first stop was the pussy willows in a tiny wetland of tinkling freshwater adjacent to Watchemoket Cove in East Providence.

Dozens of bleached-white flowers topped olive-colored new growth. The blooms looked like reversed teardrops of snow pointing toward the sky.

The pussy willows were as soft a material as I could remember touching with my fingertips.

Staghorn sumac and black willow grew in the foreground. The sumac also featured velvet-like foliage, with reddish-brown down covering the stems like the silky smooth layer atop the antlers of a male deer.

The bright, golden-bronze-and-orange young stems of black willow looped skyward. They looked a little bit like the arms of a 10-foot-wide candelabrum.

A moist, earthy pungency scented the wetland, which I left for an adjacent field rimmed by trembling aspen. The deep-red and sticky scales of the aspen's buds splayed into gray-black clusters of hair-like flowers, which ascended, as well. The field smelled of sun-heated grass.

When I returned home, Karen and I headed out to walk the Ten Mile River Greenway, also in East Providence.

Sunshine warmed our faces. Hand in hand, we followed the rise and fall of the curving path. Scanning the edge and shallow water of a small pond, we counted four wood frogs. At a second, larger pond, we found seven painted turtles basking on a log.

Re-learning the magnificence of spring is a sign of aging that I would prefer to recast as a blessing, because it allows me to savor a renewed exhilaration of the season and to embrace an accompanying sense of wonder.

As the Roman poet Virgil, said, "every calamity is to be overcome by endurance."

VALUE OF AN ANCIENT TREE
November 18, 2016

After their petite leaflets drop like golden confetti each fall, honey locust trees hold on to dangling, twisty, brown seed pods. Native to the Midwest, honey locust is a widely planted ornamental and street tree.

Some folks say the thin, winding pods look like leather straps. They remind me of salamis hanging behind the deli counters of my youth.

As a kid, growing up in the Bronx, I collected a few fallen honey locust pods in a local park late one fall. In our apartment, I extracted the seeds from the sweet-smelling pulp from within the pod and planted them. But they didn't grow.

Years later, I learned that the hard coat around a honey locust seed must be broken for the seed to germinate. You could file down the seed coat, soak the seed in corrosive liquid, or boil the seed in water and then let it swell in size in the cooling liquid.

In its native habitat, such as the stream valleys of Southern Indiana, thick-branched thorns cover the main trunk and lower branches of a honey locust. Some of the thorns are more than six inches long.

However, almost all ornamental honey locusts—like the ones we see in southern New England—are thornless forms of the tree. Honey locust is popular because it is both easy to plant and grows relatively quickly. It tolerates compacted soil, drought, flooding, air pollution and road salt. I've found robust honey locusts growing out of tree pits the size of doormats.

Many thousands of years ago, the vicious thorns on a honey locust protected a tree's foliage from giant ground sloths and other now-gone large mammals, which fed on pods that fell to the ground.

It was in the digestive systems of these animals that the hard coats of honey locust seeds began to break down. Today in the tree's native habitat, it is most often cows that eat the pods and poop out/disperse the seeds.

The other day, I stood beside a honey locust tree on traffic-rich Angell Street between Prospect and Congdon streets in Providence.

Hundreds of pods hung from the tree. I smelled the sweet scent of fermenting honey squeezed out of fallen pods by vehicle tires. It was a scent I remembered from childhood. Some of the dangling pods in the tree crown rattled in the wind.

To belong somewhere, an object either alive or inanimate must have value. I value the honey locust for its shade, foliage and pods, And, for the memory of a child, extracting seeds from sweet-smelling honey to plant in a third-floor-apartment-window-sill pot in the hope that they would grow.

PELHAM BAY AND PIZZA
January 23, 2016

New York nature nurtured us on a recent run to John F. Kennedy International Airport.

Our trip was to transport Rachel to a tour group departing for a two-week tour of Israel.

Although we were happy for Rachel that she was headed overseas, we also felt trepidation about sending her off to the Middle East.

And in the short term, we had to drive down Interstate 95, which is the region's version of running the gauntlet. A trip down that highway can freak out the fiercest road warrior. So, while on a map, a trip from Providence to Kennedy Airport takes three hours, we budgeted six.

Well, we lucked out. Within 2.5 hours of leaving home, we were in The Bronx, the northernmost borough in New York, and where I grew up.

Still struggling with a taut-string disposition, I suggested we stop off for some soothing scenery in Pelham Bay Park, which at close to 3,000 acres is the largest city-park property in New York.

You can see parts of Pelham Bay from the interstate. Among its many natural attributes, the park is where the rocky New England coastline ends in stretches of gneiss-based bedrock, rich in quartz.

We wound through wetlands, woods and reclaimed and replanted land. Given it was late morning in winter there were few people on the paths that paralleled the road, but lots of gulls and other waterfowl in the coves.

This stop-off included an extra slice of comfort in the form of pizza at a place we know on City Island off The Bronx coast.

We arrived just as the day's first pies came out of the oven. Each slice was huge, with rich sauce, reviving spices, flavorful crust, copious and gooey cheese and a nice amount of oil.

Who knew this snack would become like suet to keep our bodies warm? Back on the road we arrived at Kennedy two hours before the tour-gathering time, so we swung a little west and south from the airport to Rockaway Beach.

At City Island, comparatively gentle Long Island Sound surrounded us. Now we faced the resounding Atlantic Ocean. It was chilly, but calm at City Island. At Rockaway, there was winter wind.

On the mudflat, we walked past herring, ring-billed and greater black-backed gulls. They were tossing and tearing apart crabs, with the greater black-backed gulls physically and vocally dominating the feeding.

I found it unusual that the birds were squabbling over meaty blue crabs. Blue crabs inhabit bays and estuaries, although females often winter in the saltier water of inlets. Moreover blue crabs spend the winter in mud.

But given the relatively mild winter weather to that point, maybe blue crabs were still active in the inlets just a few blocks from the ocean side of Rockaway, and the gulls were carrying the crabs to the mudflats to feed.

Robust crab legs and other crab bits dotted the wet sand, along with hundreds of shells. In fact, there were an amazing variety of small shells in the short stretch of mud in which we walked.

Shells came from mussels; whelks; moon snails; razor clams; jingles in charcoal, gold, orange and yellow; tiny clams with bands of blue or orange; and scallops in black, blue, red or striped in a beautiful shade of dark orange. After some rooting around, it was time to deliver Rachel.

At the terminal, we said our farewells, and left, feeling like we could exhale for the first time that day.

Two doses of nature and one measure of pizza kept us on the straight and narrow. Familiarity and comfort moderated our moods, getting us through a stressful trip and preparing us for the ride home.

GETTING OUTSIDE
FOR YOUR OWN GOOD
April 7, 2019

When I was some six years old, hanging out on a Bronx street corner with friends roughly twice my age, I looked up the block to spy another band of boys, bats and belts in hand, headed to attack my buddies.

"Look," I shouted to warn of the approaching gang.

Then I took off, skedaddling up three flights of stairs to our family's apartment, as a gang fight ensued outside.

Today, I use the same skills to sense the world around me. Take last Tuesday evening on Hope and Fourth streets in Providence, when over the racket of voices and vehicular traffic, I heard a chirp.

Instantly my brain ran through bird calls typical for the time and place—house sparrow, American robin, European starling, northern cardinal. It was none of the above.

Then I remembered that the day was April 3, and the bird was right on schedule—my first osprey of the season. Indeed, I looked up to observe a large bird circling maybe 200 feet overhead. It featured a slender body and long narrow and curved wings.

"Seeing" matters deeply in both nature and human study. I think back to a stickball game during childhood, when I noticed that a teenager had a pistol tucked into his waistband under his shirt.

As I started to walk away, the young man and a neighbor, who was standing right next to me, began arguing. The teen, stinking drunk, pulled out the gun and shot the neighbor in the shoulder. The blood flowing down the man's chest looked like a map of the Hudson River and its tributaries.

My senses developed as a matter of survival. As a kid, I saw the drug deals that took place between folks shaking hands and the fingertip brushes between cheating spouses. I also grew keen to the sound of my father's voice and footsteps in our apartment.

Dad communicated primarily through his fists. Early, I learned to stay far enough away from him that he had to lunge to grab me.

Once when I was in fourth grade, dad stepped past me in our living room, and before I could sprint away, he socked me so hard it knocked the wind out of me. My mother, comforting me as I heaved, said my dad's blow was his way of showing me attention. It was his form of love, she said.

Looking back at my childhood, I can see that getting out of the apartment and into the local parks of the west-central Bronx saved me both mentally and physically.

To this day, survival remains a primary theme in my nature writing. Often, I write to give voice to flora and fauna dispensable by the next bulldozer or chainsaw.

Nature writing is also deeply sensual. You listen as a bird chirps, or as wind rustles tree crowns. You watch silvery herring climb fish ladders, or touch a moon snail crawling past your feet in shallow seawater. Seeing, hearing, and sometimes touching, smelling and tasting are all deeply personal.

Spring brings an outburst of life in which to find moments of detail to stretch out, to explore meanings and to share feelings. This time of year is so dynamic that every interaction outdoors can seem story worthy.

Dear readers, it is time to get outside, and associate with and appreciate the growing number of life forms surrounding us with each passing day.

SUMMERS OF FANTASY AND IMAGERY
June 27, 2009

Sometimes a young mind explodes in response to the freedom of June.

So it was during the days of summer school vacation long ago, when I found myself following a sun-deprived canyon between monolithic apartment buildings to a tall, narrow passageway of ancient smooth stones.

From an adjacent alleyway, I heard a young voice say "Get him," and a local gang of rough, unforgiving boys sprinted toward me.

Through the holes on the bottom of my sneakers I felt the searing breath of these juvenile thugs, as I climbed the slick rock wall straight to the top.

With the strength of a thousand street-corner hustlers, I somersaulted over the structure, as the menaces slid back one by one to the dank, putrid cement below.

On the other side, I landed on my feet in a prairie of tall sunflowers and fresh air that enveloped an orchard of cherry trees laden with fruit gulped down by birds of neon orange, purple and yellow.

Famished, I fed on plump, juicy cherries, spitting seeds in fun at striped, spangled and sequined butterflies that brightened the shadows.

Thirsty, I dipped cupped hands into the cold, clear stream burbling by the trees.

Once full, I removed my sneakers and socks to soothe my sore feet. I stretched out to observe the sapphire sky framed by feather-shaped foliage. Clouds of seafaring seals, serpents and squid drifted across the blue curtain.

Several species of small mammals, including chipmunks, ferrets, marmots and prairie dogs bedded down beside me. A soft light covered both flora and fauna, and I floated on a feather-bed-like current of fluffy foliage to a carefree sleep.

That story is fiction, of course, the product of a child's imagination in reaction to the wider and wilder world around him.

As a youngster, I needed summer time in green space, and I found it around the corner in a ribbon of rock and crabgrass called the Old Croton Aqueduct Trail. Sloping down from a sidewalk interrupted every so often by a park bench, the stony outer walls of the tunnel made for all sorts of inventive climbing adventures.

Finished in 1842, the Old Croton Aqueduct was the first extensive source of drinking water for New York City. In my part of the world, the Aqueduct ran for several miles, linking neighborhoods north to south through the west Bronx.

During my childhood summers, the Aqueduct was an escape route to solace and soul searching. I believed there were better places in the world, and that one day I would reach them via the Aqueduct Trail.

With their school year finally over, my own youngsters have begun their roaming season together and with friends. The backyard is green, and the shrubbery, compost bins and wood piles all contain secrets.

There are city parks in four directions and just a few blocks away. May the children dream in all of these places, and make the best of this most innocent and liberating time in their lives.

RHODE ISLAND

PEAR TREE PARABLE
September 15, 2007

The Greek poet Homer called the pear a "gift of the gods." To that, riders at an outbound stop of the Union Avenue RIPTA bus in Providence say, "Amen."

Because right across the street is a fruit-laden tree, which has riders and passersby asking, "May we have a pear?" in English, Hmong, Spanish, Portuguese, Vietnamese and other languages.

"It (the tree) transcends culture and language," says Deborah, whose husband, Eddie, planted the tree just inside their sidewalk fence. "Everyone wants a pear."

Discovering a lush fruit tree on the block puts a smile on the face of most urbanites. The Providence pear is a one-tree, no-fee, pick-your-own orchard.

Eddie planted the pear in Spring 2002, seven months after the couple moved into the neighborhood. Then, it was a five-foot-tall stick. Even so, it produced fruit a year later.

Today, the tree is 15 feet tall and the same length wide. Loaded down with fruit, it resembles someone struggling to hold an over-laden shopping bag in each hand.

One pear at a time, the tree has built community. Deborah and Eddie developed their "Hi neighbor, have a pear," philosophy after individuals began ringing the doorbell to ask for a fruit. People who didn't speak English pointed to the tree.

"It seems to us that in some other countries, neighbors plant, pick, eat and share more homegrown fruit than most Americans," Eddie said. "The tree has become a kind of symbol of our time in the Armory."

The couple moved into their 1870s Mansard-roofed Victorian double in 2001. Except for a wide-crowned 130-year-old Copper Beech, which takes four adults to get their arms around, the property was bare.

Eddie planted trees to provide protection from the sun and the glaring concrete and to "create a secluded atmosphere to enjoy the outdoors." At their previous home in Berkeley, Calif., they planted or tended lemon, peach, apple and pear trees.

Trees provide air, blossoms, fruit, leaves, nuts, shade and shelter. They hold the soil so powerfully that they are a metaphor for life. Trees mark both milestones and bumps in the road.

"I know that in many cultures a spiritual gift is often the planting of a tree somewhere other than where one lives," Eddie said. Fruit, as well, symbolizes regeneration. This month, for example, Jews mark the New Year by dipping apples in honey.

Eddie loves the book, The Giving Tree, by the late Shel Silverstein. The Giving Tree chronicles the lifelong relationship between one person and an apple tree, and has been translated into more than 30 languages.

For professional reasons, Deborah and Eddie plan to move some day. But they won't miss the pear, because neighbors will continue to enjoy it. "Wherever we go we will plant more fruit trees," Eddie said.

For the time being, a new parable is being written about people, trees and the human condition, at a bus stop in the heart of Providence.

Nature and
Breaking a Cycle of Violence
June 12, 2010

On an easel at Temple Beth El this morning you will find a picture of our daughter Rachel. In it she rests on her haunches, looking like a Great Plains cowboy, atop a boulder at Second Beach in Middletown.

Rachel was about 5 years old when we took that picture. She stared into the camera deeply, returning her gaze to the sea, after we snapped the shot.

As an infant, Rachel rode in a backpack on a walking tour of snowy Blackstone Park.

She remained asleep in that carrier when I slipped off riprap into Narragansett Bay, landing straight up on my feet in the muck.

Rachel's first words were an emphatic "I like it." Her most common expression was an innocent, "Again?"

So, when we lifted her into an apple tree to smell the blossoms, she asked "Again?" after we put her down. "Again?" was also what we heard in the fall after we hoisted Rachel into the same tree to hold her face against the cool, smooth apples.

Today, Rachel will become a bat mitzvah. She will sing from the Torah in a ritual synonymous to becoming a Jewish adult. Her chant, with its syllable- and word-emphasizing trope, will sound a lot like a bird's song to me.

When I was Rachel's age, Saturday's meant attending synagogue, followed by adventures with my companions to local parks or other green spaces.

Often these escapades took on the spirit of fantasy such as when we pretended to "mountain climb" the stones that sleeved the Old Croton Aqueduct tunnel.

Going to synagogue and getting outdoors were similar; chances to unwind, appreciate, heal, mourn or otherwise ponder one's place in the world.

When Rachel began her Bat Mitzvah study, we listed words that mattered to us.

They included "compassion, hope, tolerance, inclusion, responsibility, respect, kindness, goodness, mercy, loyalty and humility."

In my history, those words also apply to childhood companions whose inner lights dimmed too soon.

Because we were the only practicing Jews in the neighborhood, contemporaries beat, belittled, kicked and spat on us in the streets. At times, our home lives were not much better. Synagogue and green spaces were our sanctuaries.

One of my mates, mop-headed Steven, was stabbed on the street, the knife wrenched upward, because, one of his attackers said, "He was a Jew."

Formerly, Steven was a giddy pal, who liked to drape an arm over your shoulder. After the attack, he was sullen. I never saw him smile again.

Then there was Michael, a slight, quiet, loyal fellow. A half dozen boys jumped him one afternoon on our block, tying his hands and feet together, and dragging him through a curbside of dog feces. The youngsters chanted, "Kill the Jew."

Cheerful Michael became a frightened kid, his spirit broken.

After the attacks, Steven and Michael's families withdrew their children from both Hebrew and public school, packed up and left the neighborhood. Saturdays were never the same.

Today Rachel will wear the same prayer shawl that I donned for my Bar Mitzvah 39 years ago. Fringes and knots on that garment will tie her to my childhood pals, who never got the chance to take responsibility for their futures the way that their forebearers intended, as Rachel will do today.

Rachel will sing this morning, as freely as any bird in the forest or field. I will shed tears of happiness for her, for us, and as a witness to the breaking a cycle of harshness and violence in my life.

When Rachel and I end our daddy-daughter dance tonight at a small after-service party, should I ask, "Again?"

Otherwise, I pray that tomorrow we end up outdoors together, in peace. Again.

SEEING THE WORLD
THROUGH YOUNGER EYES
October 11, 2008

Recently I walked the two miles home from work with my eight-year-old son. I'd wanted to take the bus, but he suggested hoofing it.

"What can we do when we walk?" I asked. "We can talk," he said.

So we headed up Thayer Street in Providence, with Noah explaining the difference between *Star Wars* characters that seemed to me to come and go with each movie. As we passed Avon Cinema, he stopped in mid sentence to identify a turkey vulture soaring west to east at a fairly high altitude over our heads.

Outside Moses Brown School, Noah picked up a spiky triangular nut dropped from a copper beech tree. "Do people eat these?" he asked. "Squirrels do," I replied.

On the school grounds we heard a Killdeer. This is a type of bird in the group called plovers. We found the Killdeer standing between yardage markers on the artificial turf of the football field. Did the bird, which eats ground insects such as grasshoppers, know the ground under its feet was synthetic?

A couple of blocks north on Morris Avenue, I raised my arm to point out a patch of dill planted along the sidewalk. Noah took the gesture as "let's hold hands." He grasped my fingers in his. A huge smile on my face, I decided not to mention the dill. We walked home hand in hand.

A few days later, we escorted his sister, Rachel, 11, to a late afternoon "play date" several blocks from our home.

Along Intervale Road, the flowering dogwood trees were ripe with clusters of shiny red berries, an important food for migrating birds and other wildlife.

While Noah and Rachel recreated their most awesome soccer moves, I suggested that the two of them tiptoe toward a fruit-laden dogwood, covered in red and purple leaves.

Just before the children reached the tree, a dozen or so iridescent bronze and purple grackles exploded from deep within the foliage. The kids howled in delight.

Three hours later I escorted Rachel home. We crossed the street, where she said, "Look!" There was a slug the size of a cigar. Its sidewalk trail glistened in the moonlight between a stonewall and a strip of grass.

By habit, I guess, Rachel reached out and took my hand. She suggested that we count the different types of cricket chirps. We noted several steady songsters, a couple of slower chirpers, a lone insect that emitted an occasional "tick" sound and another that produced an intermittent sequence of "clicks."

The East Side was relatively quiet, which allowed us to perceive the irregular "chip," "zeet," or "zip" calls of migrating songbirds in the darkened sky overhead. Most songbirds migrate at night.

Near home, we stopped to admire the neighborhood's most unusual planting—tobacco. This was not the showy, sweet-smelling garden center variety, but the genuine, lettuce-leaved former staple of the Southern economy.

In the days following those strolls, I realized that opening my hand to the children opened my heart. It shrank my ego, renewed my spirit, and left me awestruck.

LEARNING ALONG THE ROCKY COAST
October 24, 2009

In the nadir of the anarchic '70s, I spent seventh grade in an all-boys public junior high school in the South Bronx in New York City. Based on my skin color and religion, peers separated me into a category they considered sub-human.

Earlier this month I spent time outside with seventh graders in the PEGASUS program at LaSalle Academy in Providence.

At a time in their lives when young people search for identity, often by slicing off cohorts into subsets of color, class, race or religion, PEGASUS engages them in a yearlong exploration of the connections and interactions that mark their place in the world.

Like a spice seller, Haley Carlisle spread samples of soil across granite bedrock at her feet, each small pile representing a layer in the cliff at Black Point in Narragansett.

Carlisle leaned through gnat-like insects dancing in her face and the dangling roots of seaside goldenrod to gently brush aside sediment surrounding a 30-pound rock embedded in the overhang.

A monarch butterfly floated past and trees swallows swooped within ten feet. "This is glacial till," Carlisle said, pointing to the samples. "The big rock is a glacial erratic. It's different from the sediment.

Glacial ice carried it here."

For their assignment, Carlisle and PEGASUS classmates served as scientists. It is one of several roles they play during their look at their place in the world.

This year, PEGASUS is responding to the question, "Who am I?" through activities that involve interacting, understanding and participating.

Answering "Who am I?" involves looking together at connections with family, government, school and the greater world, said Anne Ejnes, leader and teacher.

Studying natural science is as much about finding a phylum and family for a species as it is determining how the species connects to life around it, she said.

With a field book in one hand and a *National Audubon Society Field Guide to Seashore Creatures* in the other, Biagio DeSimone lay prone on a slab of granite examining seaweed, wrack and slime on bedrock exposed to air at low tide and underwater at high tide.

"My family visits here twice a year," he said. "I want to know what I'm looking at during those trips."

Several of DeSimone's classmates removed and returned items to a tidal pool, including crabs, periwinkles and sea stars with tube feet that undulated like the tide.

Matthew Pontikes showed me a red-bearded sponge, a fleshy creature with dozens of small, root-like, intertwined branches. Teacher Jeff Danielian oversaw the activities, designed to examine the structure of scientific inquiry. Fieldwork, research and study cut across curricular areas, from biology to communications, language arts to social studies, he said.

The students discussed their observations, answered questions and presented findings. Each group took five minutes to speak. There were no power struggles, name-calling incidents or raised voices.

Each presentation underscored the relationships surrounding the students. For example, the bedrock exposed by erosion held water fed by tides. The resulting pools harbored sea and insect life, attracting gulls and other birds.

Unexpectedly a woman fishing behind a towering wall of granite let out a shout. I left the students, climbed around the stone and found her pulling in a five-pound tautog. She dropped the plump fish into a tidal-pool crevice. The animal was charcoal-blue on the back and sides, and gray on the belly.

Beyond, on the horizon, I saw varying sized sailing vessels, plus two cargo ships.

Danielian authored the recent book, *Enriching the Young Naturalist: The Nature of a Science Classroom*. His mantra is to bring exploration and discovery to the classroom by sending students into the outdoors to study the beauty and wonder of the natural world.

Earlier that morning, Danielian had shown me a granite boulder sheared at the point of a quartz vein, revealing a six-foot-tall seam. "Most people only get to see the surface," he said, which also suggested to me how some of us view the world.

The crystal vein of pink and orange was a slice of heaven. It suggested that we are all in the same boat. We face common challenges, and we need to work together to solve our problems.

EMBRACING A
REFRESHING CHANGE
September 11, 2010

I f a cold front ever ushered in the feeling of a fresh start, it was the one that pushed Hurricane Earl east overnight Sept. 4.

Just after dawn, I walked with Woody, the dog, into a nippy, northwest wind that transported wet leaves down the street. There, we all met the day's first rays of sunlight, which burned through the low milky gray clouds that trailed the storm. The sky overhead turned robin's egg blue.

Gone was the heat and humidity that had wrapped us like a lead blanket most of the summer. Cobwebs slipped from my brain, telling my limbs to "shake it loose." So I stretched my arms toward the sky.

The sunlight hit the sidewalk, illuminating dozens of acorns that had fallen from a neighbor's red oak, which now rustled loudly.

What a cap to a wild week. School had begun for Karen, a firstgrade teacher, for Rachel (eighth grade) and Noah (fifth). I wrapped up a nine-month project at my job.

In addition, our kitchen ceiling came down one night, after leaky pipes under the second-floor bathroom weakened 4,000 pounds of material.

For now, we will use the closet-sized bathroom and shower stall on the first floor.

By the way, having two bathrooms was a luxury I realized that I took for granted. Heck, 40 percent of the world's population live without access to any toilet!

After Woody and I returned from the walk, I opened every downstairs window. The cold front flushed the rooms with fresh air.

Opening the windows disturbed a pair of goldfinches working over the heads of a 12-foot sunflower next to our house.

In addition, a Carolina wren shot out of the pink-magenta-flowered Rose of Sharon and into a deep inconspicuous tunnel in the woodpile in the backyard.

I watched as the wren popped back out of its woodpile sanctuary. The bird then hopped atop the branches, flicked its tail, spun around, chipped, squawked and jibber-jabbered like a windup toy on caffeine.

Above the bouncing wren, a squirrel, with a mouthful of leaves, climbed up the maple tree. I figured that the rodent was on its way to fortify the family nest. Indeed, winter was coming, I remembered.

With every window I opened in our house that morning, cool air would levitate the curtains. Out with old and in with the new, as the saying goes.

Inhaling the fresh air expanded my lungs and my world. It suggested that our existence was about making our hearts and minds airier and roomier for those we loved.

The wren was like sugar in my coffee–adding sweetness to life.

After slogging through the sweltering past few months, the cold front was like a do-over—the kind we used to ask for as kids. Unharnessed now, I felt like I was being given another chance to get things right.

That night, Karen and I sipped honey vodka, a homemade gift from a friend. This was a syrupy, soul-warming drink—real nectar of the Gods.

The vodka sharpened our awareness and our joy. It also fueled the discussions we needed to have—about repairing our home and our lives in the coming weeks.

Nature Is Never Far Away
October 13, 2007

On the night of Oct. 5, 2007, millions of midges swarmed over downtown Cleveland, Ohio, descending onto Jacobs Field (now Progressive Field), the baseball home of the Indians, during a playoff game versus the New York Yankees.

Players from both teams waved their gloves and hats to fend off the insects. Midges covered the sweaty neck and back of Yankee pitcher Joba Chamberlain, and entered his nose and mouth.

The type of midge that took the field is sometimes erroneously called a Canadian soldier (The real insect Canadian soldier are Lake Erie's mayflies.). The insect, which looks somewhat like a mosquito, shows up regularly during warmer months along Lake Erie. The midge appearance that night was the worst that locals could remember.

As we watched the spectacle on TV, a scent so powerful drifted through the window that our eyes watered. The night provided striking evidence that urbanites remain tied to nature. Although our story wasn't as exciting as that involving the midges, it was dramatic to us. The animal playing the lead role here was a striped skunk.

One of the most familiar species of suburban wildlife, the striped skunk is leaving its mark in our cities. It seems like almost every Rhode Island urbanite has a skunk tale.

First up is Cranston, where a woman in the Edgewood neighborhood sets out a bowl of milk for feral cats. Two blocks away, a mother striped skunk and five weaned young emerge from beneath a back porch to search for food. The party of six works its way toward the milk, using homes, buildings and other structures for cover.

Striped skunks sleep in burrows during the day. They eat a wild variety of items, from small mammals to bees to fruit. Insects make up nearly 70 percent of their diet. In some communities, skunks control the populations of lawn grubs and other bugs.

However, if the cat lady of Cranston puts out milk, striped skunks, depending upon the time of year and the resources available, will drink it.

In the Blackstone neighborhood of Providence, a barbecue halts when a lone male striped skunk waddles through a gap in the fence, literally stepping up to the plate.

Every evening this skunk comes out from under a tool shed that sits on half cinder blocks. The skunk meanders the same route through backyards, as do local children at play during the day. When he shows up, families stop their chats, put the dogs inside, admire the animal, enjoy the drama, and let him pass.

A woman who lives in the Summit neighborhood of Providence told me she found a starving skunk stuck inside her garbage can, which she tipped over to free the wobbly animal.

The woman didn't call the folks who cart away critters because she had spent childhood summers at a Matunuck beach house, where a skunk lived under the porch. Her family never evicted the animal. Instead they chose to enjoy the porch after the skunk had left for the evening.

This month I heard about a skunk that ambled into the backyard hut, called a Sukkah, where some Jews eat meals during the fall holiday of Sukkot.

A Warwick woman passed on word of a white skunk in Providence. A couple in Pawtucket said a skunk in their yard had a white tail and back stained yellow.

The striped skunk employs the well-known defense of scent spraying. Skunk scent is so potent that one neighbor told me it pulled him out of a deep sleep at 3 a.m. The man eventually fell back asleep. But his brain incorporated the odor into his dream.

The suburb-to-city spread of the striped skunk underscores that it is one of the Ocean State's most resourceful mammals. Nature is never far away. For some of us city slickers, it is right in our faces.

A Winter Woolly
February 17, 2019

The fuzzy orange-and-black woolly bear caterpillar curled into a ball atop my gloved hand.

We picked up the insect and moved it to the trailside to keep it from getting flattened on the William C. O'Neill Bike Path a half-mile south of the West Kingston Train Station in a section that passes beside and through the Great Swamp Management Area.

To the best of our memories, this was the first February woolly bear we'd found. Scientists know that these little creatures—icons of both fall and false weather predictions—can endure sub freezing conditions beneath leaf litter.

In response to cold conditions, a woolly bear goes into an insect-specific inactivity called quiescence. As part of this survival trait, the caterpillar produces large quantities of glycerol, which keeps its cells from rupturing when they freeze. Quiescence is reversible when the weather warms up. So if winter temperatures rise and fall regularly, the woolly bear will go into and out of inactivity. In spring a surviving woolly bear forms a cocoon and transforms into an Isabella tiger moth.

Our walk took place on a sunny, 35-degree afternoon in mid-February, during which a steady stream of bikers, skaters, strollers, dog walkers and others passed by.

At present, the Great Swamp is a great swamp—full of water. Where the sun shone, open water surrounded the red maples, which are ubiquitous in the giant wetland. In shadier spots, ice encased the base of the trees. Where there was a rise in elevation—even a few inches—oaks and white pines took hold, and ground pine carpeted the forest floor.

At a small waterfall, the water churned under the path in a chorus of burbles, babbles and trickles.

The Great Swamp may be a wetland wonderland, but it's probably best known as the site of the Great Swamp Fight in December 1675. Within the mire, Native Americans fought English settlers and their Native American allies in what *Encyclopedia Britannica* (EB) calls "one of the bloodiest conflicts (per capita) in U.S. history."

The battle is also called the Great Swamp Massacre, notes EB, because "Despite fierce resistance, the (Native American) fort was finally taken and burned; many elder Indians and women and children were burned alive." This was a deep, dark moment in Colonial history.

Our walk coincided with the publication of a global review that found the world's insects are on a pathway to extinction, and could vanish within 100 years. Given that insects govern our food production, pollinating plants and getting rid of bad bugs, and purify soil and water, and recycle waste through their above- and below-ground activities, the report suggests that the insect extinction will lead to the sooner or later disappearance of our own species. Simply put, we cannot live without bugs.

The study authors cited intensive agriculture, especially the heavy use of pesticides, as the main driver of the insect nose-dive. Other major factors include urbanization and climate change.

At a fenced-off cut in the swamp vegetation, where some sort of high-voltage electrical work was taking place, the forest edge hosted seven Eastern Bluebirds. In the sunshine, their backs, heads and wings were the color of blue sky, while their soft brown breasts and sides suggested the color of earth. Such shades in winter were astounding to witness, but I wondered how soon this and other bug-eating bird species would vanish along with the insects?

To the freshwater of the Great Swamp, we added salty tears.

Then I remembered the woolly bear; a tiny creature that can freeze and thaw repeatedly under the disarray of leaf litter on the forest floor before emerging into the open. That is quite a survival mechanism in our ever-harsh world. I wondered what tricks we humans had or needed to evolve, and quick, to survive and crawl out from under the mess we've made of our world.

SETTLING THE ACORN WAR
February 27, 2005

The Acorn War is over. For my family, that means we can feed the birds without fear of squirrels sacking the seed.

Like many conflicts, the Acorn War started through ignorance. In the fall of 1970, I was a 12-year-old living in New York City with a new slingshot. It was a beauty: sanded hickory handle, double-thick rubber bands, and a pouch cut from the tongue of a Converse high top. Acorns from the local oaks made perfect ammo. I hoarded every one. What I didn't understand was that the local squirrel family starved.

For the foolishness of a prepubescent boy, the Squirrel Nation exacted revenge. When my family moved from city apartment to suburban home a few years later, the local clan found its opening. In this case, it was our rotted roof shingles. The rodents' path to justice led straight to our attic.

We trapped and transported the transgressors, but they returned. We sealed the roof with steel wool, which they pilfered and used, for all we know, to scrub their pots and pans.

Now a young man, I assigned myself the task of protecting my family. I marched up the attic steps, BB rifle in hand. I shot a squirrel between the eyes, but he simply blinked and kept on chewing. I skulked back downstairs.

Today I have my own home and my own family. But the skirmishes continue. When we placed a bird feeder in the backyard, squirrels tore it down. We put it back up, protected by a plastic baffle. The squirrels chomped the baffle, and toppled the feeder. We used metal partitions, but the pests took those apart, possibly using power tools, and ripped down the feeder again.

Determined to win the battle, we bought a feeder armored with rubberized wire. The squirrels responded with reinforcements. Seven squirrels trounced the contraption, wrested the top off, gorged on the seed, and shredded the plastic. Within a week, all that remained was a metal shell, with much of the rubber chewed off, and a bit of wire.

Not feeding birds gnawed at us. When you live in the city, it's comforting to draw wild creatures to your home. We craved close encounters with nuthatches, not squirrels.

So one night I went out on a limb and snuck a small suction-cupped feeder onto the outside of the windowpane. When I drew the curtains the next morning, I faced a squirrel that had rappelled down the shingles and glass. Seeing the rat-like moth pressed against the pane, I shrieked like a schoolgirl.

That day I shelled out for a squirrel-proof feeder: a model that shuts its portals when a squirrel tries to reach in. It arrived, we installed it, and–

In a nutshell – it worked.

Don't fret. I am not starving squirrels again. Every morning, I spread birdseed across the lawn.

We settled the Acorn War the way we could, not necessarily the way we wanted, and everyone here is better for it. Come spring, I hope to report that we all wintered well.

CELEBRATING MUMMICHOG
May 7, 2011

In a memorable line from the movie, Toy Story 2, Jessie sees Woody and shouts excitedly, "It's you, it's you, it's really you!"

That was how I felt when Narragansett Bay Keeper John Torgan, of Save the Bay, held out his palm to show me a three-inch, flip-flopping olive-green backed, vertically striped fish called the common mummichog.

I contacted Save the Bay after watching something dapple the water's edge in the Blackstone Park/Swan Point cove on the Seekonk River in Providence.

At first, I thought I was hallucinating. Then, when the bay rippled on each side of me, I crouched at the shoreline and thought I saw what looked like little fish.

Even with sunglasses, I couldn't tell what was jiggling the water.

Torgan was kind enough to meet me at the site a couple of days later. He possesses a fisherman's eye, which is that well developed skill of looking at water and seeing what most of us don't.

With the tide out, we walked across mounds of salt marsh peat that were cloaked in ribbed mussels. Underfoot crackled last year's hollow stems of spartina, also called salt marsh hay. When I stepped on the mud, a soft-shelled clam squirted up.

Wearing boot-foot fishing waders, Torgan negotiated the lapping tide in places where the mud can suck you in. I stayed atop the peat.

Tall wooden rods anchored each end of Torgan's seining net. Lead weights held down the material, which was topped by floats.

Torgan gave me one side of the net. He held the other and tilted the device on a low angle, as we dropped the net into the water.

On our first couple of tries, the fish took off. But on the third seine, we collected a couple of wriggling, white-bellied, silvery barred mummichogs.

Torgan said mummichogs spend winter in the bay but become more active in spring. He called them one of the "most common and important salt marsh fish of Narragansett Bay and New England."

Mummichogs eat all sorts of shoreline and marsh matter, from plankton and decaying algae to mosquito larvae. In turn, bluefish, striped bass, summer flounder and other fish eat mummichogs, which may reach five to seven inches in length.

Herons, egrets, kingfishers and other birds like to eat "mummies," too, Torgan said.

A Native American word, mummichog means, "going in crowds," a fitting moniker for a fish known for its schooling behavior.

Besides having the kind of fantastical name you don't mind repeating mummichogs are one the hardiest creatures around.

Adapted to both fresh and saltwater, mummichogs tolerate wide variations in oxygen, pollution and salinity.

Mummichogs also possess two other adaptations to life in the shallows. First, as long it remains moist, a mummichog will draw in small amounts of oxygen through its scales, which is a lifesaver for any fish left behind by a receding tide.

Second, stranded mummichogs possess the ability to flip-flop, head over tail, from a tidal pool or puddle back into the bay.

The other visible creature caught in the net was a one-inch-long shore shrimp, which is the most common shrimp found in the coastal waters of New England.

Like mummichogs, shore shrimp prefer inshore habitats, such as the brackish waters of salt marshes, where they munch on most anything.

Thirty years ago, the cove's major flora and fauna included trash, sanitary items and dead fish. The water stunk.

Although the Bay still takes in too much sewage and storm water, its waters are improving.

One of the inspiring aspects of a resurrected Narragansett Bay is that any number of little fish might cause near-shore waters in Providence to plink and plop, as if struck by invisible raindrops.

These "bait fish" include the common mummichog and its close relative, the striped killifish, as well as the sheepshead minnow, silverside minnow, juvenile menhaden, gizzard shad and bay anchovy.

Such richness is a blessing.

"You can't have a vibrant Rhode Island without a clean bay," Torgan said. "You can't have a revitalized Providence without a clean river.

"A focus on a healthy bay and ocean is not a special interest, it is a common interest."

Every known life form on the planet relies on water. That the water around us is both getting cleaner and harboring fantastic life, is another reason to shout, "It's you, it's you, it's really you!"

ON A SANDBAR AT SUNSET
August 22, 2015

Some outdoor moments leave you breathless.

Such was the case July 31, as Karen and I, plus 70 other paddlers, kayaked at dusk into the mouth of the Narrow River in Narragansett.

Just about all of the other folks had reached the trip's mid-point, which was a sandbar, where they stood watching the moon emerge over the eastern horizon and the sun drop in the west.

I was still huffing and puffing my way along. A slow kayaker by nature, I'd paused to take notes, or just observe the surroundings. Plus, I was paddling into an incoming tide.

About 100 yards from the sand, I received an escort in the form of four common terns. The vocal birds flapped powerfully before tucking in wings and taking turns plunging into the water to catch fish.

Each bird-water impact produced a loud and lovely sounding splash, dispersing saltwater in all directions. I felt a thrill, and a sense of intimacy in sharing space with these elegant creatures.

It wasn't hard to tell why the terns were there. Small silver fish were jumping out of and back into the water. In the dying light, they looked like shiny dimes, their plops like little drops of rain.

Also, shad were in the river, and I saw two fishermen reel in large and silvery specimens in the one- to two-pound range.

That river mouth was wacky with wildlife. An osprey cried incessantly from a dead limb, as a series of great blue herons, making croaking calls, crossed in front of my path.

Multiple "chur-ee" calls overhead told me that we'd disrupted foraging semipalmated plovers. That was probably the case, too, for three whimbrels, which produced twitter calls, as the big shorebirds, with their long, down-curved bills rose overhead and away.

In addition, I heard the "tew, tew, tew," of a yellowlegs, a mid-sized shorebird, and counted three great egrets, silent, but huge, flying across the river to the south shore, where several folks sat silently, crabbing.

Just ahead, and beyond the spit, an immense orange orb rose from the sea, as if the Atlantic had just given birth. This was a Blue Moon, being the second full moon in one month.

Meanwhile, behind me, the sun was settling into a western sky cloaked in gold, purple and green.

We'd departed 90-minutes earlier, a mile and a half back, from Narrow River Kayaks (NRK), outfitters on Middlebridge Road in Narragansett. This adventure was called the Pettaquamscutt Paddle. It was an annual fundraiser for the Narrow River Preservation Association (NRPA), a 45-year-old advocacy, awareness and education group for the 14-acre watershed. NRK helped host and staff the adventure.

In fact, as a slow poke, I was thrilled that one of the NRK staffers, a friendly 19-year-old named Tyler, shadowed me like a guardian angel.

The route was classic Rhode Island—forests, coves, sandbars, islands, osprey nests, rock outcrops and more.

At one point after our departure, we stopped in the river, and positioned ourselves around NRK-owner Jason Considine, who shared ecological, geological, historical and stewardship information.

I floated beside Karen and two friendly and gracious NRPA hosts, David and Rosemary Smith. We looked at the wooded granite of Gooseberry Island, the waters and marshes of Pettaquamscutt Cove and John H. Chaffee National Wildlife Refuge, and the forests of Canonchet Farm, and summed up the spot in one word, "sacred."

The river has grown cleaner due to the NRPA's pollution monitoring, watershed-protection and other work, in concert with local agencies, municipalities, residents and businesses such as NRK.

When I finally reached the sandbar, folks were leaving for the return paddle. I rested in the kayak for a minute, and then joined Karen and the other returnees. Oh, the joy of riding a rising tide! Going back was silky smooth. Plus, NRPA and NRK had food and drink waiting for everyone.

On land, I caught my breath, toasting both the phrase that good things come to those who wait and the belief that the best way to celebrate a cleaner river is to paddle it.

Spreading Some Perennial Love

August 15, 2015

In the American Book Award-winning story, "Miss Rumphius," a little girl listens to the seafaring tales of her grandfather, who suggests that with her other hopes and dreams, she "make the world more beautiful."

That child grows up to become Miss Rumphius, who settles by the sea, and in her middle-aged years spreads lupine seeds around town. "The next spring there were lupines everywhere."

To children, who gather at her feet to hear stories of faraway places, a now-elderly Miss Rumphius, says, "You must do something to make the world more beautiful." The story suggests that the children will understand what that "something" is, as they get older.

Karen has an ex-colleague, who we call "Mr. Rumphius." His name is Mark and he teaches second grade in Providence. Weekends, Mark spends in his native Portsmouth, N.H, where he lives in a 220-year-old farmhouse, surrounded by gardens.

Recently, Karen and I visited Mark in Portsmouth. He fed us, gave us a house tour and took us around the grounds.

Every so often, Mark popped a perennial from the soil, plopped it into a moist plastic bag and added it to a collection of plants that he was preparing for us to take home and replant.

Some of the plants included black-eyed Susan, columbine, coneflower, hosta, fern, ginger, iris, sunflower and yarrow.

Besides those species, the gardens contained alum, astilbe, bleeding heart, campanula, cosmos, dahlia, day lily, fern-leaved coreopsis, German catchfly, hollyhock, liatris, phlox, poppy, rose Campion, sea thrift, zinnia and more.

Mark also tends an herb garden, and apple, cherry, nectarine, peach and plum trees.

Although we visited on a hot July day, a nearby tidal cove tugged in cooler, ocean air. That kept noontime temperatures in the mid 80s. The air smelled a mix of floral and maritime.

Digging up perennials in summer meant keeping them moist in our air-conditioned car, and replanting them as soon as we got home to Providence.

In fact, we used the plants to create a 15-foot by 4-foot garden beside the sunny wall of our garage. After hoeing the stretch of dead turf and annual weeds, we turned over the soil, set in the plants and added water. Instant garden!

Over the years, Mark has shared hundreds of garden plants with colleagues and friends around Rhode Island. Mark said that he was happy sharing, and even happier that the plants "end up with folks who appreciate them."

Just a few words about Mark's Portsmouth home: It is an early New England structure in which generations of previous owners intentionally, or not, covered up many of the original features.

Over the last few years, Mark has removed carpeting, paint, wallpaper and walls to reclaim what is a lovely look of wood and use of space.

As you might guess, the old house is full of nooks and crannies. A second-floor closet beside the brick chimney shaft, for example, was once used to store smoked meat. That closet also held a false wall, behind which escaped slaves hid while traveling the Underground Railroad.

Despite the day's heat, the house was cool. There was artwork in each room, as well as fresh flowers.

Karen and Mark are both teachers, who strive to make the world a better place.

People who give so much of themselves to others and the world around them? I can't think of anything more beautiful.

SUMMERING UNDER A SANDY CITY SIDEWALK
August 1, 2015

Among the historical and architecturally significant structures on College Hill in Providence is a set of what looks like little volcanoes jutting up from one stretch of sidewalk.

This is a colony of what is commonly called sand-loving wasps. Each insect is a solitary nester, and about three dozen wasps have excavated individual nests under this particular sidewalk.

What attracts the wasps is the tan and gritty sand below the unusual pavement—a series of large flagstone squares flanked by diagonal bricks. The wasps burrow into the sand in spaces between the stonework.

This sidewalk is also sunny, getting at least six hours of direct sunshine a day, compared to the rest of the walkway, which is under shade trees, and where there are no wasp nests.

When I found the little volcanoes of sand, I thought that ants made them. So, I contacted James Waters, who studies ant physiology and behavior. Waters is an assistant professor of biology at Providence College.

Together we discovered that these were wasp burrows. We watched each female wasp land on the sidewalk by a nest, groom, and use its front legs like a spade to repair the burrow, or lift up to chase off an intruder.

A steady flow of people walked by (the wasps zipped away and returned seconds after folks passed by), but no one noticed the wasps, which rarely sting humans, by the way.

Each female wasp looked lovely. She was about two-thirds of an inch long and relatively stocky. Her wings contained a slight sheen but were mostly clear.

With wings closed, a wasp looked black. However, she did have silver and black stripes around her abdomen and a golden rear end. Her most striking feature was a pair of large green eyes.

Waters shot video of a wasp, which I shared with James Pitts, curator of the Entomology Collection at Utah State University. Pitts said that "Tachytes" was the scientific name for this type of wasp.

Tachytes, Waters pointed out, was derived from Greek. It meant rapidity; suddenness and speed, probably a nod to a female's quick work at hunting and digging.

After some research, Waters determined that the sidewalk diggers were a species with the formal name of Tachytes pennsylvanicus Banks. The scientific word for each excavated mound on the sidewalk was "tumulus," he said.

"We were spot-on in thinking that soil quality was an important characteristic for where they nest," said Waters. "Apparently even just leaving some sandy soil bare in your backyard could be enough for a wasp to find and make it her nest."

Although each female wasp is a solo nester, it is not uncommon to find such a dense aggregation of burrows, he said.

The females hunt primarily crickets, grasshoppers and katydids. These are paralyzed by stinger injection of venom, carried, and deposited into an underground cell, or chamber, in the burrow, Waters said. An egg is then placed on the paralyzed prey, he said. A larva that emerges from an egg feeds on the insect.

Some of these underground cells hold up to a dozen prey victims, with an egg laid on just the last one delivered, noted the blog, "Bug Eric," which said there are "35 species of Tachytes in North America north of Mexico. They are among our more common solitary wasps, easily observed as they feed on flower nectar, though they flit rapidly from blossom to blossom."

Males probably do not help with digging or provisioning the nest, Waters said. However, a male does "have some interesting behaviors, including the initiation of courtship by waving his antennae over the female's face; their successful mating depends on her being receptive."

A male may also engage in what is called, "hilltopping," in which he defends "prominent landmarks to attract potential female mates."

Finding the wasps was as exciting as receiving a gift, and in both Waters and wasps, I made new friends.

In the process, I learned that humans are not the only creatures to seek sand and sun in summer. Plus I re-learned that whether you are buying a home, starting a business, or building a burrow, it's all about "location, location, location."

Fruit Flavored with Asphalt
September 7, 2018

Where I live in Providence, there are three mature black walnut trees loaded with green-husked nuts. From what I've witnessed in past years, most of that fruit will end up in the gutter this fall.

After the first frost, I hope to collect and shell some of those walnuts. It's an extensive process to remove the husks, clean and crack the shells, and extract the nutmeat. Once you've done it, however, you're rich in yummy walnuts.

But, I get ahead of myself. From the first tree and shrub fruits of the growing season, which were Autumnalis cherries in late May, followed by shadbush berries in early June, this has been a bountiful year for fruit dangling over or falling onto sidewalks and streets of the city.

In late June, neighbors said I could pick from their sidewalk-stretching raspberry bushes, and I did.

Mulberries, juicy, sweet, and almost black in color, were abundant early in July. I plucked fruit from weed trees that also fed robins, starlings and cedar waxwings.

In the second half of July, I devoured blackberries from canes that snaked over sidewalks. I ate a few black cherries, too. They tasted more acidic than anything else, but I liked them in small doses.

Peaches ripened on one squirrel-ravaged tree in August. These were small, mostly stone fruits, often wormy, but fuzzy, juicy and sweet.

August also brought red plums, covering three street trees. For weeks, the fruits went unpicked, collecting on sidewalks and streets. I gathered several solid specimens. So sweet, each tasted like a spoonful of sugar.

At least two neighbors grow sidewalk-hugging beach plums, which are small trees. This was a plentiful year for the little purple sweet and sour plums, no bigger than small grapes. So far, I've consumed about two dozen, most recently sharing a tree with a migratory gray catbird.

Presently, I am also devouring Cornelian cherries from sidewalk shrubs. The somewhat thick, maroon-colored, olive-shaped fruit is quite sour. Also ready for harvest are pears from two street trees. Those that are not mushy deliver a juicy floral sweetness.

Soon to ripen will be apples. In my neighborhood, they also fall uncollected and uneaten. The apples are more sour than sweet. Still I will munch on a few.

I am also waiting for the little, purplish fruits of a black gum street tree to ripen. These fruits are fleshy, thin-skinned, sour and mostly pit. Typically, black gum fruits mature by now. It's a late season for them.

In October, paw-paw will ripen, and I hope my neighbor, who tends a sidewalk-side tree, will share one or more of the somewhat-mango-looking green fruit. The off-white, juicy, squishy and delicate custard-like pulp is delish!

Once the harvest of fleshy fruit subsides, walnuts will thud to the pavement. I plan to cart home selected nuts for the laborious but profitable process of removing the meats. By then it will be cold outside, and I will need something to keep me busy indoors.

Caring for Creation
July 9, 2011

On a day when the sun felt like it would burn holes through exposed skin, we found profound, cooling, rejuvenating relief under a grove of Norway spruces. The alcove was a tranquil space to mop our brows.

"This is our cemetery," noted Sister Rosemarie Higgins. "It is exceptionally quiet."

For the 16-acre Franciscan Missionaries of Mary campus in North Providence, the wry and spry 81-year-old Higgins oversees a landscape inventory, planting and maintenance program based on tree donations and volunteer labor and technical assistance.

In the six years of the program, Higgins and fellow sisters have planted more than 100 types of trees, following the removal of 75 large dead, dying or otherwise dangerous trees.

Franciscans follow the path of St. Francis of Assisi, patron saint of ecology. They are called to care for creation.

"We strive to create an atmosphere of peace, and to spend our time in prayer and in admiring nature's own," said Higgins, who walks the grounds daily.

Higgins wore a gold and green RI Tree Steward pin on her white shirt, as we strolled past an ancient, deeply shading copper beech; towering tulip tree; four-stemmed river birch; bright-white-flowering Kousa; and super-sized honey locust.

Newer trees, each well mulched, pruned and watered, dotted the estate-like grounds. A plaque, noting scientific name, donor name and planting occasion, marked each one.

106

On a web-based map, the sisters named, numbered and charted the condition of each tree, which they used to keep donors up to date (picture of the tree included).

The present Rhode Island landscape is not your parents'. Ecologists say that summers are hotter and drier than 50 years ago and that trees struggle with new stressors such as acid rain and exotic insects.

Part of the genius behind Higgins's planting program is that many current varieties of trees come with traits to handle urban life ,including disease and insect resistance, drought tolerance, long life expectancy, and low maintenance.

Many of the new trees on the campus were recognizable for their value to the landscape—beech, cherry, crabapple, elm, maple, redbud and more—but they were modern, reliable varieties.

Plus, with the landscape becoming hotter, there are several up and coming species such as Carolina silverbell, a southern Appalachian native, with white, distinctive, bell-shaped blossoms.

From the shade of Our Lady of Lourdes Grotto, Higgins said that the sisters used rain barrels to collect and store water, which is distributed to gator-bagged trees via a bucket brigade and hoses that stem from a well and water tank.

The sisters also relied on a converted golf cart to lug mulch; replanted holiday flowers, such as lilies and tulips, in gardens on the grounds; and composted all discarded plant materials.

Plantings of perennials marked previous bare spots. One was a "rain garden" of piping, stones, black-eyed Susan, daisies and evening primrose that slowed and captured storm water, allowing it to trickle into the soil around some of the new trees.

Another was a lasagna garden built by Higgins and local Eagle Scouts, who layered organic materials over formerly weedy grounds, including an initial sheet of about "a ton of cardboard" that Higgins collected for reuse. Pachysandra, bee balm and coreopsis, rescued from a construction site, grew in the garden.

The plan to refurbish the property sprouted in Higgins' mind after she spent time in Upstate New York in 2005, with sisters who restored their land at little or no cost. They used trees planted as remembrances, for special occasions, or by transplanting seedlings from garden beds to other parts of the grounds.

In just six years, Higgins has created an arboretum-like campus, said John Campanini, technical director of the Rhode Island Tree Council (RITree). "It is a hidden gem of Northern Rhode Island," he said.

Campanini helped Higgins produce the property plan. "This landscape has exceeded its former glory," he said. "Sister Rosemarie even persuaded me to donate a tree for my mother."

The Franciscan Missionaries of Mary have hosted three RITree Stewards classes, in which participants helped replant parts of the property, which now serves as a field lab for (RITree) training programs.

Higgins and three other sisters are trained, qualified tree stewards.

As we rested under the Norway spruce, she said that a turkey family, poults included, emerged from a campus woodlot each evening.

Other common animals included coyote, deer, fox and rabbits, Higgins said. A swallowtail floated by. The air smelled of honeysuckle. The only sounds came from orioles, catbirds and chipping sparrows.

"We believe that the whole world is interconnected, not that we people sit on high over other creatures," said Higgins, who also admires the Buddhist philosophy of applying 100-percent concentration to the task at hand.

Higgins was embarrassed by credit I might give her in describing the tree project.

"I am truly blest and humbled by the number of good people who have volunteered their service and expertise to make this project successful," she said.

Perhaps, Higgins added, the coverage "will inspire others to participate in the care of our creation, especially when they read the age of this 'old gray mare.'"

Green Grass at the Stadium
June 20, 2015

B etween 1967 and 1973 (ages 9-15), the end of school marked the start of turf season.

My grassy second home was Yankee Stadium, where I watched some 200 games over seven summers. Back then, the Yankees were mediocre at best, and usually the stadium was two-thirds empty.

I attended games with my father and two brothers. A family friend worked security and opened a gate beside the ticket turnstiles to let us through. I'm not boasting about freeloading, I'm just explaining how we got in.

Although I remember bright green grass, images show the Stadium turf as somewhat washed-out. The turf was cut in long convex strips between the infield dirt and outfield fences. Like its ballplayers and fans, the grass looked thin and tired by the end of the season.

Still, the greenery was inviting, especially on sunny days. Where we lived two miles north of the ballpark grass was rare. There was parkland but it was primarily eroded or overgrown.

Moreover, the stadium was a relatively safe place outdoors compared to our neighborhood, which was undergoing a violent transition over those years.

As part of the arrangement of sneaking in, we sat in the upper reaches of the grandstand, where no ushers checked tickets. One evening, as we trudged up the ramp, I stomped on a mustard packet. Like a line drive, the ejected stream of golden brown mustard shot across the ramp and onto the shin of my dad's pants. He didn't see what happened. But us three boys did.

My father was stern. When he found the stain later, he demanded to know who caused it. We stayed mum, which dad took as an admission of guilt. One of you, he said, "would pay."

Besides getting to see real grass at Yankee Stadium, I learned about nature in other ways there. Later in August, for example, migrating common nighthawks by the dozens picked off insects around the light stations at night.

During weekend day games in September, migrating monarch butterflies floated or flapped past the grandstand, as did some migrating hawks.

On May 27 this year, I took the afternoon off to attend a PawSox game at McCoy Stadium.

I bought a general admission ticket and sat in the grandstand behind home plate.

In the bright sunshine, the grass was a healthy, lush and welcoming fern-green color that evoked the memory of sitting in old Yankee Stadium.

A warm breeze cocooned me on the sunny, 80-degree day. The sky was a royal blue and puffy clouds mushroomed in it.

Because I had to pick up Noah from high school, I left the stands after five innings.

On my way out, I bought a hot dog, spreading yellow mustard atop it. Then I stopped to watch the game for a couple of minutes.

When I finished the dog, I discovered a thick yellow streak of mustard running down the front of my shirt.

Wiping off the condiment, a fool's smile spread across my face. You see that day was also the third anniversary of my father's death, and visiting the ballpark was an act of observance.

How appropriate that airborne mustard signified both the rendering of my garment and payback for blemishing my father's pants long ago.

GARDEN SNAILS IN THE BIG CITY
May 18, 2018

Pretty much all of the natural world delights me. But if I were to create a list of favorite creatures, the garden snail would be near the top.

Finding a snail, not only away from the seashore, but in the city, amazes me. I have stumbled upon snails in various gardens in Providence, including near downtown. In such built-up environments, you'd think the snails would get crushed, paved over or otherwise rooted out completely.

These urban snails feature whorled shells in shades of light green and/or tan interspersed by brown stripes. Our garden snails are European natives, which like many species of plants and animals, ended up elsewhere through human activities.

My first snail sighting of this season took place on April 26, when I found two, each about the size of a nickel. Garden snails hibernate in winter in moist, leafy areas. They emerge in spring, when they mate and lay eggs, which take a few weeks to hatch.

Newly hatched snails, which are transparent, feed on their own eggshells. They develop in size and color during the spring and summer; their shells growing with them.

Primarily, garden snails eat plant materials, algae and fungi, but they also graze on animal droppings, and inorganic material, such as limestone and cement to obtain calcium for their shells. Most of their feeding is benign or beneficial. Nonetheless, some gardeners and garden suppliers equate the creatures with their shell-less cousins, the slugs, which consume growing leaves, fruits and vegetables.

Garden snails mate, forage and are otherwise more active at night, when the air is usually the most humid or damp. But some garden snails come out during the day, particularly to feed.

Summertime is when I find the garden snail population at its peak. Often, they are the young of the year, and tiny. The wetter the weather, the easier it is to find the snails and the more of them I get to see. In dry summers, land snails may shut down activity or go dormant until it rains.

I want to make clear that I find garden snails only in shaded spots. My guess is that they make their way there as the sun moves behind buildings or other structures.

Some snails are in such plain sight that I've loitered beside these slow-goers to protect them, as students, lawyers, bureaucrats and other two-legged city dwellers rushed past in the routines of everyday life.

The typical garden snail in New England moves slower, averaging some 50 yards an hour. That, I would say, is more my speed.

WHEN ROBINS MEET AND MATE IN MUD
April 13, 2018

When I found a pair of Americans robin collecting nesting material in our backyard, I wondered where they would gather the mud to fortify the nest. You see, our backyard soil of loamy fine sand doesn't turn muddy. Pinch that gritty material, when it's wet, and it crumbles. The soil simply lacks the clay and organic matter to stick together.

I found an answer to this mud mystery in the webpages of the Cornell Laboratory of Ornithology. There I learned that when a female robin builds a nest, she does it from the inside out. The female presses "dead grass and twigs into a cup shape using the wrist of one wing. Other materials include paper, feathers, rootlets, or moss in addition to grass and twigs.

"Once the cup is formed, she reinforces the nest using soft mud gathered from worm castings to make a heavy, sturdy nest. She then lines the nest with fine dry grass. The finished nest is 6-8 inches across and 3-6 inches high."

Worm castings! Who knew? When earthworms rise to the soil surface they leave behind tiny mounds of black, granular, humus-rich material, which are also called castings.

Worm castings are rich in humus and biological material and even a bit of oil from a worm's alimentary canal. A casting, even when formed from loamy fine sand, sticks together.

It was roughly two weeks ago that a male robin showed up in the backyard and took to singing. He did this to establish territory.

Next, a female showed up. As a result, the male sang even more, and also chased the female around the landscape.

A robin pair chooses a nest site typically on the lower half of a tree on "one or several horizontal branches hidden in or just below a layer of dense leaves," notes the Cornell Lab. Robins generally nest twice, and sometimes even three times in a single season. From the time it's built to the time the young leave it, each nest is used for about 5 weeks. A new nest is built for each new brood.

Watch, and you might catch sight of robins carrying building material to the nest site, which is otherwise uncannily difficult to find. Because leaves are not out yet, the breeding season's first nest is often in an evergreen such as a rhododendron, juniper or cypress.

By the way, the female carries the mud. Sometimes that muck darkens her breast feathers. Building a nest involves the female making hundreds of trips, with beakfuls of mud, which she uses to curve, deepen and strengthen the nest bowl.

From the sound of it, the robins in our backyard found what they needed to build a new life. Each morning, the male sings well before dawn. In the evening, he sings faster and more elaborately, long after the sun has set.

EXPERIMENT TURNED FOREST
March 16, 2018

The sun appeared, and so did we.

On a bright but nippy late-winter morning, Karen and I ducked into Lincoln Woods State Park for a walk around Olney Pond.

We hadn't trekked that route in more than 10 years, and it was a pleasure to re-learn that it contained such attractive scenery, with the best views of shoreline rock outcrops occurring in the north and west quadrants around the pond. There was also a great deal of giant boulders all about the woods.

As we circled the pond, I noticed a prevalence of tall oaks, primarily black, white and red. I identify black oak by its charcoal-colored blocky bark. Red oak bark displays gray muscle-like striations. A white oak trunk is lighter gray, plus its bark starts to shred about 20 feet up from the ground.

Speaking of shredding, we also noted the occasional hickory, with its shaggier bark. There was also a lot of black birch, which has a blackish trunk broken into plates on larger trees. Younger black birch displays a somewhat unusual smooth, brown-red-black bark.

Where the route dipped in elevation, we found wetter soils and lots of red maples, with their gray bark and soon-to-open flower buds.

The craziest looking twigs belonged to sassafras trees. Those twigs were the only green ones out there, with some of the older branches looking somewhat orange in color. A few sassafras twigs also grew in a twisty manner that reminded us of pretzels.

The State of Rhode Island Division of Parks & Recreation provides a detailed online history of Lincoln Woods. From it, I learned that a 40-

acre woodlot, now part of the park, was where industrialist and inventor Zachariah Allen, "began an experiment in silviculture" in 1820. Silviculture is the controlled establishment and sustained cultivation of trees to meet a range of outcomes, from wildlife habitat to timber.

The land, when Allen bought it, was a "worn-out pasture," for which he hoped to restore "lost fertility." His theory, that "vacant land may be profitably improved by planting trees," proved correct, as his records showed decades later that he made a profit on the trees grown there for "home building, commercial construction, and furniture making."

A *Journal of Forestry* article, published in 1946, called Allen a "pioneer in applied silviculture." Indeed, the state's website notes that some forestry experts think that Allen's silviculture endeavor "was the first such effort in the country."

Here we are some 150 years later, and there is a 627-acre state park on the site. Learning some of its history made me wonder if any of those oaks, maples, birch and sassafras that Karen and I observed were ancestors of Allen's attempts to revitalize some of the land.

Nature, of course, is under constant change, whether humans touch it, or not. Ecosystems alter, and nothing we see outdoors now will remain the same. Even the large boulders in the park will crumble, albeit slowly, some day. Still, I can tell you that what we saw on a 45-minute walk around the pond looked wonderfully lush to us.

Taking Myself to the River
April 23, 2011

Every few seconds, the shadow of a northern rough-winged swallow passed over me.

Three birds dipped, dove, twisted and turned above the little river that ran through the valley and under the Providence roadway to the sea.

The swallows return every April to nest in a tunnel wall after spending the winter in Mexico or South America.

Usually I sped through this intersection on the way to work or to pick up one of the kids from school.

Today was atypical. I left work mid-morning to visit Noah and his fifth-grade classmates. They explored buoyancy and stability by building mini boats out of food containers.

At lunchtime, I attended the funeral for a man who loved to hold hands with his young grandchildren.

Mid-afternoon, I returned to Noah's school, where he read a poem to the school assembly.

The small, brown, insect-eating swallows gave "squib, squib," calls, as the birds rose above the roadway only to dive back down over the gurgling water.

Two of the swallows were territorial males. They were vying over a female to mate, lay eggs and raise a family beneath one of the busiest intersections in the city.

Beside me, a box elder tree grew out of stonework that channeled the river. Box elder is a maple. Its seeds germinate in rocks and waste places along waterways.

The waxy film that covered the tree's smooth, stout, telescoping twigs gave the branches a shiny green to purple color.

Across the river, lime-mortar stalactites hung over a fieldstone wall. In the coal-black muck below, water lapped in and out of a Styrofoam cup, filling and emptying it repeatedly.

The river, affected by tides two miles to the south, smelled of the sea.

Behind me, RIPTA 72, 52, 53 and 11 buses deposited clumps of high school students. They dispersed into hand holding couples, strolling along the river toward downtown.

Just above the water, a small skull pendant dangled from a necklace chain.

A one-way utility sign and its pole sat on the river bottom. The arrow pointed east.

A few weeks ago, a man placed in a casket today asked if I would take his family to a natural area I had written about. We never got the chance.

It was unfathomable to me that now he was gone. Death hoodwinked us again.

Filling my sad day with children mitigated the confusion and grief.

At the school assembly, Noah spoke confidently on the subject of self-sacrifice and spiritual change.

In observance of our human bonds, the children of a first-grade class celebrated making and breaking bread by draping arms over shoulders and churning in opposite-moving circles.

If you allow it, life will refill the pockmarks in your soul similar to the way that trees sprout from the cracks in cement.

Before me, an American goldfinch, common grackle, mourning dove and northern mockingbird sang from such trees. A pair of song sparrows dropped from a branch to pluck insects from the river rocks.

Thin clouds spread overhead like a Japanese fan. A rainbow halo of water droplets circled the sun. As a cormorant sped south, a great blue heron, looking like some ancient creature, flapped slowly east.

Beneath the shadow of the swallow and besides the soothing waters, I could feel grains of renewal congealing within me. One day, I realized, my cup would indeed "runneth" over again.

Return of Birds and Bees
April 9, 2011

The words "long," "cold," "rough" and "silent" sum up last winter. For many folks, it was worse.

In our family, five loved ones left the living.

This spring is about grieving, healing and maximizing returns.

For those of us who find renewal in the outdoors, April is when a mental checklist kicks in. It is critical to our feeling of wellness, to regaining balance, to knowing that "all is good and right," to check-off that robins have returned. Are the chipmunks chirping again? Check. Is shadbush in flower in the woods? Check.

Come back to me, my loved ones, just like you do every spring, we think. Look, it is the first mourning butterfly of the season! Check. A Northern flicker, chipping sparrow and Eastern towhee are back and singing! Check, check, check.

The parallel, of course, is the physical checklist of April, such as the data organizer that we are using to mark off possible deductions for our tax return.

Like the spring weather, we are very late with our return. This week we will rummage through receipts and forms, looking for opportunities to get back some of what we put in, so that we may survive fiscally for another year.

Clothes donated to charity? Check. Contribution made to public radio? Check.

In terms of nature, maximizing the return means not only noting what comes back, but also working to protect it, so that we all have something to look forward to in the future.

I am humbled when I hear of folks who spend April and beyond monitoring the arrival and activities of least terns, piping plovers, and other endangered or threatened species.

These volunteers carry another kind of clipboard and checklist. Are the birds back on the beach? Check. Is the "Keep off the Dunes" sign in place? Check. Did the birds begin courting? Check. Have they scraped a nest into the sand? Check.

Every volunteer who cleans and monitors bluebird boxes and bat houses, every landowner who refrains from mowing to allow grassland birds to nest maximizes the returns of spring.

This past winter, we hung a small bird feeder, filled with black oil sunflower seed, on a hook off the side yard.

Only one species visited the feeder—a pair of black-capped chickadees. The feeder is about 15 feet from a chickadee nest box that we posted last year after the neighborhood's dead and dying street trees were removed.

For the second straight April, chickadees are investigating the box. Yesterday, we watched the pair go in and out. Will they nest?

Suddenly, whether the little creatures find safe haven is even more important than the size of our tax return.

Maybe that's what happens when your heart is heavy. One minute you're cleaning a flowerbed. The next, you're sitting on a garden bench, teary eyed, cheering on chickadees.

At this moment, what matters most to us is to maximize the return of the chickadees. Each bird may weigh just one-third of an ounce but their survival feels priceless.

I am reminded of the following words. They come from the song "Millionaire Waltz" by Queen:

Bring out the charge of the love brigade
There is spring in the air once again
Drink to the sound of the song parade
There is music and love everywhere

Give a little love to me
Take a little love from me
I want to share it with you
Come back, come back to me
You make me feel like a millionaire

Unwinding Along the Upper Bay
March 12, 2011

Some lunch hours I drift away from work to spend some time raising and lowering a pair of binoculars.

On my latest breather, I ducked out to the bay, where I experienced one of the more-exciting waterfowl shows of the season—700 scaup collecting into a diving, swirling raft.

Scaup are ducks that winter in our waters, where they may flock by the thousands.

I stood on the East Providence side of the upper bay across from two 400-foot tankers and a 6,500-car-capacity Autoliner cargo ship docked in Providence.

In flocks of six to 60 ducks, scaup flew up toward the area of the northern-most gas tanks, roughly the latitude of Rhode Island Hospital.

This flight lasted almost 10 straight minutes. The scaup landed in a circle in the middle of the bay. As their raft grew, it morphed into an oval, which eventually stretched nearly the length of a football field.

From a distance, male scaup look black, white and gray and females brown.

The ducks reminded me of marching cadets, as they swam north into the current and then turned at the top of the oval to head south.

Meanwhile, some of the birds dove, while others flew from the back to the front of the flock, keeping the oval intact.

When a drilling rig began pounding the East Providence shoreline, the scaup congealed into a tight circle that began floating downstream.

As they moved south, the ducks formed look-alike rows within the circle. They looked like marshmallow Peeps packed into an Easter basket. Then the birds broke into three distinct rings atop the water.

With the scaup out of view, I inspected other waterfowl bobbing like apples on the bay.

I counted one pair of hooded mergansers, 10 bufflehead, 11 red-breasted mergansers and 15 American wigeon. The latter were very close to the shoreline of the East Bay Bike Path and produced excited-sounding whistles as they paddled away from my approach.

As I stood alongside a brushy edge of vegetation, at least four American tree sparrows foraged on the ground, articulating the occasional "tseet" call.

Two loons, their long necks extended fully, flew into an early afternoon wind, as did a red-tailed hawk, sailing by in the aerodynamically superior shape of a teardrop.

Early March is when you have a pretty good chance of spotting our national bird cruising the upper bay. On and off during this escape I'd looked up with no luck.

Then, I saw it. Directly overhead was the Autoliner of raptors—much larger than the red-tailed hawk.

A bald eagle takes five years to reach maturity. This flat-winged, dark-brown-bodied individual, with an off-white head and some white in the tail, was diagnostic of a fourth-year eagle.

Although the bird flew with the wind, it also adopted a teardrop shape, speeding off toward the Iway.

As I walked down the bike path, the three circles of scaup, looking like a trio of in-and-out-stepping square dancers, reconstructed, deconstructed and then finally reformed their oval just north of the rocky shores of the Squantum Association.

Industrial sounds dominated the bay, with metal on metal booms, clanks, clunks and groans drowning out the sounds of birds.

While the Coast Guard Cutter Bainbridge Island cut a path north toward the tankers, I trotted my non-aerodynamic frame up the trail to the pull-off lot on Veteran's Memorial Parkway.

I drove back to the office de-compressed by a simple walk by the bay, and ready to dive back into work.

Eden in the Capital City
October 30, 2010

Most of us would describe our streets in terms of their intersections or by the types of homes on the block.

Elva and Bob depict their Providence thoroughfare in the context of current and former trees such as the giant pin oak in their backyard, which they invited me to visit.

When the couple bought their home in 1974, they discovered colossal trees up and down the street, leading Elva to dub it "Avenue of the Giants," after a well-known redwood grove in northern California.

Besides the pin oak, the couple's 50-by-100-foot property contained a lilac, pussy willow, two crabapples and two climbing roses.

A blue spruce grows in a side yard. Since 1974, the tree has doubled in height. Elva and Bob said that the native wildflower false Solomon's seal appeared in the "crabapple" corner of the yard after they stopped raking there.

Over the years, the couple added a grape arbor, apple tree, herb garden, raspberries (at present, ripe with fall fruit) and the native wildflower Solomon's seal. They also planted a spicebush and "squeezed a plum tree into the east side of the yard between the pussy willow and one of the crabapples."

Their latest planting is a hops arbor, featuring vines of small puffy, artichoke-looking fruits that sway in the wind.

As we walked the property, it occurred to me that Elva and Bob's landscape belonged to a quilt of hundreds of home gardens and grounds in a neighborhood, bracketed by larger green spaces—North Burial Ground, Lippitt Park, Blackstone Boulevard and Swan Point Cemetery.

Urban green patches, like Elva and Bob's, serve as pathways and crossroads for migrating songbirds, resident breeding birds, raccoons, skunks, squirrels, and other visiting or local creatures moving within or through the landscape.

Although not as inclusive as the rural natural world, this urban cover of greenery is still dense, vibrant and diverse.

Over the herb garden, a one-inch-diameter grapevine curled up from the ground, twisting into a stout square shape, and turning up into the apple tree. This natural "sculpture" looked like a giant bent paperclip suspended in space.

Elva showed me where cardinals sheltered their young in the cone of foliage created by the grape vine snaking through the apple crown.

"Each morning, the cardinals spend up to three hours at a stretch in the backyard," she said. "This year, the couple brought three fledgling chicks here."

Cardinals are the inspiration for Elva's garden diary, which she calls, "The Red Bird Chronicles."

Of the backyard, Elva says, "This is our Eden." Lording over it is a 134-inch-circumference pin oak tree.

Thirty-four years ago, when an enormous branch broke off the right side of the pin oak, the forester who trimmed the tree estimated that it was 75 years old. Since then, three professional foresters have visited the pin oak, and none have contradicted that estimate, which suggests that the tree is now about 110 years old.

Pin oaks are relatively short-lived. The oldest specimens usually last 90-120 years.

Typical pin oaks feature symmetrical, almost pyramidal crowns. This tree is the shape of a fan—with a much-wider-than-usual canopy.

Uncharacteristically massive limbs winnow down into grayish bark, which Elva says, "flows like liquid."

At the tree's base, Elva showed me a meaty explosion of fruiting Hen of the Woods fungi, known for its fabulous flavor. Squirrels had chewed up the mushroom's outer layers. In the morning, squirrels break off and eat the tan colored fronds, she said.

Despite its landscape prominence—and a mix of gold, green, orange and yellow foliage this time of year—the pin oak is hardly a one-tree ecosystem. Several other giant trees remain in the neighborhood, including even-larger-circumference black, red and white oaks just one block east. A lush backyard garden complements each oak.

Besides a birdbath and wooden chimes, Elva and Bob's yard includes a Japanese Buddha under the spruce. The Buddha's hands are folded into a position symbolizing wisdom.

This is appropriate, Elva says, given that the Buddha received enlightenment under a tree.

That day, I received ecological enlightenment. I believe that we must think globally but protecting the planet starts locally. Elva and Bob's backyard represents how to start saving the world one garden at a time. The couple embraces and enhances the natural world around them.

Visiting "Eden" left me hopeful, refreshed, and feeling like I was part of something much larger.

Nature in One Thread
September 22, 2007

To catch the blues, or shed them, visit the Providence River, where the shoreline buzzes with the tapestry of life.

Our family's most important time there was during the afternoon of Sept. 18, 2001, when we strolled the East Bay Bike Path, between Veterans Memorial Parkway and Watchemoket Cove.

We sought relief from the heartache, anger and confusion of 9/11. Ten family friends died on 9/11. We grieved for lives lost. Our sense of security was gone. We had difficulty sleeping, and could not imagine what world awaited our children.

The sky was a light purplish blue. There were no clouds. The temperature was in the mid 70s. A northwest wind delivered the stink of decaying shellfish and the creosote smell of rotting timbers.

Hundreds of bees produced a humming sound, as they collected pollen and nectar from blue, gold, magenta, pink, red, white and yellow wildflowers.

Migrating swallows crisscrossed overhead, as did migrating terns. Atop a red cedar crouched a green-backed heron. Snowy egrets and a great blue heron worked the cove shore.

Our party included my wife, four-year-old daughter, two-month-old son and me. At a former railway trestle we watched a fisherman fight a bluefish. The olive-skinned man wore a brown floral-patterned button-down shirt. In one hand he grasped a light saltwater fishing rod. He held a 16-ounce can of beer in the other hand. His gelled, pitch-black hair, with gray speckles, held steady against the breeze.

By the pull and running of the line, he estimated the fish to be about three pounds. When the blue began leaping, the fisherman put down the beer. Then he asked our daughter to help bring in the fish. We guided her past shining green poison ivy, laden with white waxy fruit. Some leaves were a vivid red. "Thank you," we said to him.

Bluefish invade the bay later in summer, following schools of baitfish. Off the trestle, thousands of shimmering baitfish thickened the aquamarine water. Every so often, a bluefish, its back skimming just below the surface, would launch through the tiny fish. Some of the baitfish jumped out of the water, their silvery sides twinkling in the sunshine.

The fisherman had enticed the blue to strike a jig. As the hooked fish leapt out of the water, our daughter and new friend pulled the rod with both sets of hands.

The fish lost. It had a blue-green back, silvery sides, a large mouth and conspicuous teeth. The fisherman said it was time for our daughter to move back. A bluefish will bite off a finger, he said, working the fish free and releasing it.

We thanked the man again, and waved goodbye. Walking back to our car, we took in the panorama. It occurred to us that this fisherman had turned to people who needed care—us—and by sharing had made our lives better.

An industrial whistle on the Providence waterfront blew at 3 p.m. That was our wake-up call. We felt a little more hopeful. Looking at the children, we remembered that they would provide continuity between that day and the world ahead. The trip gave us back the sight and light to see the world more comfortably.

Last week we rode the bike path—our September sojourn to the river for renewal. The threads of life were again the color of bait, birds, fish, flowers, insects, people, sky and water, all woven from a single loom.

Millions of Menhaden Move On

November 7, 2015

On an overcast 60-degree morning in late October, whirling gulls whacked the Seekonk River in Providence in an effort to snare small silvery menhaden.

As fish skipped over the water surface in ripples, gulls landed atop the river, opened their wings, hopped, and dunked their heads to grab menhaden.

Multiple cormorants also dove for fish, while two great blue herons, standing about 200 feet apart in shallow water off mudflats, hunted as well.

I first saw the menhaden in mid-August along the east bank of the Providence River. The tiny fish traveled in pods so dense that they resembled ghostly black paisleys. Sometimes older and larger menhaden swam by.

"Peanut bunker" is the common name for young menhaden, said John Torgan, Director of Ocean & Coastal Conservation for the Rhode Island Chapter of The Nature Conservancy.

As individuals, young menhaden are defenseless. But "there is strength in numbers," he said. Traveling tightly together makes it harder "to get picked off."

This fall, millions of menhaden sought refuge in Rhode Island estuaries from larger predators such as striped bass and bluefish. An estuary is the tidal mouth of a river.

Around Providence, for example, "there were three different year classes of menhaden," Torgan said, and they attracted many predators, such as sizable bluefish in the near-10-pound range.

Top to bottom, Rhode Island was full of fish. On a September visit to Watch Hill, for example, Karen, Noah and I stood in warm, clear, chest-deep water, surrounded by thousands of swirling baitfish.

Every so often, a false albacore, a green-silver predator in the five-to-15-pound range, would attack a pod, sending sunshine-sparkling silver fish into the air.

The last few weeks have been "a time of abundance in our back-yard," both "spectacular and extraordinary," said Torgan. He attributed the richness to cleaner rivers, particularly "getting the sewage out," "a lot of state and community conservation," and "better regulation up and down the East Coast."

At various stages of their lives, menhaden filter feed on micro-scopic plants, called phytoplankton, and on zooplankton, which are tiny creatures along with immature stages of larger animals.

In turn, menhaden serve as prey for bluefish, striped bass and other coastal fish; humpback whales; plus gulls, terns, osprey and other birds.

For people, menhaden is a prime source of omega-3 fatty acids, which our bodies need to function, and which provide several health benefits. Each year, millions of pounds of menhaden are collected and processed into fish-oil, as well as high-protein feed for livestock.

In 2012, after coastwide populations of menhaden neared historic lows due to decades of overfishing, the Atlantic States Marine Fisheries Commission capped the commercial catch.

"We don't have all the data yet, but conservation measures appear to be working, with more menhaden in various sizes in the Bay than people have seen in years," Torgan said.

Many menhaden have moved out from local waters in recent days, and are heading south and west along the coast. Although most menhaden are migrating to the Carolinas, some will remain in local waters, prey for striped bass, which Torgan catches in January and February in the Providence River.

A generation ago, the Providence River was polluted. It stunk. Now, Torgan fishes local waters with his 9-year-old son and 82-year-old dad.

"To share this resource across generations, I never thought I'd see the day. The menhaden story underscores the connectedness of life, where a lowly fish determines the abundance and diversity of the ocean."

For almost three months, local waters bubbled with baitfish. Bluefish tails slapped the surface in chase, while menhaden jiggled and plopped in coatings so thick they resembled jelly.

On my trips to the Providence and Seekonk rivers, I never saw another person stop to look at the fish, which were so close, so mesmerizing, and as Torgan put it, "otherworldly."

Mathematics of Mother Nature
November 29, 2014

O
n Sunday afternoon, November 16, 2014, my 17-year-old daughter, Rachel, and I relearned that two plus two sometimes equals 22.

Rachel slid her fingers into the black, compost-rich soil of a large green clay pot on our patio. She looked a little like a doctor delivering a newborn. "Not yet," was her status report.

Suddenly, Rachel's signature widespread grin formed. To that nonverbal communication, I replied, "Work them up gently, slowly."

Forearms well into the pot, Rachel loosened up and surfaced crooked red tubers about the size of jumbo shrimp. Each sweet potato trailed one or more thin, twisting roots that curled up upon release.

All told, Rachel collected 22 soil-caked little vegetables. These were the offspring of four budding leftover sweet potatoes from last winter's farm share.

In spring, we had buried two potatoes in the pot. A few days later, we planted two more. The four were about the size of hefty pears.

Once planted, the budding sweet potatoes sent up drought-tolerant, bushy, twisting vines of ivy-like foliage. We wound that foliage around a downspout beside the patio.

One year, by the way, we planted sweet potatoes that also produced white-and-purple, morning-glory-like blooms. Sweet potatoes are a member of the morning glory family.

Typically, farmers harvest sweet potatoes in early fall before the vines blacken. We wait until after the first night or two of temperatures in the 20s. This one-pot harvest coincides with another hard-frost-fueled event—the annual gingko leaf drop.

Most trees that drop leaves do it in dribs and drabs. In contrast, gingkos release all of their fan-shaped leaves in a matter of hours.

Right after harvesting the sweet potatoes, I visited a gingko around the corner. The previous day that tree's crown was thick with golden-yellow leaves.

Now, every last leaf formed a warm-yellow carpet surrounding the trunk. The leaves appeared to glow in the sunshine, contrasting beautifully with the tree's grayish-brown furrowed bark and spur-rich gray-tan twigs.

I walked over to a second gingko. Once again, I found a golden blanket of foliage that seemed to circle the gray tree trunk. Quite fetching.

Leaves that fall from trees have stems called petioles, which scar-up in fall to protect soon-to-be exposed tissues from disease and other agents. This scarring process starts with leaves at the top of the tree.

As fall deepens, treetop leaves fall first. Remaining leaves scar-up and tumble away, too, in a process often accelerated by a hard frost.

Gingko petioles form a protective layer together when nighttime temperatures fall into the upper 20s. Often in the dark of a new day, the golden leaves shower to the ground.

I like the uncertainty of such November phenomena. When will the first frosts arrive? How hard will they be? Will one or both of our kids help with the sweet potato harvest? Will we ever actually see the ginkgo leaves drop, or just find them on the ground? All good stuff, and whether you're 7, 17 or 57, easy to dig.

FIGURING OUT A FOX
July 2, 2016

When the red-winged blackbirds chorused in distress from the utility wires above the road, we figured that a hawk had arrived.

But the four of us, on an evening stroll along an East Bay beach, should have looked down instead of up.

An adult red fox was walking down the road. This eye-catching creature was orange-red, with a bushy tail tipped in white. Its legs were dark, fading to black by the feet. The chest was white up to the muzzle.

What did the fox want? At this hour before sunset in early summer, four cars, with occupants, were parked in the sand just off the road.

Besides our quartet, the beach also hosted a woman and child, flying a kite in the shape of a killer whale.

Meanwhile at the water's edge, a total of five people, two individuals, and three together, fished. Just offshore on the Sakonnet River, a windsurfer dashed west to east.

By nature, red foxes are shy. They hunt at night, sunset and dawn. Sometimes foxes contract rabies, but that's not common. Anyway, if the sight of a fox makes you squirm, then clap your hands or shout. The fox will take off.

Abruptly, the animal turned off the road and onto the sand. From our angle, it appeared to walk toward the trio fishing—two men and a woman. They were casting beside the riprap at the end of the beach.

Halfway toward the water, the fox stopped. Then it dipped its head into a shallow depression in the sand, coming back up with what looked like a black box the size and shape of a Belgian waffle.

The animal turned and walked back over the beach and roadway and directly into the thicket atop the dunes. Gone.

I strolled over to the fishing folks. All three were reeling in scup. Scup school around structures such as rock. The relatively flat, silvery fish with white bellies and blue hues sparkled in the pre-dusk sun.

What did the fox snatch, I asked? "Meat," said one of the men. Earlier in the evening, there was a barbeque on the beach, and when the picnickers packed up, they tossed a chunk of charred meat onto the sand, he said

"That cooking smelled good," he added, and all of them nodded in agreement.

Red foxes are called omnivores, because they eat both plant and animal matter. Mice, rabbits, birds, snakes and beetles are all fox food. So are cherries, grapes and acorns. Foxes also consume roadkill and other carrion.

Based on our observation that evening, we will add barbeque to the list of what a fox eats, and the beach to the inventory of places where you might see one of these fetching creatures.

A Sweet September Sea

October 4, 2014

Karen and I swam with the fishes.

At Watch Hill, we stepped into 68-degree waves on an 80-degree morning at the end of September.

The aquamarine water was so lucent that we saw the bottom of the ocean, even when we stood in chest-high water.

In it, we also saw fish, maybe a foot long, and oriented perpendicular to the waves that rose over our heads on approach. The fish looked like blue specters in the green sea.

When a wave crashed, we yelped, dove amid bubbles, re-found our footing, and waited for the next impact.

Retreating to knee-deep water, we witnessed, maybe 100 feet offshore, a sphere of the sea, the size of a baseball batter's circle, boiling, with herring-type baitfish under attack from bluefish.

Out of this cauldron leapt the occasional prey, with the backs of predators skimming the bubbling surface. The spot looked like a patina of silver sparkles in the sunshine.

Suddenly, and literally out of the clear blue sky, a large dark bird lowered in, its yellow talons barely touching the water, and grabbed a plump, foot-long fish.

This flat-winged raptor, with dark head and tail, and bits of white around the body, was an immature bald eagle. The bird flapped its way toward the Watch Hill Lighthouse, its victim showing a lot of bright-white flesh in the late-morning sun.

We walked back onshore, where a witness to the eagle-fish encounter said that he'd also spotted a seal near the simmering sea earlier that morning.

Karen retired to our towel and I strolled through a narrow path of seaside vegetation fragrant with goldenrod. The fluttering shadow of a monarch butterfly passed over me, and then another.

Any monarch sighting these days is a sign of hope. Loss of both habitat and food has led to the disappearance of monarchs in much of North America over the last 10 years. In fact, some biologists estimate up to a 98-percent drop in monarch numbers. The butterflies migrate south through Rhode Island this time of year.

On the path I found a wooly bear caterpillar crossing between the walls of vegetation. Tips of black framed the warm-brown body of the little critter.

As folks walked to and from the beach, I guided them away from stepping inadvertently on the insect, until it vanished into the greenery.

Wooly bears look for food and then search for sheltered spots to hibernate for winter. In spring they spin cocoons, emerging in two weeks as Isabella tiger moths.

Legend has it that the wider the middle section of a caterpillar, the milder the coming winter. Since, the wooly bear I found was mostly brown, a mild winter may be on tap. But don't bet on it.

Back on the beach, I walked the shoreline, examining and admiring the myriad of flat, colorful stones amidst the little bodies of crabs and shells of the tide line.

Watch Hill beaches feature some of the flattest and most-oval stones along the state's coastline. In fact, the rocks remind me of the kind that I find around the Great Lakes or in streams and rivers in other parts of the country.

Sometimes on the Watch Hill beaches I also find good numbers of round, thick stones. They suggest colorful, speckled bird eggs of varying sizes.

After such an exciting and lovely 90 minutes on the beach, all of the rocks on the beach were lucky stones, as Watch Hill was ripe with living energy.

Or, in the words of two 13-year-old boys, who caught a bluefish after casting from the beach, "That was pretty awesome."

SEEKING-OUT THE LADY OF THE LAKE

July 12, 2014

In the second full week of summer, Karen and I strolled around a seven-acre pond, with its co-owner, a woman, who with her husband, has lived alongside the natural body of water for the past 36 years.

The pond, a few miles east of Providence, might qualify as a small lake, given there are a few houses around it between stretches of vegetation.

There was a lot of bird song, when we arrived. Sleek cedar waxwings whistled from tall white oaks, gray catbirds mewed from surrounding thickets and several ruby-throated hummingbirds exchanged "chee-dit" calls around a feeder.

From adjacent woods, a rufous-sided towhee repeated its diagnostic "sip-your-tea" call, while an ovenbird called, "teacher, teacher, teacher."

Since our host did not want to be identified, I will call her lake lady. She spoke intriguingly of life around her.

For one thing, lake lady said that she wished the hummingbirds could speak, so she could ask them what it was like to spend the winter in Mexico.

Jewelweed grew thick by the shore. Later in summer, those plants will produce seed-filled pods that will pop between a pinch of thumb and forefinger. Lake lady called jewelweed, "nature's bubble wrap."

Multiple dragonflies hovered over the water. Lake lady said there were "a gazillion dragonflies," plus the tree "frogs were in good voice." The forest was "mosquito heaven," she said.

The three of us walked around the property, where views of the water changed every few feet. When the road veered away, thick oaks, elderberry shrubs and ferns shielded the pond from view.

Below some white pines we found a dead Eastern painted turtle. Its deep green shell, known scientifically as a carapace, was cracked. To me, it seemed awfully hard to snap a turtle shell like that. My guess is that a vehicle ran over the turtle, which walked off the road and died.

A few feet farther we found another dead painted turtle. This one was crushed into what looked like bathroom floor tiles. Lake lady shook her head, and used her foot to brush the pieces off the road.

Recently, a large snapping turtle was run over. Lake lady found the dead snapper, which was filled with eggs.

Here and there, we saw little boats along shore. Plus there was a neighbor, swimming. The water was "pretty deep in the middle," we learned.

A great blue heron visited sporadically, while mallards raised a four-duckling brood this year.

A couple of days before we showed up, lake lady's husband saw a fisher, which "ran back into the woods." A fisher is a long, slim-bodied member of the weasel family, with short legs, rounded ears and a bushy tail.

Then, on a canoe paddle after we visited, lake lady and her husband discovered bryozoans, or moss animals. These are massed colonies of individual creatures called zooids.

Each zooid features "delicate feeding tentacles swaying slowly in the water catching food," notes a University of Massachusetts website, which says that the fossil record for bryozoans extends back 500 million years.

"We observed round blobs ranging in size from tennis ball to soccer ball, and found them just under the surface of the water near the edge of the pond," said lake lady.

In the fall, a "couple of dozen ducks" and an "armada" of Canada geese," occupy the pond. If mid-winter conditions are right, the ice-skating is good, although eight inches of snow often ends up "on top of perfectly smooth ice," lake lady said.

The "cheerful sound" of a "gazillion peep toads" (spring peepers) marks the onset of spring, as do the arrival of wetlands-seeking red-winged blackbirds, and the appearance of box, painted and snapping turtles.

Last winter, snow kept people from skating on the frozen water, lake lady said. Plus the peepers were late, first calling at the start of April.

After such a lengthy winter, however, the arrival of peepers "was a sign of hope." Moreover, all of the "green now growing" around the lake was joyous, she said.

Yes, we agreed, life on the pond hummed along swimmingly.

WHEN FALL FEELS LIKE SPRINGTIME
November 21, 2009

L ast week, on a day when the-mid November temperature approached 70 degrees, I stopped to observe upper Narragansett Bay, which looked as still as a bedspread.

That night, my father told me of a November morning 34 years ago, when he and his cousin, Stanford, set out from a New Rochelle Marina into Long Island Sound to catch the last of the season's migrating bluefish.

A Manhattan plumber to the stars, Stanford lived in the leafy suburbs with his family, drove a motorcycle and owned a boat. I still remember holding onto his leather jacket as we raced around the block on a Harley.

Stanford used his 24-foot craft to fish the Sound. Sometimes he invited my father, Ed, who lugged home glassy-eyed creatures for my mother to clean and fillet.

Besides the Staten Island Ferry, the only boat I ever sat in as a youngster belonged to Stanford. One afternoon, when I was a teenager, he pulled into a cove off the north shore of Pelham Bay Park. We swam out to climb aboard. A few minutes later, I jumped back into the water to avoid heaving from seasickness.

On a November day when the temperature in New York hit 75 degrees, Stanford and Ed, shirts unbuttoned and hats off, took the channel out past small islands toward a cloud of gulls about two miles offshore.

The birds were attacking silvery baitfish stirred up by a school of bluefish.

A migratory species, bluefish move south along the Atlantic through fall. They travel in schools that feed in a one-of-a-kind, bird-attracting, water-broiling fury.

In summer, feeding bluefish attract birds, such as terns, which swirl over the bubbling water. By November, with the terns having migrated, it is primarily gulls that concentrate above the feeding fish.

Stanford outfitted my father with a powerful saltwater fishing pole and line tipped with a jig-lured umbrella rig—a multiple-armed contraption that suggested a flashing school of batfish.

The men reached the gulls, and bluefish hit all six lures of my father's line. Short, powerful and proud, my father would not let Stanford help him reel-in 30-plus pounds of fish. By the time Ed pulled the blues aboard, two had fallen off.

Stanford steered toward the next swirl of gulls, which the men spied farther out in the Sound. The birds hovered adjacent to Execution Rocks Lighthouse a mile north of Sands Point.

As the men raced toward the birds, the boat hit a patch of floating branches, lumber and other debris, and then the submerged peaks of a rocky reef.

The impacts shook the craft, damaging the propeller and shaft. Around the men, dense, excited gulls suggested that the bluefish were indeed active below.

Elsewhere on the Sound, the water was calm and clear of other craft. Most pleasure boats were out of the water for winter. Ed and Stanford's fishing frenzy ended abruptly.

Stanford brought the boat back into the marina. There, he removed the shaft and propeller, which the two men drove to City Island for repairs.

My father and Stanford still see each other once and a while, acting as rowdy as they did in the '30s and '40s, as children in Brooklyn.

The conversation with my father reminded me that our hunger for everyday moments and pursuits, such as fishing, watching the bay, or checking in, are what keep us going.

Just to be alive is a miracle. Suffusing life with love and the will of friendship is a blessing.

SITTING WITH SEVERAL SPECIES OF BUTTERFLY
July 21, 2012

On a sunny Sunday afternoon in summer, I lazed on a lounge chair in the shade of a red maple at an outdoor pool in Seekonk.

Some 30 minutes after dozing off, I opened my eyes to find a butterfly whizzing back and forth over my feet.

The butterfly was a red admiral, which eventually settled on the hard, white plastic edge of the seat.

The two-inch butterfly opened dark-chocolate-colored wings wide to reveal an orange band and a white spotted pattern on each forewing and a black-spotted, orange margin on each hindwing.

My lounge chair bordered an open forest adjacent to the swimming pool, plots of perennials, and fields of thistle and goldenrod. There were lots of edges between the fields, forests and open green spaces— good butterfly-watching habitat.

The admiral departed, as I stood up. That's when I noticed what looked like an especially attractive leaf on the forest edge foliage.

That leaf was a painted lady butterfly.

A relative of the red admiral, both species belong to the lovely named genus of butterflies called Vanessa.

Slightly larger than the red admiral, the painted lady showed off black-tipped, white-spotted forewings that blended back into a pattern of orange and black.

The painted lady remained stationary but began beating its wings together rapidly. The action reminded me of a cymbal-banging monkey toy.

I turned away and after just a few steps found a third, dark and small erratically flying butterfly, which seemed to challenge me for a puddle of water in a sunny spot.

I stepped back and the little butterfly landed at the puddle's edge, opening its wings.

Called a common sootywing, the butterfly looked half the size of the red admiral. The sootywing's outer forewings contained some white spots. Otherwise, the butterfly was dark.

I returned to the chair to loll again, like a seal on a rock.

In this spirit of idleness and wonder, I didn't get worked up when a 3-inch purplish butterfly whooshed by before I could identify it.

But I did note that a black swallowtail flew past. This was a large, spotted, iridescent beauty. I also saw my first two monarch butterflies of the season.

Eating dinner by the pool the following weekend, I watched an Eastern tiger swallowtail butterfly zip by the picnic table.

When I shared the sighting with dinner partners, an eight-year-old, named Henry, told me that an Eastern tiger swallowtail landed on his big toe when he got out of the pool earlier in the day.

Henry's eight-year-old buddy, Noah, confirmed the occurrence and added that the butterfly's bright colors and large-sized body and wings suggested that it was indeed an Eastern tiger swallowtail.

The exchange reminded me that butterfly admiration/watching is ageless.

That evening I returned to my chair under the red maple to continue loitering. Chilling out allowed me to close my eyes and think about nothing. It also unlocked my senses to the beautiful creatures that shared the same space.

Dozing off to images of real butterflies dancing in my head, I thought of the saying, "Sometimes I sit and think, and sometimes I just sit."

A Dolphin in the Seekonk River

December 19, 2015

S tanding with others on the School Street Pier in Pawtucket on a late afternoon at the end of November, I felt like one of the disparate people in the movie, "Close Encounters of the Third Kind," united after witnessing a UFO.

At the pier, we stood in amazement before a dolphin, which surfaced less than 10 feet away, exhaling in a loud, sighing hiss from its blowhole.

Mother of God! I was in Pawtucket, just south of where the freshwater Blackstone River becomes the long tidal estuary called the Seekonk River.

Although December was two days away, the much-cleaner-than-it-used-to-be Seekonk River remained full of menhaden. And small schooling fish were a dolphin's top prey.

Near eight feet in length, the active, dark-looking dolphin surfaced regularly. Every so often, the mammal leapt out of the water, returning in a splash.

Each surface break produced rings atop the river that grew large as they traveled outward. The six or so of us standing on the pier used those rings to note the mammal's movements as it swam out and across the waterway.

Eventually the dolphin moved north under the Division Street and I-95 bridges and into downtown Pawtucket.

Earlier that afternoon, I had received a picture of the dolphin via email, sent by a reader named Will. When I reached the School Street Pier, Will was gone, but I joined other folks who'd also heard about the mammal.

Among the people there were Thyra and Mike, local volunteers for the Mystic Aquarium's Animal Rescue Program. After receiving word of the dolphin, the Aquarium asked the couple to check on the dolphin's status.

Mike used the *Guide to Marine Mammals of the World* to identify the creature as a short-beaked common dolphin.

These are "energetic, boisterous animals often seen breaking the water's surface at high speed and frequently bow-riding in front of large vessels," I read later on the website of Whale and Dolphin Conservation (WDC).

The dolphins "typically travel in large social groups numbering between 10 and 50 animals, and occasionally, thousands of individuals. They are very acrobatic and can often be seen breaching and somersaulting through the air."

According to WDC, the short-beaked common dolphin occurs in most tropical and temperate areas of the Pacific and Atlantic oceans, declining in some places "due to by-catch in illegal driftnets, prey depletion from overfishing, chemical pollution and habitat degradation.

WDC said the maximum length for the species was just short of 9 feet and top weight was about 330 pounds. Estimated population worldwide was three million.

Next morning, Mike visited the pier but saw no dolphins. Maybe it "found its way back to the Bay with the outgoing tide," he suggested. Mike added that he'd named the dolphin, "Flippah, in honor of the local RI accent."

Five days later, the media reported a dolphin swimming in the Providence River downtown. Pictures were taken, crowds gathered. Maybe this was Flippah.

After witnessing the dolphin, I thanked Will for alerting me. Will said that after sending me the image, he went to his Providence home, got his wife and their young child, and returned to watch the mammal. I probably just missed them.

It was cool that Will was able to share the dolphin's presence with loved ones. As local waters get cleaner, I hope head-of-the-bay dolphin sightings become commonplace for our kids and their children.

For now, such extraordinary encounters seem out of this world.

Over the River and Through Beautiful Woods
March 22, 2008

Thrashed by 40-mile-per-hour-winds, the green, pretzel-shaped twigs atop a stand of fifty-foot-tall sassafras trees rocked back and forth like a gospel choir. A black-capped chickadee worked its way around a rotted cinnamon-colored sassafras sapling, probing a trail of holes left by woodpeckers.

Below, five-year-old Aran marched through a puddle churning up a layer of red maple leaves. On this chilly March afternoon, the little girl wore a hooded pink and white winter coat, sky blue pants and blue boots trimmed in red.

The trees swayed and Aran played on a wet, wooded slope within the Town of Narragansett's Canonchet Farm property. She and brothers Jack, 7 and Brendan, 4, accompanied their mother, Tara Flaherty and 11 other adults on a public walk designed "to introduce people to the beauty and possibilities" of the site, said Kathie Kelleher, secretary of the Friends of Canonchet Farms.

Dense forests of oak and maple and stretches of amphibian-rich wetlands surround two sun-swept fields on the 160-acre property. Former granite quarries now serve as vernal ponds–small temporary bodies of water, which last long enough each spring for the birth and development of frogs, salamanders and insects.

Igneous rock, which bubbled to the surface millions of years ago, and sedimentary rock, formed from sediments compacted under pressure, dot the landscape.

Locals talk about the coyotes that bark and the owls that hoot from the Farm at night. Deer are common, and fox sighted regularly.

Soon, the mating calls of spring peepers will fill the air, I'm told. Each June, Kelleher spies female snapping turtles searching for sites to lay eggs.

"I am a strong believer in 'no child left inside,'" said Tara Flaherty, one of 10 founders of the Friends. "Lives of children are too structured indoors. They need free unrestricted time outdoors."

Seven-year-old Jack said he was raising frog eggs at home. "It takes three summers for an egg to turn into a frog," he said.

"Three summers mean three years," noted Aran, who leaned against my shoulder, as I squatted to chat. All three Flaherty children nodded their heads.

Pointing to sassafras, tour leader Tom Fortier explained that the tree's thick fleshy roots often generate sprouts that grow into new trees. Given room to flourish, one sassafras tree may surround itself with a colony of clones. Researchers have found sassafras trees a mile apart joined by the same root systems, he said.

Sunshine bathing the tree canopy cascaded down to a network of historic, lichen-covered stonewalls, separating the property from Pettaquamscutt Cove and the Narrow River, which are overseen by the U.S. Fish and Wildlife Service. A gap in one of the walls marked a former road through which horse-drawn wagons once hauled salt marsh hay.

Narragansett Town Council appointed a committee to draft a master plan for the site to present in April, said Charles Lee, Friends vice president. The Friends formed in 2007, with the goal of managing the property, in collaboration with the Town, "for the enjoyment of present and future generations," he said.

In less than six months, the Friends have grown to 192 members and raised $20,000—more than three times the Town's annual budget for the property.

"Canonchet Farm is a place where people who enjoy being in natural places can hike, observe and learn about our coastal environments," said Fortier, who is president of the Friends. He is an arborist, horticulturalist and organic landscaper.

As safe haven for plants and wildlife, filter for pollutants and living ecological laboratory, the land speaks for itself.

If you are more interested in history, the property was once part of a plantation owned by Thomas Mumford, a Narragansett Planter. It was a colonial farm, and one-time home of former Rhode Island Governor William Sprague and his wife, Kate Chase Sprague, "the belle of Washington." Her father served as Secretary of the Treasury under President Lincoln, and later as Chief Justice of the Supreme Court. South County Museum currently occupies a small portion of the site.

"I see the Friends volunteer effort to protect, manage and learn from this wonderful resource, as a gleam of hope," said Fortier. "I believe that stewardship is the only legitimate human role in nature. Here is a piece of public land in stages of regeneration, standing at the edge of a growing population, which could get involved in its stewardship."

Flaherty's father grew up on the west coast of Ireland, where property ownership was coupled with a moral and ethical responsibility to care for the land.

"We learned from him to respect and appreciate walking in the woods. My father taught us that land was sacred. You passed your land on to your children.

"I am hoping that the town will approve the master plan, so one day we may pass on Canonchet Farm to our children."

Praise for the Pawpaw
October 31, 2015

O f all the fruits I've tasted, pawpaw ranks at the top in terms of my desire to taste it again.

Pawpaw is the largest edible fruit native to the United States. It has a bit of an apple taste, and a bit of a banana essence.

With each bite of pawpaw, the spirits of other fruits, such as mango and pineapple, waft through my mouth and nose. I find the taste complex and enticing.

A pawpaw fruit comes from a pawpaw tree. It is a relatively small tree—think dogwood-sized—with large, almost tropical-looking, deep-green leaves. The species is found primarily in states between the Gulf Coast and Great Lakes, and as far west as Nebraska.

I first ate pawpaw in the 1970s in Indiana. When I lived in Ohio in the latter half of the 1980s, I reacquainted myself with the fruit, collecting it in early fall from thickets growing in the deep, rich soils of riverbanks.

Back in those days, I called pawpaw the "Indiana banana," although it goes by other names such as "American custard apple."

Earlier this month, my neighbor, Andrew, who tends a creative and colorful home garden, was kind enough to offer me a pawpaw from a tree in his arboretum-like backyard. I couldn't remember the last time I had eaten a pawpaw, maybe in the early '90s.

Pawpaw fruit ripen in clusters. Each fruit is pear-sized, or larger, and shaped somewhat like a mango. The skin is thin and light green. Hold a pawpaw in your hand, and you feel its heft.

The inside of a pawpaw is creamy off-white, juicy and delicate. This squishy, custard-like flesh surrounds large seeds that look like giant, dark-brown lima beans.

I eat a pawpaw by gently slicing around it, and then peeling off some of the skin. Then I slice, slurp or spoon out the slippery creaminess from around the seeds, nibbling and sucking remaining flesh from skin and seeds.

In plain words, I gorge myself in a primitive fashion, whenever I eat a pawpaw. The experience is moist, gooey and probably gross to anyone watching.

By the way, pawpaw's fragrance is almost as powerful as its taste. Our kitchen is about 120 square feet, and just one pawpaw quickly filled that space with a commanding smell similar to that of overripe apples.

Smelling and eating a pawpaw not only excites my senses, but evokes memories from the '70s, '80s and '90s. The experience includes a feeling that I can best describe as, "fall is coming along the rich rivers and streams, and I can't believe nature produces this exquisite fruit."

As a food and a staple, pawpaw was once well known. Then pawpaw seemed to vanish from the culinary radar. Now, it is making a comeback. For growing pawpaw here in Southern New England, Andrew deserves credit for out-of-the-box thinking.

Pawpaw is evidence that not every exotic food has to come from a faraway place. To me, eating pawpaw adds an extra-special thrill to the chill of fall. It is one of the few fruits (I feel similar about Macoun apples) that leave me longing for their scent and their taste this time of year.

BAD BEHAVIOR ON THE BEACH
July 28, 2012

During my 18th year and the Bicentennial of our independence, 1976, my summer job was to clean the men's locker room of Van Cortlandt Park Pool in the Bronx.

All seasonal workers also took turns toiling one 4 p.m. to midnight shift. The job entailed serving as garbage collector and watchman after the pool closed at 6 p.m.

My shift came after a 95-degree afternoon. As darkness enveloped the property, lights atop tall concrete stanchions illuminated the blue waters.

At about 9 p.m., people began climbing over the perimeter fences.

Once inside, folks swam, drank or toked. Out of the darkness, a bottle sailed over the fence and smashed poolside. Several more bottles came crashing in. A few people began scaling the light pillars on this powerfully hot and humid night.

I locked myself in the concrete bunker of an office and called the police.

This memory most reminds me of what my family and I experienced on a Saturday evening recently along the Rhode Island shore.

We're daytime regulars at a beach and nature preserve that we think is some of the loveliest coastline in Southern New England. The beauty of this area attracts many visitors, and almost all of them respect its recreation and protection rules.

Over the last 20 years, The Nature Conservancy has increased its public awareness programs of this coastal pond/barrier beach ecosystem, offering all sorts of family events and educational programs, particularly with the opening of a new family education center.

Moreover, well-meaning and hardworking staff and volunteers oversee these properties. Local residents also keep the beach clean. Stewards trained by The Nature Conservancy help protect the plants and animals.

I believe all of those good folks went home at 5 p.m. on Saturday.

We arrived just after 6 p.m. As we laid out a beach blanket, some people sat down behind us. They planted an American flag and then tossed trash alongside us. A person to our right threw an empty cigarette box and a napkin into the surf.

I got up and collected the garbage.

Unleashed dogs ran back and forth between sand and surf. Scanning up and down the beach, I counted 21 canines. Posted signs state that dogs are not allowed.

This stretch of shoreline boasts some of the region's greatest success in attracting shorebirds, such as the federally protected and globally rare piping plover, to breed. The Nature Conservancy has managed the piping plover nest areas for more than 20 years, and the plovers have made significant progress.

Protecting breeding birds from people with pets is key to nesting success in this beach-dunes-saltwater-pond ecosystem.

We packed up and left the beach to walk into the preserve, passing two people, dragging out bags of trash. Kudos to them.

Unleashed canines, followed by their owners, sauntered past the large white sign prohibiting dogs and declaring the area home to breeding piping plovers.

Although The Nature Conservancy has witnessed significant progress in the attitudes of visitors toward following restrictions within the preserve, both restrained and unrestrained dogs have a negative impact on adult piping plovers, especially flightless chicks.

Deep inside the nesting area of the state-threatened least terns, we observed a couple of dozen children and adults playing what looked like tag, racing back and forth alongside the fence lines and Keep Out signs.

Clearly upset, the terns crisscrossed the skies, shrieking "zreep" alarm calls.

When I called The Nature Conservancy a few days later, I learned that the piping plover nesting success was somewhat below average this summer.

"Among other variables, it can also be related to the amount of people traffic, and especially to those people that bring their dogs," said Jeanne Parente, Operations Administrator.

And despite a summer of disturbances, the terns had produced 17 chicks, she said.

A few years ago, our son, Noah, found his first baby flounder and one and only seahorse in the preserve's salt pond. From the same waters on Saturday we collected several floating plastic bags.

Many law-abiding folks visit this area. It is the anarchy and filth of the unlawful few that are the opposite of pristine. This lack of respect for boundaries contradicts the spiritual and ethical principles that define what we can become as a society.

It felt like 1976 again. I was garbage collector and watchman, retreating from human misbehavior.

Besides my sorrow for the shorebirds and terns, I felt bad for the workers and volunteers, who would return the next morning to assess the damage and clean up the mess.

Maybe the one difference between 1976 and 2012 was that this time I failed to call the police.

LIFE-CHANGING SALAMANDERS
June 28, 2014

Not everything was better in the old days.

Use Google Maps Street View to find the 90-year-old Bronx apartment building in which I grew up. The 3-D, 360-degree scene will show you a five-story walkup, with a quiet courtyard, on a clean street with small street trees and lots of air conditioners in the windows.

Forty years ago, that same courtyard was a mini-arena for gang fights, and the gutter was a garbage patch. There were no trees, and no one I knew owned an air conditioner.

Back In 1974, if you could have zoomed into a certain corner third-floor window, you would have found a teenaged me (sharing a bedroom with three brothers), dreaming of open spaces and the flora and fauna that called them home.

Now imagine my joy in finding that after 15 years of reviving the soil, replanting the little landscape around our Providence home (the gardens were neglected for a long time), and providing other enhancements, such as a birdbath and a woodpile, we hosted our first family of Eastern cottontail rabbits in 2012.

Then in 2013, we discovered a redback salamander under one of the logs in the backyard, where the rabbits hung out.

The redback salamander is Rhode Island's most common amphibian and the only one that lives entirely on land. It eats insects and spiders, and improves soil by tunneling, which mixes in nutrients that plants then pull into their roots more easily.

So far this spring and summer, we've become a way station or home for three more species: Eastern chipmunk, chipping sparrow and the plant, jewelweed.

The salamander's presence may account, in part, for the chipmunk's arrival. Salamanders are among the many things that chipmunks eat.

The glade-like look to our backyard may help explain the nesting chipping sparrows. A pert, petite bird with a rusty cap and black line through the eye, the chipping sparrow breeds where trees intersperse with grassy areas. Most often found in open forests, and in parks and along roadsides, the birds sometimes nest in backyards, especially where there are trees and feeders. This year, we left up the black-oil sunflower and thistle seed feeders. Voila!

Arrival of the native jewelweed is another indicator of improving conditions. Most often, I find jewelweed in rich, shaded, wet spots, particularly along streams and small rivers. Its coming suggests that after years of adding plants to the garden and compost to the soil, we've turned the sunbaked dust into something closer to shaded, creek-side earth.

On jewelweed leaves, moisture beads up, reflecting light and looking like little crystals. Juice in jewelweed contains a fungicide and anti-inflammatory that soothes a fresh mosquito bite or a brush with poison ivy. Jewelweed's trumpet-shaped flowers are orange and spotted with red. Those flowers become swollen pods that burst into coiled shreds and edible seeds at the touch of a finger.

We're going to have some backyard fun with jewelweed!

For a kid who grew up in concrete, certain species become larger in meaning than they might to others. Folks who've lived a lifetime around chipmunks and salamanders may not understand my delight.

I can still recall, when as a teen, I discovered my first salamander. The amphibian was under a log in upstate New York. The experience was like unlocking a door to a new world.

Each new native plant or animal at our home is a milestone and a chance to marvel.

Some things in life do get better. And in this case, I *am* living the dream.

Finding a Fortune Together in the Sand and Surf

June 30, 2012

O n the second-to-last Tuesday of school, I visited 18 first graders on a field trip from maritime-based Paul Cuffee School in Providence to the summer home of their reading teacher, Lauren, and her family on the Kickemuit River in Warren.

The adventure celebrated completion of the classes' multiple intelligence unit. For several weeks, the young people had pursued eight areas of knowledge such as "art smart" and "math/logic smart."

Swashbuckling was the celebration theme. As part of a "word smart" lesson the previous week, the class had read "Pirate Girl," in which pirates kidnap a young girl, named Molly, who proves more than the buccaneers can handle.

To the sound of gulls and surf, the first graders marched from bus to shoreline, singing, "We are the pirates; Paul Cuffee pirates. We are so smart, in so many ways. Let us tell you how."

Then they rotated among three centers. One was the boat and shoreline, another was the ramp and dock, and a third was a sandy strip, with "treasure" buried under wooden Xs.

Looking like a string of ducklings trailing their mom, six children in life vests followed their classroom teacher, Karen, who also happens to be my spouse, toward a paddleboat, pulled just onto a sandy shore.

The first graders settled into the boat, which Karen pulled into waist-deep waters. There she asked the children to scan the horizon for pirates.

Onshore and out of site, Pirate Nanny (Lauren's aunt in character) tossed a corked bottle into the waves.

Suddenly one of the children, Jasmine, spotted the bottle. And, it contained a note! As the kids chattered breathlessly, Karen steered the boat over.

With peers, Beyanca and Dashelys, Jasmine popped the cork and out slipped a note. "Help me," it read. Pirates had captured Molly!

The first graders called out for Molly, scanning the sea and shoreline.

With the boat now in shallower waters, two kids jumped out to search for the fictitious Molly. The others, using nets distributed by Pirate Nanny, looked for signs of life under the water's surface. This was a "nature smart" activity.

Walk slowly and scoop fast, Pirate Nanny told Jahdiel. The little fellow informed the rest of his mates that schools of fish zipped along the shoreline, and the rest of the kids grabbed nets.

Fiona splashed over to show me two small shrimp, which she dropped into a collection pool of seawater on shore.

Besides containing all sorts of shells, the pool also held these living creatures: rock crab, blue crab, conch, mussels, clams, periwinkles and mummichog.

Before the end of the visit, all life in the pool would go back into the sea, Fiona said.

The clang of an old-fashioned chuck wagon triangle dinner bell signaled a change of centers. Lauren's mom, Susan, helped transition the children from site to site.

At the dock, I found another group of six kids. "Word smart" placards were taped to parts of the structure. Lauren and math teacher, Becky, reviewed the words "ramp," "raft" and "cleat," with the children. For some youngsters, this was their first time on a dock.

In a screened porch behind the sand, teaching partner Christian, helped "art smart" Anthony, Dillan and Philip color bandanas blue, orange and green, while "people smart" and "self smart" Genesis, Magdiel and Skyla compared pirate tattoos, the content of treasure bags, and discussed working together to find kidnapped Molly.

After lunch, the children ate a crab cake—a giant donut in the shape of a crustacean.

Then they danced in the sunlight and breeze. They swayed and leapt, swooned and stretched their arms to the sky. This was "music smart," and joyous to observe.

OUR LITTLE CHICKADEES
June 14, 2014

Just before Memorial Day weekend, Karen and I became grandparents. Oh, thank you for your warm wishes! We're excited, too. And to our closest friends, sorry we did not tell you first.

One thing: We never determined how many grandchildren we gained: Four, maybe five? But oh how their parents loved them, bringing those babies a caterpillar every three to five minutes for hours a day.

Our "grandchildren" were a handful of black-capped chickadees born in a box on a pole outside our kitchen window. A chickadee box features a 1 1/8-inch hole size that restricts invasive species, such as house sparrows, from claiming the container.

On our street, house sparrows may have a dozen active nests. The sparrows are persistent in attempting to wiggle through that chickadee nest hole.

Once, a female sparrow tried to squeeze inside the box, but appeared jammed. Her jiggling, plus gurgling calls, reminded us of Flick's flapping and cries of "stuck" when his tongue adhered to the frozen flagpole in "A Christmas Story."

Our chickadee grandchildren arrived exactly when we needed an avian fix. Let me explain. May is when hundreds of thousands of migrating birds, sing, rest and chow their way home to Rhode Island or northward. Such tireless efforts are devoted to one thing—breeding to perpetuate the species.

Morning after morning this past May, flycatchers, vireos, warblers and other migrants sang or called from the greenery in our neighborhood.

However, Karen and I were busy with work and family commitments. As a result, we spent just one hour in May devoted to birdwatching.

By the end of the month, when morning calls came just from the usual nesting birds, I felt grief at missing the migration.

But then the little chickadees began squeaking from the box when mom or pop brought home a bug.

With every inchworm and spider meal, the little peeps grew stronger, as the parents took turns rocketing back to the hole from nearby tree branches.

Their box sits about 8 feet off the ground just outside our kitchen window in a small clear space amidst a little forest of small native trees that include black birch, gray birch, black walnut and red oak.

After a couple days, the bawls of the baby birds sounded like the high-pitched trills, sighs and whistles of cedar waxwings, fruit-eaters which had returned to our neighborhood in small numbers at the end of May to feed on Yoshino cherries, the first fruit of the season.

Those cherries, by the way, are more pits than flesh, with a cyanide-like aftertaste. The birds like them, though.

Over the next several days, the little chickadees began sounding, well, like little chickadees, with gurgling and whiny "dee-dee-dee" sounds when food arrived.

Then, some 15 days after we first learned of their presence, the brood, plus their parents vanished.

Parent chickadees feed their young for 3-4 weeks after fledgling. Subsequently, the family splits up, with babies dispersing from where they were born and raised. Chickadees typically produce one brood per nesting season.

In recent days, we've heard the family in the trees around the house. With the youngsters still asking for food, and with chickadees making so many calls anyway, the clan sounds like a chickadee convention.

My grief over missing migration subsided, mitigated by time spent with the grandchildren, our little chickadees.

A NOD TO NATIVE PLANTS
June 2, 2012

Often, you don't run into native plants in the built-up landscape. That wasn't the case for some college students last week when they drove a rental truck into an American elm street tree at the corner of Brown and Benevolent streets in Providence.

Taking the turn too tightly, the driver gouged open a section of the tree, driving a corkscrewed strip of gleaming six-inch-wide metal into the trunk.

The resilient tree stood its ground. The square box atop the truck twisted into a diamond shape. The box top crumpled backward like a wad of discarded paper.

When a tractor-trailer tow truck pulled the rental off the elm, the ground below it was covered in busted strips of white and yellow paneling, with a smattering of shattered bark and broken branches. The tree looked much like it did before the crash.

There is something tough about native plants, and that is partly the reasoning behind why our family uses them to landscape our property.

Once upon a time much of what is now our Providence neighborhood supported a forest of beech, birch, maple, oak and pine.

When we replant a native species, we re-link that ancient chain. These trees are adapted to local soil, slope and sun. Some start slow, but they almost always do well.

Our nod to natives also honors what we consider our family tree—species that grew for millennia on land we now occupy. Those trees were our ancestors, and replanting the latest generation is a tribute to their memory.

For our home, we've either purchased or replanted about a dozen native species to form a flowery, shady, fruit- and nut-producing fence line someday. Those natives include black walnut, gray birch, sweet birch, pin oak, red oak, white oak and shadbush.

Sometimes squirrels do the planting.

The red oak, for example, showed up on the property border almost 10 years ago. Like most other oaks, the seedling grew slowly, maybe a foot in height a year.

This spring, the oak seemed to explode upward and outward, spreading its branches like multiple sets of open arms.

The oak's appearance in our Providence yard was divine. Birds also poop out seeds that become seedlings on our property. Each spring, we find that bird droppings the previous year delivered us small mulberry trees, which, while we love mulberry for its fruiting ability, get pulled out, as we prefer other, tidier, fuller-growing species. Red mulberry, by the way, is a native.

In late spring we enjoy some of the most glorious flowers of our native trees. A few blocks away, on Blackstone Boulevard, for instance, towering tulip trees are now in bloom.

Tulip tree leaves form fully before the flowers open. The trees are also called tulip poplar but they are a type of magnolia. Each of their late May/early June blooms are hefty, upright, orange-based, yellow-to-light-green masses of nectar-yielding, pollen-producing parts.

Noticed the green pollen on your car these mornings? The last few days that pollen was so thick that I used the wipers to clear it off the windshield. Maybe some of that pollen on my car came from local tulips!

At this time of year, as trees branch out and plants bear first fruits (think strawberries, for example), kids end the school year and many of us lessen our workloads for the summer. It is a good time to take stock—a spot in the season for some deep breaths to help us to rejuvenate and to blossom.

How are we equipped to bear fruit? Spend time with loved ones. Show kindness. Give to charity. Share.

I would like to think that we humans are as tough as street corner elms. We absorb some blows during the year, but we have what it takes to rebound and continue to mature.

So Long to a Crabapple
January 28, 2012

The only evidence that a lovely crabapple once bloomed outside my office building was a snow-covered, military-helmet-sized mound of golden wood chips.

The snow reminded me of the tree's dazzling white flowers each spring. On warm spring days, the perfumed scent of crabapple blossoms filled our open-windowed workspace. Those flowers massed into a bee-covered brilliance, eventually forming thousands of small fruits, which robins and other migrants gulped down every fall.

Winter is a good time for tree pruning and removal. It is when you can most easily visualize a specimen's structure and minimize its stress, such as the flow of sap and resin, and the spread of disease.

Last week, the trees around my office were pruned or removed. Besides dispensing of the crabapple, crews took down a large, dying sycamore maple, with its widow- and widower-making branches dangling from the canopy.

That sycamore maple once shaded our building from the worst late day summer heat and sun the Providence sky could muster. However, its time had come.

Also felled was a long-in-decline little leaf linden. It was a mostly hollow trunk, in which someone had once poured concrete. I think the foresters and facilities folks are still pondering how to remove the last of that material-filled trunk.

The final tree to get the axe was a hackberry. This mid-sized, warty-backed specimen was flush with dead and dying branches.

The crabapple's removal, though, was a mystery. My first reaction was powerful—the tree was an innocent that deserved to live.

What was wrong with the crabapple, I asked the landscape architect, grounds superintendent and lead groundworker?

The tree, they said, had simply grown too big for its space. Planted decades ago just five feet from the building, the crabapple had zero room left to grow. In the garden, size mattered.

"Did you ever smell the tree?" I asked. "Listen to its bees? I lived with that tree for 15 years."

I'd known these folks for years. They were good people.

We couldn't keep the tree under control, one person said, adding, "It was a plant out of place." Besides, new plants will come later this year, as will new benches and a change in the walkways. This nice space will grow even nicer, they said.

Somewhere inside I understood. To maintain a garden you must remove what no longer belongs. Still, the death felt like an amputation.

In the twilight, I re-visited the snow-covered chips. Overhead swirled the coal-black shapes of crows that roosted nearby each night. I dug into remnants of the ground-up stump, plucking what looked like a set of pinky-sized firewood logs. They smelled like apple.

Back inside, I showed the splinters to a coworker, and mourned the snow-white, sweet-smelling, trunk-twisting tree.

"What crabapple?" she responded. Although my colleague had worked a half-dozen years on the other side of the wall from the tree, she could not recall it.

In my office, I spread out the crabapple slivers like a deck of cards. Then I shuffled them into what resembled a miniature funeral pyre, sniffed the wood one last time, shut off the lights and headed home.

Expanding My World at the River

June 9, 2017

I t was hard to visualize that the winding path beneath my feet was an overgrown, dumping ground not long ago.

But Joan, a lifelong and now elderly resident of Olneyville, said that she remembered bushwhacking through that brush and trash decades earlier alongside the first folks determined to create a trail that would reconnect the Woonasquatucket River with neighborhood residents.

Those "visionaries," as Joan called them, used machetes to cut through the overgrown vegetation.

Joan's tale prompted Elizabeth, a relatively new Olneyville occupant, to share that this stroll—the 3rd Annual Paul McElroy Bird Walk—was her first along the river.

Compared to Joan, everything was new to Elizabeth, a Certified Nursing Assistant, who moved to Providence from the Dominican Republic two years ago.

So, for example, when Elizabeth saw a female mallard on the Woonasquatucket, she said that the bird reminded her of a yaguasa, a type of duck that inhabits the Isabela River, in her hometown of Santo Domingo.

And, when we sniffed the creamy fragrance of black locust flowers, Elizabeth said that the smell reminded her of vetiver, an alluring scent derived from a plant related to lemongrass.

The walk along the Woonasquatucket River Greenway bike path honored the late Paul McElroy, a supporter of the Woonasquatucket

172

River Watershed Council (WRWC) and the Audubon Society of Rhode Island.

Decades of dreaming, planning and labor led to completion of the first on-road segment of the path in 2002, with the work ongoing in several forms.

For example, we visited a fish ladder, finished in 2009, in Riverside Park. The ladder allows "fish such as shad and herring, which migrate from saltwater to fresh to spawn, and eels, which migrate from fresh to salt to spawn, to move up and down the lower river," notes the WRWC.

Indeed, just two days before the walk, 26 herring used the ladder to continue their trek upstream to breeding grounds.

We also found meadows; where there was once environmental contamination, and woodlots, formerly home to rubble.

As a result, we uttered an "ooh, aah" at a large mat of native phlox, a wildflower with blue blossoms, in the floodplain, and again at the vivid orange plumage of a male Baltimore oriole, foraging for insects in the treetops.

We heard a tree frog calling near a small wetland and watched a belted kingfisher hurry past, its rattling call louder than traffic on nearby U.S. Route 6.

That we could experience these wonders, while making new friends, was the result of the courage and dedication of those who came before us, plus the hard work of the folks who continue to revitalize this waterway and surroundings for all of us to discover and enjoy.

A Natural Place to Meet Neighbors
September 19, 2009

For a week, the Russians came. So did former residents of the Soviet Bloc and a few Turks.

The destination was a row of Cornelian cherry trees on Brook Street in Providence.

Folks pulled up in cars, vans and station wagons; they walked over from neighborhoods or came by bus, to maintain an old-country tradition of collecting the clustered, maroon, olive-shaped fruits of Cornelian cherry to make jelly, syrup or pies.

Most visitors were at least 50 years old. One couple spoke in English, until I approached. Then, they switched to Russian, when I asked what they made with the fruit.

Keeping one's mouth shut to strangers is also an old custom from life in the former Soviet Union—a tradition that may be hard to break.

One smiling fellow said his family called the jelly, "kizil." A woman said she used one pound of sugar to every two pounds of fruit after the berries, which she called "cornel," pronounced "CORE-Neal," with the accent on the first syllable, were steamed and strained.

Cornelian cherry, also known as *Cornus mas*, is native to central and southern Europe and parts of western Asia. It is planted widely elsewhere in temperate climates.

The invasion of the Brook Street trees caught me by surprise. I thought I was alone, spying the ripening berries over the summer, anticipating their tart taste by the end of August. The chewy fruit may crunch like a cranberry, when you bite it, and each berry contains a large pit.

Indeed, when the first significant handful of fruit turned deep red I collected some, continuing on my way, spitting seeds into shrubbery and flowerbeds, imagining those pits would give rise to new trees.

The next day, I found people amidst the foliage. As I revisited during the week, I noticed that several harvesters were wearing improvised buckets—former margarine tubs held by strings slung around necks like binoculars.

I learned about Cornelian cherry almost 30 years ago when I met three elderly women in babushka headscarves collecting fruit from trees adjacent to what is now called the Russian Mission to the UN Residency, which is in the Bronx.

None of those individuals said a word to me. One woman shared a berry, puckering her lips to warn me that it was tart. The fruit was sour, but pleasing. I still feel like we were being watched.

Cultivation of ornamentals or their spread as invasive plants—think of dandelion flowers for wine and leaves for salads—allows us to observe and to learn about other cultures. Sometimes we also get to make new friends.

In the early 1980s, I met a Chinese family collecting ginkgo nuts from the pavement near the intersection of 122nd Street and Riverside Drive in Manhattan. The father, mother and pre-teen daughter told me that the fruit fell from the trees after the first major frost.

The trio wore yellow dishwashing gloves to handle the outer covering—a pinkish-orange, vomit-smelling pulp—which they would remove before washing, and then roast the greenish nuts on an oiled pan.

The next two autumns, I saw the family, when I donned the same style of gloves to gather some ginkgo nuts, which I cooked, and found delicious. I learned from the family that the nuts were also used in desserts and drinks.

One of the oldest living species of trees, the ginkgo is a living fossil, with specimens dating back more than 250 million years. The tree is tolerant of air pollution, possibly because it evolved when Earth's atmosphere was dirtier from volcanic eruptions.

Ginkgo leaves are different from the net- or parallel-veined foliage of other deciduous trees. The veins of ginkgo fan out from the bottom toward the rim of the leaf, resembling ancient pine needles fused into one butterfly-winged shape.

Today, an extract from ginkgo leaves composes some of the world's most popular medications.

After the frost arrives, I will visit a fruit-laden gingko near the Pawtucket/Providence line. Stop by and say hi, I will be the guy wearing yellow gloves.

Ravens Over City Skies
February 24, 2017

On a typical February afternoon (cold, but sunny) in Providence, I loitered at the vehicular-and-pedestrian-busy intersection of Smith Street and Academy Avenue.

Any minute, I would meet up with our son, Noah, who was about to leave high school at the end of the school day.

A bird moving south to north and roughly 200-feet overhead caught my eye. It was big, black, with a huge beak, and a clearly visible long, wedged-shaped tail.

The bird floated across the intersection in a flap-free flight that suggested a relatively powerful command of the airspace.

This was one of my all-time favorite creatures, and not an everyday city sighting in New England. The bird was a common raven, in its characteristic silhouette and raptor-like flight, and it flew solo, which ravens often do.

In this half of the Western Hemisphere, ravens are most often found in the West, from Mexico to Alaska, and to our north, particularly Canada.

For many years, a small number of ravens nested in northern Rhode Island, noted a friend, who tracks bird records in the Ocean State.

About five to six years ago, ravens also nested in South County, she said, plus in a few more places in Rhode Island, including some of our urban terrain.

That uptick in the number of nesting ravens leveled off. And today, it is uncommon, but not impossible, to see a raven over Providence.

Compared to a crow, a raven is much larger. Typically, a raven holds its wings out and glides more often in flight than a crow, which flaps much more frequently than does a raven. Raven wings also look slimmer, longer and narrower than those of crows.

Among cultures, myths and religions, the raven is a guide, messenger, omen, symbol or some other character associated with luck, secrecy or other traits. To many folks around the world, ravens have personalities!

From berries to roadkill, ravens eat pretty much anything. Maybe it's because they eat decomposing flesh that many myths portray ravens as intermediaries between life and death.

As a person rooted in the urban Northeast, ravens remain special to me. In our part of the northern hemisphere, I generally think of ravens as representative of where I've seen them, primarily the mountains of New Hampshire, New York and Vermont.

To me, the raven symbolizes both majesty of the air and mystery of the rugged outdoors. That remains true, even if I happen to see a raven soaring above one of the busiest intersections in the Ocean State.

LENDING HERRING A HAND
May 10, 2008

Amidst the fear and disbelief of these challenging times, I found hope among people who believed that their actions counted for something in our rapidly changing world.

At the second annual Scoop the Herring Day in East Providence, I watched a human fish ladder transfer hundreds of schooling, streamlined, fork-tailed, green and silver, plankton-feeding, six- to eight-inch fish. Teams of three or four volunteers moved the herring from the brackish Seekonk River into freshwater on the other side of Omega Dam, where the Ten Mile River thundered into Narragansett Bay.

Omega Dam is one of several water power structures first erected about 150 years ago along the Bay. The dams inadvertently prevented millions of sea-run freshwater populations of river herring and shad from spawning. Born in freshwater, the fish migrate to upriver birthplaces each spring after spending months at sea. Shad show up in the Bay later in spring.

Against the pressure of the waterfall and high tide, Armando Medeiros swept an improvised, 10-foot-long PVC-pipe-and-steel-reinforced scoop net at the base of the dam.

After snaring a group of five herring, Medeiros handed the net to a second volunteer at the top of the steps, who gave it to a third man on the embankment. He walked the device over to the pond, dipped and twisted it, releasing fish into freshwater.

"That was a lot of physical exertion, but you knew you were doing something good," said Medeiros, his head glistening with sweat. He came to the Scoop with colleagues from the Rhode Island Saltwater Anglers

Association, and his daughter, Amanda, 19, who sat on an abutment, clipboard in hand, keeping a herring count.

Medeiros handed the net to volunteer Gita Holske, "five feet tall on a good day," who climbed down for her first-ever scoop. After several minutes, Holske raised the device, which contained three squirming fish. She relinquished the net and raised her arms in triumph. When Holske reached the top of the stairs, her daughter Neela, 2½, handed her a dandelion flower.

For 40 years, a local fisherman, Paul Bettencourt, transferred herring from the Seekonk into Ten Mile River, keeping the run sustained in a small, yet important way. A few years ago, the Massachusetts Division of Marine Fisheries released additional herring into Turner Reservoir upstream.

Scoop organizer Keith Gonsalves joined Bettencourt two years ago. Gonsalves founded the Ten Mile River Watershed Council, a Rhode Island-based preservation, protection and education group. He reached the Scoop by kayaking the river from Freedom Green, along with 10 others. All told, the event attracted about 75 volunteers.

"Once we passed the houses on Central Ave., the river turned very quiet," he said. "You wouldn't have known if you were in East Providence or on the Wood River in South County."

On the way to Omega Dam, kayakers saw two white-tailed deer behind Agawam Hunt, while snapping turtles slid off logs into the river.

"The trip gave us an outdoor experience," Gonsalves said. "Now we get to see these beautiful fish. I'm glad everyone got to see something special today."

A conglomeration of federal, state and local agencies, plus protection and restoration groups and angler organizations, have worked together over the past eight years to get ramp-like fish ladders for herring and shad built at three sites on Ten Mile River at a cost of more than $2 million. The last hurdle before beginning construction is the approval of some of the state monies.

Wenley Ferguson, Habitat Restoration Coordinator for Save the Bay, has worked on the project since 1996. "What has encouraged me is the ability of a fish-run restoration project to reconnect people to the river in their backyard and to reconnect those rivers with Narragansett Bay," she said.

Certainly, folks at the Scoop passed along more than herring. Neighbors, as well as individuals from agencies and groups, shared consideration, kindness and responsibility for the world. As that world shrinks, it is comforting to know that locals still retain a core human quality of cultivating hope through teamwork in an endeavor important to them.

"When I began kayaking 17 years ago, with some of my buddies, we found that no one was taking care of the Ten Mile River," Gonsalves said. "Here was a public resource in our backyard that you could paddle for hours. This water is more valuable than just moving away our sewage."

Once, a lone fisherman hoisted herring over a roaring dam. I met a dozen of Gonsalves' relatives at the Scoop. That day, a village did the work.

"This volunteer effort is about saving a world," said Gonsalves' wife, Deb, "one fish at a time."

FAREWELL, SUGAR MAPLE
June 24, 2006

This summer the street tree in front of our home will die. It is a sugar maple, maybe 50 years old.

The maple's sparse leaves have curled brown. The crown has died back. The silvery bark of the dead limbs sheds and drops like paint chips off an old home.

The tree lived, and will breathe its last breath, within a three-foot-wide slice of sandy earth and stones. Elsewhere in the urban landscape of New England, sugar maples make excellent specimens or shade trees in sites with ample root and crown space such as lawns, parks and backyards. In the sugar maple's natural wooded habitat, across eastern North America, it prefers moist, fertile soil.

Over the years, our maple took its fair share of hits from bike tires, Wiffle Balls and water balloons. But those embarrassments pale before what many Providence street trees endure, surviving salt, sand, sideswipes and other shames of living within sidewalk slivers.

This summer, Providence is conducting a street tree tally, the first such census since 1988. The City expects to find about 30,000 street trees. The new tally will identify urban forest trends and changes, and will assist the City's effort to create a street tree management plan.

Dozens of volunteers are helping count and qualify the current crop of street trees. Their tallies vary dramatically. One 11-block count found just five trees, and one of those specimens was dead. In contrast, a 15-block count across town showed 87 trees, only one dead and one stump.

Back in the 1980s, when I taught environmental science, I visited fifth graders in Bushwick, Brooklyn. The children were stunned to learn street trees were actually alive. We walked through the neighborhood until we found a young, battered, but still living little-leaf linden. The youngsters ran their hands along the smooth gray bark and fiddled with the heart-shaped green leaves.

Our sugar maple provided us with shade, color and wildlife habitat. While it grew, the tree took carbon dioxide from the air through photosynthesis, and when mature and leafy, it produced as much oxygen in a season as 10 people inhale in a year.

This tree was a looker, too. Its lobed, medium-green leaves developed fiery orange fall color. We will miss the maple's stunning gray plates of blocky bark covered in dark green mats of moss and silver-dollar-sized patches of lichens.

One evening recently a screech owl occupied a hole high in the tree's trunk. The bird's somber wails were a Mourner's Kaddish.

In the book, *A Tree Grows in Brooklyn*, a weed tree represents hope, joy, knowledge and perseverance. The tree, commonly called Tree of Heaven, or Ailanthus, reflects the resolve of the tenement dwellers it shelters.

Soon, the sugar maple that shaded our newborn children and protected us from countless Nor'easters will end up as a check mark in a tree tally. Later, foresters will cut it down and grind away the stump. No trace of the tree will remain.

It sounds sappy, but this maple, a humble servant and a touch of beauty in our daily lives, will live on in our memories.

THE LITTLE VALLEY THAT COULD
October 17, 2009

When I needed a safe place during childhood I snuck into a nearby garage, snuggled in my own thoughts and dozed off. I think of that haven, when I visit the Moshassuck River. Cool, damp, serene, sometimes smelling of oil and gas, home to Roger Williams and the Industrial Revolution, it's the "river where moose watered" long ago.

The Moshassuck, with its beginnings in the tiny streams of Lime Rock near Lincoln, slices through a valley once the natural course of the Blackstone River until ice jammed it eons ago. Look west from College Hill to the 180-foot summit of Windmill Hill to witness the Moshassuck's natural corridor.

It is "an old, old path," said Greg Gerritt, founder of Friends of the Moshassuck, an advocacy, protection and restoration group. The valley was a main line before, during and after the Revolution, when manufacturing was king in Rhode Island, and the river served as industrial sewer for mills, metal works and textile factories.

Today the Moshassuck shares the valley with hundreds of home and commercial properties, and major routes, including Interstate 95, Amtrak and MBTA rail lines, and North Main Street. At least 29 roadways cross the river across several communities.

Last week, I ran into Gerritt on my way to the river. We walked over to Collyer Park. Although the whine of interstate traffic dominated, I could still hear the water rippling over fallen trees.

We stood under a red maple on the stonework of the channeled bank. Sunlight pierced the crimson foliage, illuminating the river bottom. The summer algae and sewage smell were gone.

Gerritt said that in about 10 years, completion of the Narragansett Bay Commission's combined sewage project would finally rid the Moshassuck of human waste.

In Collyer Park, the Friends of Moshassuck has transformed a field of invasive Japanese knotweed into a budding river bottom forest of red and silver maple, sweetgum, red oak, river birch and white ash. The trees produce shade that suppresses the knotweed.

Japanese knotweed spreads rapidly into dense thickets, particularly along shorelines, withstanding drought, flooding and high heat. It can reach 10 feet in height, with broad, oval, pointy tipped leaves.

I've watched the trees planted by the Friends spread from atolls into growing riparian forest, and the knotweed underneath begin to wither.

A trail of thick black plastic, dotted with the lemon-yellow land snails that congregate on it, winds through the new forest, which produces a fruit cereal display of gold, orange, red, purple and yellow in late October.

When a train in the valley discharged a three-second wistful warning whistle, I thought of our restructuring world in which so many people live in constant fear and uncertainty.

Restoring the health of local environments is a way to repair the world, Gerritt said. "If we don't heal ecosystems, we won't make it on this planet."

Once, the Moshassuck fueled the greatest nation on earth. Then the river was left to die.

Still, the not-always-pretty Moshassuck flows to the sea. From its banks, Gerritt has seen menhaden, suckers and sunfish, fox, muskrat, and herons.

Repair work by the Friends of the Moshassuck reminds me that mending can take a long time.

I once found refuge in a dark garage. There is light along the banks of the river, where a group of people believe they can transform the survival of an individual resource into a meaningful community for all.

I believe that if you give animals, plants and the landscape a chance, they all return.

Snow and the
Forgotten Landscape
December 20, 2008

T he first snow of the season saluted everyday creatures and features.

From the backdoor, I stepped into a thin layer of bright packing snow adorned by tiny crisscrossing tracks. These were left by dark-eyed juncos, a common bird at feeders, where they typically forage on the ground, twittering in small flocks.

Juncos are a mix of gray, white and brown, with dark eyes, pink legs and white outer tail feathers. Nicknamed "snowbirds," juncos arrive in October from northern breeding grounds and leave in April. In summer I find them in high-elevation forests in New Hampshire. Here they poke around cars in the driveway.

The snow also displayed a straight set of larger tracks. The five-toed prints in a set of four—two in the front, two in the back—belonged to the prolific and adaptable gray squirrel.

At least two bushy-tailed squirrels occupied a nest in a neighbor's maple. Both squirrels looked gray, but their coats held hints of black, brown, orange, silver and white. Each had thick-looking white belly fur and white ear tufts. Their nest, called a drey, was made mostly of leaves and twigs, and featured thin strips of clear plastic.

Snow clarified routine items of the landscape. The drey, for example, was there for months. But I felt like I was seeing the snow-topped structure for the first time. Frosted oak branches looked stout. A red cedar, dusted by powdered sugar, appeared wispy. Spirea shrubs called

187

"snowmound," looked like they were flowering, which actually happens in late May.

This first snow quieted the landscape. I could hear the tinkling of landing flakes, and I looked up to watch them float down. This left me feeling giddy. I understood why kids make snow angels, snowballs and snowmen.

The call of a black-capped chickadee broke the silence. Three birds, accompanied by two titmice, two nuthatches and a downy woodpecker, moved through the trees. One by one, members of an equally sized flock of tail-flicking juncos entered the backyard, heading for the shrubbery.

A squirrel dropped from a branch to a wooden fence, exploding the topping of snow. Another squirrel scolded me. The short grunts and high-pitched whines caused the birds to stop and quiet down.

I stepped back inside, where I was reminded of winter's sobering effects. From the kitchen, I observed a heavily breathing goldfinch, clinging to a wire-mesh feeder. The bird appeared ill, and hanging on to life.

I thought of people holding on to someone or something tightly during the current economic climate. Our family may put seed in a feeder every couple of days, but more importantly we help fill boxes with cereal, rice, canned goods and other items. On Christmas Day we will deliver meals to folks alone and hungry.

Snow lights up the landscape, making the mundane seem miraculous. May the load lighten for the average Joe and Jane, starting now, with the first snowfall of the season.

ORCHID OF WOODLAND SHADE
June 23, 2012

One of the most beautiful, unusual and abused blossoms shows up in late spring.

The flower of pink lady's slipper hangs like a pink dinner biscuit from a single green stalk centered between two green leaves.

Pink lady's slipper is an orchid of the shaded forest, where the soil pH and nutrient levels are low. Depending upon the location, the plant is listed as endangered, rare, threatened, but always commercially exploited and vulnerable.

That is because people regularly dig up the flower. Given the plant is protected, carting off pink lady's slippers is almost always illegal.

Plus, it's futile. Unless replanted adjacently, pink lady's slipper will not reproduce. It takes a locally present fungus to crack open a pink lady's slipper seed. The fungus also attaches, and delivers food and nutrients, to the seed, which lacks its own food supply. A maturing plant then allows the fungus to absorb nutrients from its roots.

In a corner of Newport County, we visited a husband and wife duo, tending 25 acres of forest that contains dozens of pink lady's slipper.

The land is a combination of purchased, inherited and donated-to-land-trust-in-preservation woodland, with an agreement that stipulates no publicity for who donated the land or for its location.

Karen, our 14-year-old daughter, Rachel, and I admired the pink lady's slippers, growing singly, in pairs or in clumps of three plants. The blooms looked like hot-pink pillows.

The flower's sweet smell attracts insects. A robust bee, such as a bumblebee, can force itself inside the slight opening in front of the flower. But the flower smell is a pollination ruse, as the blossom contains no nectar. To squeeze back out, the bee will brush past the pollen-producing reproductive organ, called a stamen. Thus, the bee exits with pollen stuck to it.

If the bee visits another pink lady's slipper, it brings along the pollen. The second flower may use that pollen to make new seeds.

Crouched beside a group of flowers, Rachel pointed out a camouflaged toad no bigger than her fingernail. I was amazed that she spotted something so secret and small.

Ahead, skunk cabbage, with great leaves, covered the swamp floor.

There was also Jack-in-the-pulpit in the woods, and Indian pipe will appear later in summer.

An American redstart, a wet-woods warbler of striking orange and black, repeated its "tsee, tsee, tsee" call. I also heard the high-pitched "ke-eee" cry of a broad-winged hawk, which is a species that breeds in uninterrupted forest.

Our hosts showed us a corner stack of rocks—an old time property marker. There, we examined pre-bloom clusters of mountain laurel flowers. The woods were full of these little stars of pink, which would turn white after the flowers opened.

Rachel called our attention to a small hole in the ground near the stones. Was it a sign of chipmunk, she asked? The property also harbored other creatures, such as coyote, deer, fox and turkey. Deer feed on pink lady's slipper.

The property's main trail was once the route of a two-wheeled, firewood-hauling oxen cart in the late 1800s and early 1900s. You can still see the wheel ruts.

When people and organizations partner to protect and maintain natural areas, it means walking a line between conservation and preservation.

That effort takes commitment, fortitude and concern for the past, present and future.

Our hosts, and their partners in protection, did a good deed.

Together, they safeguarded the habitats, distinctive flora and fauna, and historic features that define who we are and where we live.

It is much easier to sell, clear and pave. In this forest, that would mean goodbye to the pink lady's slippers and all of the other species and relics of times gone by, coexisting with it.

A Brush with Royalty

July 31, 2011

Karen and I saw a blood red dragonfly on the edge of a hay field in Tillinghast Pond Management Area.

The dragonfly powered past our shins as we examined small white, urn-shaped flowers of wintergreen and a swarm-like cluster of green fruit on a bayberry.

Neither of us could recall ever seeing a dragonfly the color of pomegranate juice.

In July, flora and fauna reign at Tillinghast Pond.

At an observation deck over the water, dragonflies sped back and forth, including one that was neon blue. Striders propelled over still water.

In this calm, biting flies abounded. Insect spray on our skin and clothing repelled the flies, which stayed close, pinging off our hats like raindrops.

Bullfrogs grumbled, as a great blue heron flapped silently over a patch of flowering lily pads, their fringed petals and yellow centers blinking toward the sky.

Pollinated by beetles, lily pad flowers open in the morning and close by evening.

When a Nature Conservancy preserve as great in size as Tillinghast Pond—1,800 acres—harbors lily pads, you might find signs of the robust mammal that eats them—beaver.

Sure enough, we saw several chewed tree stumps, chips and sticks in the woods.

Soft, waxy stands of Indian pipe speckled the forest. This pale plant lacks chlorophyll. A fungus transfers the chemical product of photosynthesis from tree roots to those of the Indian pipe.

We also found several stands of Indian-pipe-related pinesap, also called false beechdrops. This fleshy yellowish plant is parasitic of oak and pine, drawing nutrients more directly from their roots.

Carpets of scarlet oak seedlings lined the woodland trail. Scarlet oak is a species of upland, sandy soils, germinating best beneath somewhat open canopy.

How curious that at this point on the walk the only bird singing was a scarlet tanager.

A mature male scarlet tanager is an arresting, velvety red, with black wings. That's if you can find the bird, which works the forest canopy brilliantly to remain secretive.

Red was also the color of tall, abundant, bowl-shaped mushrooms. Some of the colorful tops of these fungi were as wide in diameter as a compact disc.

Some of the mushrooms came in purple, and we even found a green one.

Chewed in several places, it looked like a huge, spongy four-leaved clover.

The woodland aromas were of pine or humus. Every so often, a light breeze carried the scent of lily pad flowers.

Wild blueberries provided sustenance at several spots, including at the foot of a rock outcrop that looked like a Mayan visage.

This great stone head included a ridged brow, pointed proboscis and jutting chin. A dangling vine looked like hair growing out of its nose.

The hay field edge was particularly rich. Wild strawberries were abundant in spots. We found several swamp milkweed plants upon which small butterflies clustered. There was also sweet fern, with its fragrant-when-crushed-foliage.

At one point, a string of tiny frogs or toads leapt together into the hay, as if starting their own sack race.

Several times in the field, we displaced a common buckeye butterfly.

When still, a buckeye appears brown. But each forewing contains two orange bars and two eyespots, one held in a white band. The hindwings have two eyespots, with the upper one being the largest and containing a magenta crescent.

Karen said the natural scenery, especially the wide fields and great pond, was the stuff of Monet paintings.

I thought Tillinghast was as close to natural royalty as we've found in Rhode Island. Maybe we should have bowed our heads and offered a "Your Majesty," on the way out.

WHEN TIDES PROVIDE A WAKE-UP CALL
September 22, 2012

Who knew that each wave offered the chance for growth? On what began as a cloudy fall-like morning, Karen and I settled into chairs on a drying mudflat, before a receding tide and beneath charcoal, flat-bottomed clouds through which visible rays of sunlight hit the sea.

Then, she asked, "Do you want to swim?"

As a child, swimming was a hoot until I began to lose my eyesight in grade school. Soon, taking a dunk terrified me.

When I was 12, the summer camp director threw me into seven-foot water to force me "to learn to swim." I fell straight to the bottom, saved by a swimming instructor.

Two years later, while treading water in a swimming class, both of my legs cramped and I dropped like a wrecked boat. My brother, a certified lifesaver, swam down, put me in a headlock and brought me up and out.

For the following four decades, I avoided deep water.

Now, Karen reached for my hand. She asked me to trust her. I removed my eyeglasses and placed them carefully atop the folded towels of the beach cart.

By this time, sunshine had parted the clouds. Together, we stepped into the sea. We walked in above our ankles, and then our knees. Karen said the fastest way to overcome hesitation (and shaking!) was to submerge, when we reached waist depth.

As a decent-size wave descended, I let go of her hand and dove.

Underwater, I watched the wave pass overhead. The ocean was green, clear and full of bubbles.

When I emerged, we whooped like kids. Man, it felt good. And one thing about the setting—it provided limitless waves to test again.

Depending upon the ripple, we dove in, under or with the curl. I felt warm. Sure, I couldn't see very far, but I felt safe. I had fun.

Before I left the water, Karen retrieved her smartphone to snap off pictures.

We retreated back to our chairs, as happy as any recent moment in memory.

Karen wrapped me in a towel and we sat together in the now full sun. I remembered that wonderful feeling from early childhood of returning from a swim to the beach blanket, getting swathed in cloth and drying off under warm rays.

I dozed off into a brief, but deep and satisfying sleep.

When I awoke, I put on my glasses and considered what had happened.

A normal morning grew into an extraordinary day. In the time it took for one wave to follow another, I'd found faith and courage, and confronted, in my own way, my mortality.

Each wave delivered strength and reminded me of something more within me.

What a way to wake up to what was inside and around me. No matter what our age, we could change. We just had to really want it— from our core, our mantle, from every cell in our system.

I mentioned this to Karen, who reminded me that throughout our lives, we possessed capabilities we could enhance. People were resourceful beings, she said, with great—often hidden—powers of character.

Alive, and improved, I thought of lyrics from "Land of Hope and Dreams," a song by Bruce Springsteen.

"And I'll stand by your side. You'll need a good companion now, for this part of the ride. Leave behind your sorrows. Let this day be the last. Tomorrow there'll be sunshine. And all this darkness past."

The tune ends, "... Dreams will not be thwarted ... Faith will be rewarded."

Looking around the beach, everything seemed the same. Goldenrod hosted monarchs. Sanderlings skedaddled from the tide. A fisherman cast for stripers. But I had changed.

Five days later, writing this tale, I can't wait for the four of us—Karen and I, and our two children, Rachel and Noah—to visit the beach and ride the waves together. That would be a hoot.

Refuge Shows Small Is beautiful
December 6, 2008

If your sense of place includes a tide-slurped salt marsh, surrounded by forests and fields, then I have a landscape for you.

David, a friend who hikes and kayaks across the Northeast, turned me on to Touisset Marsh Wildlife Refuge, a 66-acre property of the Audubon Society of Rhode Island.

Touisset is tucked into an eastern corner of Warren, along the Kickemuit River. David keeps coming back to the refuge, which is just 25 minutes from his home in Providence.

"What draws me there is feeling like in one loop of the trail I have visited so many landscapes, all packed into one small area," said David. You encounter "stonewalls, fields, the bridge over the creek, the little cove, the river itself," and more, he said.

On a clear 30-degree morning, I followed narrow lanes to where the air smelled of tidal flats, mown hay, cow manure and wood smoke.

Rimming a Touisset trail were elderberry and sumac shrubs, and American elm and bitternut hickory saplings, with twigs displaying bright sulfur-colored buds.

From a stretch of bittersweet and mutliflora rose, white-throated sparrows sang their "Oh sweet Canada, Canada" songs. The males glistened in the bright sunlight, with white throats, black and white head stripes, yellow eye patches and gray chests.

Out of a small woodlot of Eastern red cedars, a Carolina wren boomed its "tea-kettle," song. The loud little bird featured a buff body with reddish under-parts and white eye-stripe.

Sensitive to frigid conditions, Carolina wrens took a hit during severe winters of the late 70s. But their populations are now stable or coming back.

Three deer watched from a fencerow, where trees gave way to windswept grasses, streams and flats. A huge glacial boulder sat in a field of soon-to-be hay.

Scientists call this a high salt marsh. It's off the water, home to unique sea grasses and plants, and influenced by tides and their irregular flooding.

On a boardwalk of weathered, lichen-festooned, rough-hewn wood, I crossed paths with a semi-retired builder, named Raymond.

He had lived in eight different Bristol County homes during his lifetime. But when Raymond stopped full-time work, he built a home across from Touisset preserve. "The nicest place I have ever lived is here," he said.

We stood alongside Chase Cove on a trail that flooded at moon tide, said Raymond, who performs trail-maintenance volunteer work at Touisset and other refuges. Roughly twice a day tides swept the shoreline cordgrass and sea lettuce mats. The cove was about six feet deep. Raymond said he has crossed it on cross-country skis in winter.

A horseshoe crab shell, covered in ice crystals, twinkled at our feet. Raymond showed me where oysters grew amidst ribbed mussels attached to plant roots and under rocks. He also pointed out the peak of a large conch just off shore.

About 50 yards out in the water, buffleheads, the smallest diving ducks in North America, bobbed between white caps. The male birds sparkled, with white sides, black heads and backs, and white head-patches.

Nearby, Brant, geese of the ocean shore, produced soft croaking calls.

I parted ways with Raymond on a lane lined with black cherries. There, a hairy woodpecker flew ahead of me, belting out a rattling call.

The bird landed on a tree, releasing a string of sharp "peek" calls. Then it drummed rapidly.

After years of declining locally, hairy woodpeckers are returning to former haunts.

My encounters with conches, oysters, a wren and woodpecker underscored a preserve's primary role—to protect habitat important to flora and fauna.

We are all organisms in need of pristine habitats to thrive. I expect I will join David, Raymond and other life forms of the New England landscape in coming back to this picture-postcard place.

The Rewards of Standing Still

April 25, 2015

On a sunny, warm morning in a grove of oaks, Karen and I stood listening to early-in-the season spring migrants including chipping sparrow, pine warbler, Northern flicker and Eastern phoebe.

A single high note hit our ears. It belonged to a brown creeper, a small russet-and-white species that spirals up tree trunks, foraging in bark crevices for insects and spiders and their eggs, or pupae.

With a slender body, down-curved bill and long, stiff tail, used for support and balance, a creeper looks like a piece of bark, or a leaf, come alive.

Once a creeper reaches the top of a tree, it flies down to the bottom of the next one to restart its hunt for food. This morning, the creeper dropped down from the canopy to land at the base of the black oak beside us. The bird began to spiral, and then sing.

Male and female creepers produce a high-pitched, reedy call of varying short length, particularly while foraging.

We've heard the call, but we'd never heard the song. According to the Cornell Laboratory of Ornithology, only the male creeper sings, "and usually on breeding grounds, though sometimes during migration as well."

The Lab describes the song as a "a jumble of high, thin notes that lasts up to 1.5 seconds. It's sometimes likened to singing the phrase *trees, beautiful trees.*"

Well, the song we heard coming from that little bird was a lovely, little tune that produced a visceral reaction within us, like that yummy feeling when you get from a hug or a kiss. Maybe this was because the song was new to us, or that we shared an unusual moment, or that the experience was so intimate.

Providence, where we stood, was not creeper breeding grounds. The species nests within the interior of mature coniferous forests, and up to an elevation of 4,500 feet in the eastern U.S.

The brown creeper has a unique, almost-hard-to-believe nesting strategy. The species builds a hammock-shaped nest *behind* a loosened flap of bark on a dead or dying tree.

An old friend, who worked as a land manager in New Hampshire, once told me that he considered it a sign of great luck to find a creeper nest. In 10 years on the job, he found a nest, by accident, just once.

In fact, it was not until 1879 that naturalists discovered the one-of-a-kind nesting strategy of the brown creeper.

Here's one more cool fact about the species. According to whatbird.com, a group of creepers are collectively known as a "sleeze" or a "spiral."

The male that sang beside us was as crisp and bright a looking creeper as we'd ever seen. The contrast between the wings and the breast were especially sharp, with the bird appearing to contain a thin strip of near-chestnut brown at the wing-belly border.

Just being outside that spring morning was good enough. Hearing the one-note creeper call made the outing high quality. Seeing such a handsome songbird created a special moment. Standing side by side with the singer was unique.

SHINY OBJECTS IN SPRING
April 11, 2015

S ome folks see flowering crocuses, and announce the arrival of spring. Others say spring comes when a robin sings.

For me, it's officially a new season when Greg Gerritt, founder of the Friends of the Moshassuck and author of the Prosperity for RI blog, shares news that Eastern painted turtles in the North Burial Ground pond in Providence have emerged from hibernation.

On April 2, Gerritt reported some ice on the pond. One day later, Eastern painted turtles were sunning themselves, he said.

At the pond, I showed up on Sunday morning, April 5. It was breezy, but sunny and about 50 degrees. This was a bright moment in a spring where rain or snows seem to show up every few hours.

Three Eastern painted turtles were on a stout, semi-submerged log. The dark, smooth, flattened shells of the reptiles glistened, but I noticed that the shells dried quickly in the sun.

These were hefty turtles. Each shell looked close in diameter to a Frisbee. All three creatures featured yellow stripes on their necks.

Bird-wise, the pond was loud and frenzied in activity. The two most numerous and gregarious species were newly arrived migrants, common grackles and red-winged blackbirds.

Plus, it seemed like an influx of birds had bolstered local numbers of American goldfinches and dark-eyed juncos. They twittered and sang, with noisy, colorful flocks filling some of the smaller evergreens.

Speaking of recent arrivals, the most numerous and recognizable bird was the quietest. In grassy areas around the water, I counted more than 50 American robins. They stood like ornaments among the gravestones.

The pond also hosted one rusty blackbird. Sized between a grackle and a red wing, the bird featured an unusual pale-yellow eye and a call that sounded like a rusty hinge opening and closing.

Rusty blackbirds breed in boreal forests and winter in the Eastern U.S. Over the last 60 years, their numbers have dropped about 90 percent, although anecdotal evidence suggests a gradual decline over some 100 years.

This is the second year of a project called the Rusty Blackbird Migration Blitz. The 38-state, data-collecting effort is designed to determine the migratory requirements and habits of rusty blackbirds.

The most beautiful bird at the pond was a fox sparrow, which rustled out of the shoreline brush. The bird darted into the upper branches and sunlight, and I could see its red-and-gray head and richly marked brown flanks and chest.

Then, I remembered the turtles. When I looked back, the sunshine had strengthened on the log, and each turtle had extended its head, neck, tail and feet. Turtles are cold-blooded, and they warm up in sunlight. Eastern painted turtles are known for basking in large groups.

Last fall, when people bundled up, turtles put on extra fat, slowed down, burrowed deep into the mud, and hibernated.

Turtle blood modifies during hibernation to allow the reptiles to withstand cold temperatures. As a result, turtle body temperature drops to just a few degrees above freezing, much lower than for most other hibernating creatures.

This year, around the start of April, the reptiles warmed up, awakened and slowly became more active.

In that way, I felt like a turtle; entombed over the winter, but now limbering up. Instinct led me out into the sunshine, although learned behavior taught me to wear sunblock.

WOOD'S WINTER GIFT
January 30, 2016

For many New Englanders, burning wood is instinctive, special and even ritualistic.

I have a friend in Massachusetts, for example, who likes the relatively sweet smell of red-hot white birch. He has a comrade in New Hampshire who sets aside white birch to burn in the fireplace when his Bay State buddy visits.

These two natives know that white birch doesn't give off a lot of heat compared to other local species of wood. It also burns fast and produces a short-lived bed of coals. But its smell is satisfying.

When Rachel was a toddler, I pulled her around the neighborhood after storms in a wooden-sided red wagon to collect limbs from fallen trees for use as firewood. I kept a folding hand saw in my back pocket to cut wood, so that it and Rachel fit in the wagon.

What we collected came from several types of oak, as well as flowering cherry, flowering pear, crabapple, linden, sugar maple, ash and a lot of Norway maple.

Sometimes we'd come across limbs already cut and stacked by the curb for the taking. On one such occasion, we snared dogwood. Another time it was a chainsaw-piled stack of sweetgum.

The best burners included oak, ash, sugar maple and dogwood. They were high-energy-content species, releasing more heat per load than the other wood.

Once on a visit to New York, my father, may he rest in peace, insisted that I take home the sawn limbs of a black cherry tree that grew along the driveway. I did, and we burned it the following year. That black cherry gave off a good amount of heat and had a really nice aroma.

Then, on a visit with Karen's family in Ohio, her dad gave us two five-gallon buckets of split firewood from fallen apple trees. That apple was fantastic to burn. It was dense, hot and produced a lovely aroma, plus a great-looking and long-lasting bed of coals.

On the other end of the burning spectrum, linden did not produce much heat. It also burned relatively quickly.

Sweetgum and Norway maple were two species that needed extra months to dry out. They burned relatively fast while offering a low to medium amount of heat, and both types were tied for producing the most fireplace ash of any species that we burned.

Alas, we rarely use the fireplace in winter. A few years ago a specialist cleaned and relined the chimney, redid its mortar and added a cap. This upkeep and upgrade was vital for safety reasons.

But as a result, we discovered that when we opened the new and improved flue, the natural draft was so powerful that it not only provided a constant airflow up the chimney, it sucked the heat out of the house.

As a result, we only use the fireplace when outside temperatures are moderate.

It seems to me that almost anywhere I walk in winter, I smell wood burning. Could be in a fireplace. Might be in a wood-burning stove. I'm told that wood pellets produce aromas, too, with oak smelling the best.

From fruits to nuts, oxygen to shade, trees offer many life-sustaining gifts. Even from a twig headed for a fireplace or stove, I derive inspiration and feel a sacred connection.

STEPPING INTO A NEW SANCTUARY
March 31, 2017

One way to contemplate a nature preserve is from one of its trails—what do you find there? Another approach is the big-picture view—why was this property conserved?

Karen and I entered King Preserve via its Boston Neck Road lot and trailhead. The park-like setting harbored twisted, gnarly, lichen-covered trees that reminded us of the talking trees in the children's television series, "H.R. Pufnstuf."

With each step, the crisp, clean air quieted.

The woods grew rich in vernal pools. These seasonal bodies of water provide habitats for wetland plants, such as sedges, and creatures, such as frogs and salamanders.

Some of the wetland trees included black gum, red maple and sassafras. When the landscape rose just an inch or two, we found tall oaks, many of which grew out of mossy humps that looked like Fire Swamp scenery from the movie, "The Princess Bride."

The thick wet forest, containing shade and moisture, combined with the pure air to create excellent growing conditions for lichens.

Gray, green and silver lichens covered branches and stones. Some lichens grew so thick and shaggy that they fell in clumps from tree limbs.

At various points, the serpent-like roots of yellow birch trees crossed the trail. Yellow birch is eye-catching for its smooth, shiny, yellowish-bronze bark, shredding into strips.

Beyond the wetlands grew an occasional American holly. This conical native evergreen, with relatively broad, green and spiny leaves, produces fruit that ripens in fall. Birds gobble it down in winter.

We walked for an hour into the preserve, but we reached just its midpoint. This was because we found so many astounding features to study along the way.

The trail actually culminates at the shore of the Narrow River. This waterway is actually an estuary, a tidal outlet of lower Narragansett Bay. It's also a primary clue to why The Nature Conservancy (TNC) purchased the property, with funding from The Champlin Foundations.

The preserve, named for the late Dave King, the first executive director of The Champlin Foundations and a conservation leader, sits at a key spot in the watershed of the headwaters of the Narrow River, said Scott Comings, TNC's associate state director.

King Preserve is a "connecting piece for conservation land on either side," he said. The preserve "brings together almost 1,000 acres of watershed property for the Narrow River."

The estuary hosts one of the state's most productive runs of river herring, said Comings. It is also home to many other aquatic species, and serves as an important wintering ground for a variety of waterfowl, he said.

Instituting the trail system and property boundaries involves an ongoing partnership among multiple conservation groups and public agencies, said Comings.

In addition to its ecological importance, the site is a Rhode Island microcosm, he said. "In a relatively short walk, you can see so much, such as wet areas, upland forest, coastal shoreline, the Narrow River and more."

From our boots-on-wet-ground perspective, King Preserve induced a child-like feeling of adventure and discovery—that type of delight we can experience outdoors, when our time, and our landscape, are unstructured in exploration.

THE PLACE TO LORD OVER THE CAPITOL CITY AND BEYOND
December 15, 2012

I n Sunday morning sunshine, I sat with Woody, the Shih Tzu atop Neutaconkanut Hill.

At 296 feet above sea level, the hill is the highest point in Providence.

Acting the role of Mufasa in the Lion King, I turned to the little gray and white dog, and pointed toward the city. "One day," I said nonsensically, "all of this will be yours."

If you want a seriously wide-angled view of Rhode Island's capitol and suburbs, you will get it from this 88-acre park, which once marked the northwest border of land that Roger Williams acquired from Narragansett Sachems in 1636.

Our trek up the hill began on the Pinnacle Trail. To the right was a small forest of non-native, but naturalized black locust trees, some hosting tightly wrapped, thick-stemmed poison ivy vines lush with reddish, tendril-like hairs.

Dense, ornamental undergrowth to the left harbored wintering white-throated sparrows. Several birds broke out into signature "oh-sweet-Canada-Canada" song.

"White-throats" breed across Canada and the northern Northeast and Midwest.

We turned right onto the Pond Trail. As we climbed its stone steps, the flora transitioned to native elm, with its gray-brown bark of flattened ridges and intervening furrows, and black cherry, marked by small raised-edge black plates.

More natives appeared, particularly red and white oaks with wide girths. I also found lots of young hickory, with its gray, smooth, somewhat diamond-patterned bark, growing across the ridge.

Two-thirds of the way up the hill, we met a man coming down. He said that his name was Miguel, and that he had climbed Neutaconkanut earlier in the morning to watch the sunrise.

Miguel wore a blue mid-season jacket, blue jeans and black shoes. His hair was thick and raven colored. Miguel's eyes were the same hue.

A regular visitor to the summit, morning was the quietest time to visit, he said. Once, Miguel said he sat on a rock, and two coyotes walked past, sniffing the ground near his feet, but appearing not to notice him.

Miguel saw that I carried a small book—my reporter's pad. He showed me his book, a fairly compact red-covered tome, marked by a large gold cross and the words Libero Catholica.

Near the top, I admired the various crown, twig and other shapes of the forest against the blue sky.

There, we turned north toward the meadow. The forest edge was full of birds. They included more white-throated sparrows, plus a black-capped chickadee, tufted titmouse and white-breasted nuthatch. A hairy woodpecker released both a resounding "peek" call and a ringing "rattle" call from the woods.

On the other side of some boulders, a Carolina wren belted out an array of warbling calls and what sounded like burps. American robins foraged on the ground, as northern juncos trilled.

The warm sun felt like springtime. The meadow grasses appeared amber, and the white birches looked chalky.

Thicker-twigged aspens, with their pointy red, resinous buds, flanked a little forest of gray birch. Beneath grew a spread of bayberry.

Every September I lead a nature walk for college students across College Hill on the east side of the city. Invariably, when we reach the Roger Williams statue in Prospect Terrace Park, someone asks about the forested ridge to the west.

That is Neutaconkanut Hill. I tell students without a car that they can reach the park via the 19 Plainfield/Westminster RIPTA bus.

I like how Miguel summed up Neutaconkanut Hill. When we chatted earlier, he looked out over the undulating ridges of forests, spread out his arms, and said, "The trees, the rocks, the sky; here, it's all good."

Making Way for Kids in Search of Shapes Outdoors
December 9, 2016

W hen my wife Karen told me that she was bringing her first grade class to the pond in North Burial Ground in Providence, I asked to meet them there.

Every other week last year, Karen took the same youngsters, then in kindergarten, to the pond to study it.

Now the children were learning geometrical shapes, and Karen was taking the kids back to the pond to use its natural setting to extend classroom lessons.

On an overcast 40-degree morning on the last day of November, 11 first-graders, plus two teachers, from the nearby Jewish Community Day School of Rhode Island (JCDSRI), arrived at the pond.

Before setting out, the teachers urged the students to take their time searching the landscape, and to look "very hard," in order to find "some of the very cool" objects there.

To record their findings, the students shared iPads. So, when Millie found a black fungal ring on a fallen maple leaf, Meitel snapped the shot. After BenL showed his mates a square of bark on a tree trunk, Natan took the picture. And as Aden pointed out a triangle in a canopy created by crossed branches, Eden captured the image.

The visit crossed disciplines, said Karen. Linking math and art, for example, she and co-teacher, Sarah, pointed out sides and corners within shapes, and spaces that surrounded shapes.

Sarah also shared the Hebrew names for shapes. Triangle, for example, was pronounced "meh-shoo-lahsh."

For me the trip was a chance to observe six- and seven-year-olds connect with nature

On a grassy slope beside the pond, Zemer examined the triangular corners of a red oak leaf. Malcolm held up a cylindrical fallen branch. The tall evergreen across the pond was "one large cone," said Bentzi.

And, when Eshel found an oval-shaped growth of lichen on a boulder, BenS took a picture of the entire stone for context.

Geese poop, the class decided, was cylindrical. Gray birch not only had triangular leaves but triangular marks on its bark where branches fell off, said the kids.

As for the narrow seedpods hanging from a catalpa tree, those were "100" vertical lines, noted the children, who added that the pods dangling overhead looked "spooky, like long fingers."

The outing was also an opportunity to ponder the unseen, such as when students learned that the tiny, perfectly round holes on the bark of a sugar maple tree served as entrances and exits for beetles that lived under the bark.

The kids came and went via a little white bus driven by a JCDSRI employee named Peter, who helped the teachers usher the kids aboard.

The scene brought to mind the book, "Make Way for Ducklings," in which Boston police shepherd Mrs. Mallard and her brood to the pond in Boston Public Garden.

Here in Providence teachers and protectors led a line of little ones in fun and joyfulness in a landscape filled with an abundance of detail.

Witness to a Wayward Songbird
October 7, 2016

As we watched the Northern wheatear, Karen and I smiled amidst whispered words of bliss and feelings of elation.

A little songbird, the Northern wheatear is "the only North American representative of a widespread Old World genus in the thrush family," according to the Cornell Lab of Ornithology.

This was the first wheatear we'd ever seen. The bird breeds across Earth's northern reaches. It winters in Sub-Saharan Africa.

To reach Africa, wheatears that breed in the eastern Arctic migrate through Greenland and Europe. Western Arctic wheatears migrate into Siberia and then angle across Asia to Africa, sometimes traveling more than 18,000 miles round trip.

In terms of size and weight, the Northern wheatear is the migrant champion of the avian world.

Every few years, an off-track wheatear winds up along the New England coast. In the second half of September, a wheatear appeared in Sandwich on Cape Cod. A few days later, a wheatear showed up in Colt State Park in Bristol. Maybe it was the same bird.

The wheatear in Colt State Park hung around the parking lot near the statue of the late Senator John Chafee. When Karen and I exited our car, a fellow birdwatcher pointed out the bird, which was on the lawn near a low wall of stone along the outflow of Mill Gut Pond.

The Northern wheatear is six inches in length. It weighs one-twentieth of a pound. The little bird in front of us was an appealing buff-brown color, with a white eyebrow. Its tail contained some black feathers, including a visible blackish edging.

When the bird stood on the lawn or on the wall, the wheatear bobbed its tail. When the bird flew, we could see its distinctive white rump.

We watched as the wheatear pecked at insects either in the grass or when the bird was atop the rock wall. Every so often, the wheatear chased after a bug in a relatively high-speed flight. The bird sort of zipped, cartoon-like, from one spot to another.

To us the wheatear's black legs looked long and its black feet appeared large. We noted how it used those legs and feet to stand along the edge of the flat granite stones atop the rock wall. Gripping the granite lip, the bird would lean over the edge, appearing to look down.

This behavior reminded us of a red-liquid, glass-bulb, drinking-bird toy, which is supposed to mimic the motion of a bird sipping from a liquid source.

Seeing this Old World bird on its way to Africa made the planet appear a little smaller and more intimate. The encounter seemed to release chemicals in our brains that resulted in feelings of joy. It was a satisfying experience, with our euphoria lasting for several days.

A Fish That Is Both Charming and Chum

October 19, 2007

In the Golden Age of films, Busby Berkeley choreographed complex dance and musical numbers in the shape of geometric patterns framed by the camera at unusual angles such as overhead.

On a hot afternoon in October I thought of those elaborate productions as I watched legions of menhaden swim in circles, figure eights, snake lines and other shapes. The foot-long fish, mouths open, with silver sides and forked tails, reminded me of Berkeley's showgirls, with their headdresses, fans and other set dressings.

My vantage point was the Providence River, between the Frank Licht Judicial Complex and Textron World Headquarters. Later that week, I read in the Journal that an unexplained upsurge of menhaden had led to similar shows in the Blackstone River, as well as the Moshassuck and Woonasquatucket rivers, which join to form the Providence River downtown.

To my right, a blond-haired woman wearing white-rimmed sunglasses leaned over the railing. In Pawtucket, she'd watched the fish in the Blackstone for weeks, noting that they traveled up the river as far as the Apex dam. Her neighbor, who fished from under one of the bridges, ate everything he caught, she said, including the bony, oily, often foul-tasting and sometimes foul-looking, plankton-eating menhaden.

The breeze blew warm, salty air into our faces. Bus, motorcycle and truck engines roared through the intersection of Memorial Boulevard and Westminster Street. When the light turned red, alternative rock, country or hip-hop blared from open windows.

Still, you could hear the intermittent slap of water that accompanied an undulation of the menhaden conga line.

Past us walked RISD students and lawyers on cell phones. A ring-billed gull appeared to maneuver carefully on the water, like a swan boat in the Public Garden, as the bird followed shifting fish.

When I read about menhaden, I learned that until 1900 or so, the manufacture of menhaden oil, derived from the fish, was a major industrial pursuit in the town of Tiverton. One angling blog called menhaden "lowly," urging local fishermen to pursue two species that feed on it— striped bass and bluefish.

In my left hand, I held a printout of a series of emails from a colleague, a magazine editor and former environmental reporter, who first saw the menhaden in late September, while walking to work from the Providence Train Station. This led him to the Internet to learn more about the fish.

He wrote, "These may be just fish milling around from the bay; an important food for other fishes, primary source of fish meal, and probably the fish the natives threw in their cornfields for fertilizer. Source for fish emulsion, I imagine."

In his final correspondence he noted, "This is a great drama, and it is happening right under our noses."

A man with sandy-colored hair peered over the railing. The fish, he said, were a reminder that he was bound to his work on a beautiful afternoon. His preference was to collect a few menhaden, set them onto a treble hook and head out past the hurricane barrier to fish in the bay.

The sun's angle changed and the menhaden began shimmering like a mirrored kaleidoscope design. The routine was easily worthy of the operatic and symphonic music I'd heard at this same spot during Waterfire.

As the menhaden swirled beneath floating leaves and a lost Barbie doll, her black hair splayed on the water's surface, all I could add was "Wow!"

Our Calling:
Recovery and Responsibility
June 6, 2009

The garter snake on the Gano Street sidewalk curled into an 18-inch S shape, its head pointed toward the chain link fence, thin pile of rotting leaves, damp cigarette box and deli container top from which it had emerged.

I'm no Saint Francis of Assisi, but I did feel a responsibility to keep the snake from venturing any farther into where folks tread in both directions. So I moved my foot slightly and the snake slipped back into a grassy, fenced-in collection of overgrown wooden pilings, a nice place for an urban reptile to reside.

Maybe I had in mind the woman who stood with four others, including two children, that same Friday evening, and who said that God hated me. Then she pulled out an Israeli flag and blew her nose in it. The woman was part of a touring church group spreading the "good word" that God detested homosexuals, Israel, Jews, Obama and America.

What a coincidence. Before running into this quintet, I had been thinking about our accountability for all creatures, based on a Yale study I'd heard about earlier in the week, in which researchers showed that spoiled ecosystems rebounded if people protected them. Polluted waterways and ripped-apart forests examined in the study recovered not to pristine states but to environments that once again supported webs of life.

The Yale study brought to mind my view of the Providence River, which I walk across once a week, via the Point Street Bridge. From that perch, I may observe the occasional striped bass or bluefish, or swirling school of menhaden. Closer to the walls that frame the river, I note crabs, shellfish and tens of thousands of silvery baitfish. The water never looks clean to me—mostly cloudy and occasionally malodorous—yet it is purer than it has been in decades.

If recovery and responsibility are our calling, then the work is daunting, as we live in an age of extinction.

Worldwide, birds, fish, insects, large mammals and other species are disappearing, because we are depleting and diverting fresh water, and transforming the Earth through agriculture, forestry and construction.

We are also spreading diseases, such as the chytrid fungus, which is wiping out amphibians worldwide.

And what can we do in response to the new report by the Global Humanitarian Forum that finds climate change kills more than 300,000 people a year? Isn't it our responsibility to not only protect and restore the natural world, but to change our behavior to become more sustainable—to bike and walk; compost kitchen scraps and yard waste; reduce, reuse and recycle; and so on? Adopting a more sustainable way of life would set up circumstances not only for local ecosystems to rebound but would also cut back on the carbon emissions that fuel climate change.

Protecting our natural resources puts the lives of all species in our hands. Interfering with the natural course of events makes us redeemers of life on earth.

The woman from the church organization said that I was going to hell.

She even said that I would eat my own children. But I see the world differently. We are responsible for each other. In this frail world of relationships, we are all tied together. Nudging the garter snake back into the grass—versus, say, stomping it to death with my heel– was one small fulfillment of that vow.

A Good 'Schvitz'

October 12, 2017

For a seashore known for its rocks and minerals, Moonstone Beach had even more cobbles and less sand and mud than my wife, Karen, and I could recall when we visited on the last Sunday in September.

Our trip to the beach came near the end of two weeks of strong surf, fueled by tropical weather. My guess is that weeks of pounding had left the piles of rocks stretching from the dunes to the 6-foot-tall waves that continued to drub the shoreline.

We'd left Providence, where the dew point temperature was more than 70 degrees. That air was uncomfortably sticky.

Moonstone felt no different. There was no breeze off the ocean. So, we sat on the beach and sweated, cooling off by stepping into waves, but only ankle deep lest we risk getting swept out by the currents.

The water, by the way, was at its warmest, yet it was still refreshing.

Amid such calm stickiness, there were bugs. Bees in particular, and they kept landing on me. At one point a bee visited my neck and then crept under my shirt, while another landed on my eyebrow, crawling into the space between my eyelid and glasses.

Karen helped me gently shake out and swipe away the insects. They, or others, returned, and the only way for me to avoid them was to head back to the water.

On one such stroll, I noticed a mound of oval rocks, including one that was the size and shape of a small chicken egg, but maroon in color.

Like a bird bringing back a shiny or eye-catching object to attract a mate or adorn a nest, I collected a few of the stones to spread out in front of Karen.

A few days after our trip to Moonstone Beach, I explained the sweating-and-cooling experience to neighbor and friend Andy, who recalled a Yiddish phrase his father used, "shveys vi a khzir," or "sweat like a pig" in English.

I remembered my father's father, talking more than 50 years ago of a Russian steam bath, where folks went for "a good schvitz." Although spelled differently, shveys and schvitz are the same word, meaning "sweat."

A bathhouse schvitz was good for the body and mind, our ancestors believed. First, you sweat, and then you either douse yourself in cold water or plunge into a pool of ice-cold water. From there, you repeated the process.

Go have a schvitz, I could hear my grandmother telling my grandfather long ago. Well, I guess Karen and I did just that. And it was good.

BIRD BONANZA AT ONE PROVIDENCE PARK
June 9, 2019

Most weekday mornings after I drive Karen to work, Woody the Shih Tzu and I head into nearby Davis Park, off Raymond Street in the heart of Providence.

Davis Park is a multi-use rest and recreational greenspace. It contains a playground, two ballfields, a basketball court, various tall shade trees, and a community garden.

For me, the best part of Davis Park are its woods and thickets that rim the rear of the property. This greenery acts as an oasis, particularly for migrating songbirds.

Take spring migration, an urgent time for birds to return to breeding grounds, stake out territories and attract mates. While some species migrate during the day, most songbirds fly by night.

Folks in Rhode Island who track migration say that birds flying overhead at night look for dark areas below, which are typically parks, within the lights of cities. Such black blobs suggest places for the birds to drop in and to find food to fuel their passage.

For the past two weeks, I've enjoyed an abundance of morning bird songs in Davis Park. I've listened to warblers, vireos, wrens, flycatchers, thrushes, orioles, sparrows and more.

At the end of May, these experiences peaked. On May 30, I heard a raspy "we-be" call coming from the thick undergrowth. This was the song of an Alder Flycatcher, which is an uncommon spring migrant in Rhode Island. Maybe 10 of these birds are heard or seen in the state each spring.

The next morning, I found an even rarer species. Near that same thicket, I heard a rolling, two-syllable call that sounded like "cheery-cheery-cheery." This was the song of a Mourning Warbler.

I recorded the tune, sharing it with bird experts, who confirmed my ID. So far this spring, about a half-dozen Mourning Warblers have been reported in RI. Some springs, none are found.

I took Karen to the park to search for the rare birds. We didn't find either one, but we did hear and see some colorful species such as the orange-flashing Baltimore Oriole and the butter-colored, red-striped Yellow Warbler.

At the park, we also followed fly balls of young men practicing baseball, and watched a middle-aged man sink jump shots. Kids squealed from the playground, as shovels slid through compost in the community garden.

I believe that urban parks are vital to flora and fauna, including people. Parks provide wildlife with food and shelter, and space for plants to grow. For people, parks are communal spaces in fresh air. Often our parks offer idyllic features such as woods and fields, thickets, streams, ponds, rock outcrops and more.

Urban parks are places to unwind and reconnect with the natural world. In city parks, we come together, in unity, in community.

Davis Park is an oasis. If you haven't visited it, then I suggest you act like a migrant songbird on a spring night, and drop in.

New Hampshire

LESSONS FROM FIELD AND STREET
September 6, 2008

Each of the past four years we have spent a weeklong summer vacation in the Lakes Region of New Hampshire, drawing strength from bald eagles, inspiration from towering hemlocks, and serenity from clear waters.

There this summer I saw a poster for the Fresh Air Fund, which mentioned hosting young people from my childhood neck of the woods, the Bronx.

With all I've read recently about the summer of 1968, I can tell you that 40 years ago I could have used a Fresh Air Fund experience.

In 1968 my parents had no money to send me anywhere but to the streets, and in that Bronx summer, what you witnessed you never forgot.

Forty years ago, for example, I watched a drunken teen-ager, a kid with whom I had once sat on the corner and traded comics, pull a gun and shoot a hunk of shoulder out of a man, standing next to me, after the two of them argued over a fair-foul call during a stickball game.

Later, while awaiting trial, the teen-ager said he would kill me if I testified against him. Then he asked if I wanted to sit and read comic books again. I was 10.

That summer of 1968, if I had been among the New Hampshire lakes, I would have done something similar to what my family has enjoyed over the last four years: floated together on purple tubes in clear coves, watched white puffs of clouds swell above distant mountains and roasted marshmallows over glowing campfire coals.

But instead of enjoying the calls of loons out among the islands, I listened to the final words of a blond boy, whose face all the girls loved, dying on the sidewalk under my bedroom window one night from a wound ripped open by a rival gang member.

I also heard a sound that any parent fears—the dull thump of a speeding car hitting a tiny girl who had dashed out from between parked cars during a downpour. I watched her broken body slide more than 100 feet down the rain-slickened road.

In my young life, urban nurture too often meant death. Nature, meanwhile, has symbolized healing, renewal and life.

Our New Hampshire vacations began in 2005 based on the generosity of a family that allowed us to rent a lakefront cabin at the last minute so my daughter could begin her recovery from heart surgery. (Today she is mended and healthy). What we received would become a version of our own Fresh Air Fund experience.

To us, the two-room cabin, with its small bathroom and kitchen alcove, felt like the Vanderbilt Mansion. From a nearby pier of stones, my two youngsters learned to fish for bluegills, sunfish and smallmouth bass. They also taught themselves tennis on the property's court; their accompanying giggles and howls caused a family of foxes in the surrounding woods to yip in response.

On the cabin's wooden deck, a place with more daddy long legs than timbers, we watched openings, created by fallen trees, fill in with ferns, hemlock, oak and pine. From granite steps leading down to the lake, we followed meteors slice through a sky of 10,000 stars.

This past summer, we witnessed the first powerful cold front of the season sweep across the lake with forking bolts of lightning worthy of Zeus, leaving in its wake crisp air and a moonbeam across the water.

The rain that hammered the roof drowned out sound in the cabin and reminded us that most of the world lived in similar thin-roofed structures and how lucky we were to know that we could return to a home in Providence, which was insulated and warm.

The flute-like song of a Swainson's thrush serenaded us during walks in the forest this summer. The musical notes suggested that land would sometimes call out for people to be worthy of it. The family that has owned this property for generations has guided its management with a plan that has resulted in a sanctuary for plants and animals, as well as a sanctified place for folks passing through it. This is the opposite of the split-second street violence, in the form of the Saturday night special and switchblade, which took away life around me in 1968.

From the clear air and rich shade of the forest, I thought of Deganawidah, who led the formation of the Six Nations Confederacy. Of the future, he said, "Think not forever of yourselves, O chiefs, nor of your own generation. Think of the continuing generations of our families, think of the grandchildren and those yet unborn, whose faces are coming from beneath the ground."

Faces cannot come up through bloodstained asphalt and concrete. I saw a lifetime of such pavement in the summer of 1968.

Tranquility Among Wailing Loons

August 28, 2010

Word among kids on the block was that Smiley was so straight and civilized that he would take a bullet for one of us.

Smiley was about 18, when he showed up on our West Bronx street in the summer of 1966. He was uncommonly friendly. That may be why youngsters accepted and looked up to him so readily.

The ever-present grin on Smiley's face complemented his lean frame and the odd way that he walked—long strides off his toes.

Smiley was also serene, compared to the street's aggressive teens.

Their signature behavior was to gather loudly by the curbside and smash soda bottles. The accumulated glass would reflect the sky like placid water.

One late summer night I heard loud music and wild laughter coming from an apartment full of those adolescents.

I listened as the hooting morphed into noisy, angry shouts in the building's courtyard. I got up and looked out the window. Just like in the movies, there were screams, and then a deep, resonant pop.

This event sprang to mind last week, as my family settled down for the night in our rented lakeside cabin in New Hampshire.

Outside, waves slapped the riprap. The four of us quieted down to listen, as a common loon emitted a long howl. Elsewhere on the water, another loon called, followed by a third and then a fourth.

What we were hearing was the "wail," the extended cry that common loons use to contact one another.

230

Other loon calls include tremolo, yodel and hoot.

Tremolo is the loon's laugher-like alarm, uttered when danger approaches. Loon pairs sometimes tremolo together, and it is the only call that loons make in flight.

Male common loons yodel to declare or defend territory, primarily during the breeding season. A yodel may also suggest danger.

A loon hoot is a soft call. The birds hoot between mates, adults and chicks, or among social groups living on or visiting a lake.

A born insomniac, I've always listened to sounds of the night. As a child, I could tell the thud of a man's shoes versus the clack of a woman's high heels; or the cry of a baby from the whine of a cat; and a fire truck compared to a police car or ambulance.

The loud pop that I heard 44 years ago was an unfamiliar noise. But I would hear it again and again in subsequent years, as our neighborhood became a free-for-all.

It was a gunshot. That night in 1966 an off-duty police officer living across the street had demanded that the teen-agers end their noisemaking.

When a drunken adolescent stepped toward him, the officer fired, but Smiley jumped between them. The bullet blew out Smiley's stomach.

It took all autumn for Smiley to recuperate. The officer was suspended from his job.

The book, *The Common Loon; Spirit of Northern Lakes*, by Judith McIntyre, contains the text: "Loons hoot during ritualized social gatherings and on the fall staging grounds. Hoots are also used by one loon as it approaches a group or enters the territory of another loon."

Hooting was a hallmark of the territorial teens that convened at a shrine of broken glass two generations ago. If I close my eyes, I can still hear their howls. The recollection triggers anxiety.

I hope that in the years since Smiley indeed took a bullet for one of us that he re-discovered the feelings of serenity, which is what I experienced, as well as sweetness and wonder, listening to loons last week from a cabin in New Hampshire with my family.

231

Mystical Moose

December 3, 2011

Moose may be the largest land mammals in New Hampshire, but I am the state's biggest sap.

In the last 10 years, our family has visited New Hampshire at least a a dozen times. Each visit we've looked for moose.

If these outings were a box score, we would be 0 for 12.

New Hampshire Fish and Game says moose occur in all 10 counties in the state, and that there are at least 6,000 moose in the Granite State.

"Moose," said Fish and Game, "are hard to see at night. They are 6 feet tall at the shoulder and your headlights will often only reveal their legs, which are the same color as the pavement. Their height also means that if you hit one, the bulk of a moose will fall on your windshield and roof."

We've seen innumerable "Moose Crossing" signs, and other warnings that urge drivers to "Brake for Moose: It Could Save Your Life."

These signs work for us. We slow down and scan the road cautiously.

In summer, for example, when moose gorge on aquatic plants, we cruise along the bogs, lakes, ponds and streams from North Conway to Jackson to Bartlett, and between Moultonborough, Tamworth and North Sandwich.

No moose.

Fish and Game says a healthy moose will eat 40 to 60 pounds of browse a day. Indeed, moose is an Algonquin term for "eater of twigs."

In fall and winter, we nestle into the leaves, twigs and buds of aspen, birch, fir, maple and willow along what locals call "moose runs" outside Rumney, Woodstock and Franconia.

Zippo.

Last weekend, we went straight to the highest-density region of moose in New Hampshire—the Great North Woods.

Three days at dusk we sat amidst wetlands and adjacent stands of small to mid-sized softwoods and hardwoods.

Chill, said the locals, and your patience will be rewarded. But it got dark, and we got cold. Another zero.

So we cruised side roads of the National Forest. Into the night, the four of us drove the sloughs between Littleton, Whitefield, Lancaster and Groveton.

Zilch.

Finally, we headed north through clear-cuts and burns, covered by rich browse, and past beaver flows and islands of young trees.

Here by the border with Quebec, we heard that moose stepped out of premier habitats to lick road salt from wet highways. Again, another lost trip. We saw "rien," which is French for "nothing."

Our wish to see a moose began a decade ago, when we watched a video about the mammals. A narrator said that adult moose stood six-feet tall and averaged 1,000 pounds.

Nearsighted creatures, moose possessed keen senses of smell and hearing, the narrator noted. Bulls had dark brown or black muzzles and could grow 40-pound antlers of long tines and wide, curved palms. In contrast, cow faces were light brown, and cows had white patches of fur just under their tails.

I can't believe we bought this "bull." To us, moose remain fictional creatures like dragons and unicorns, vampires and zombies.

How curious that a New Hampshire slogan reads, "Make memories every day in the White Mountains of New Hampshire—a place you'll never forget."

Really? I can't stop thinking about the place. This yearning to see a moose is driving me nuts.

PECKS AMIDST PRODUCE
October 10, 2018

Karen and I exchanged pecks amidst produce at Rosaly's Garden and Farmstand in Peterborough, NH.

We were in Southern New Hampshire, celebrating our 25th wedding anniversary, visiting farm stands and state parks.

Rainfall brought on the autumn crops, said Beth, who worked behind the counter. Lettuce was the only vegetative victim of the moisture, with several varieties rotting in the field, she said.

At Rosaly's we found so many types of fruits, vegetables and flowers that the stand looked like a late-harvest museum. Also, we got a kick out of the veggie and fruit names such as sweet dumpling squash, cha-cha green kabocha squash, lunchbox peppers, indigo kumquat tomatoes and pinto gold fingerling potatoes.

Posters touted low-price bulk orders—bushels—of squash and potatoes for root cellars. A root cellar employs earth's natural cooling, insulating and humidifying properties to store food through the winter months. It denotes a closer-to-the-land life, as did the outhouse at Rosaly's, situated beneath a row of trees. The clean, fresh, little building was outfitted with toilet paper in a plastic box to keep chipmunks from shredding it, and aromatic cedar chips for odor control.

On that sunny morning, you could see brilliant tree colors beyond the farm's fields. The foliage looked like fruity cereal. In the foreground stretched rows of Rosaly's zinnias in pink, red, orange, yellow, white, as well as assorted blends and shades.

We filled the car with local peaches, apples, carrots, corn, squash, shallots, peppers and more (such as a freshly baked berry pie). Yes, peaches were still arriving from area orchards, Beth said.

That afternoon, we hiked up a rocky and very wet trail through hardwoods and conifers toward the top of Mount Monadnock. But we were just strolling, so despite the richness of the dense woods, lush in yellow birch, hemlock and ferns, we meandered back down to the car after climbing just a quarter mile.

The next morning in N.H.—still not looking to hike much—we drove up to the summit of nearby Pack Monadnock. The air was chilly and waves of misty fog floated past.

Atop this high point, the visibility was maybe 100 feet. There were few people up there among the spruce, mountain ash and slabs of granite, and we enjoyed the tranquility.

Our favorite moment was when we heard birds chipping from within the fog-shrouded spruce. Karen pointed to movement on the lower branches. We watched a tiny, wing-flicking songbird—a quarter-ounce-weighing, smaller-than-a-chickadee, Ruby-crowned Kinglet—emerge from the mist before flitting back into the foggy foliage.

Before heading home to Providence, we re-visited Rosaly's, in part, to replace what we had already eaten (peaches, apples and cherry tomatoes).

This time, gray skies muted the colors. Autumnal moisture drew a rich smell from the soil, and we found somewhat different produce selections—fewer pumpkins, but more potatoes, for instance.

Although the growing season winds down in autumn, some fall crops (apples, squash, pumpkins and more) explode in September and October. This is also true for the fare of winged and four-legged fauna, with first frosts often softening and sweetening wild fruit, such as crabapples, for creatures to devour.

If your senses—sight, sound, and smell—are locked in, you will find that the landscape changes nonstop, revealing something new with each visit.

I think that the same is true for relationships. If your emotional senses are sharpened and in-sync, then you will find that daily interactions are rich in words, gestures and actions. Like a spectacular sighting on a mountaintop, these are moments at which to marvel, too.

Spring Wings
April 7, 2017

From where we stood at the University of New Hampshire (UNH), you wouldn't know it was the last week of March.

A foot-or-so of snow blanketed the landscape in Durham, NH. Ice covered freshwater ponds. The peak temperature that afternoon was 35 degrees.

Except, a turkey vulture floated over campus. Turkey vultures return north in spring. Given vultures eat carrion (rotting flesh and meat); you don't usually see them when and where snow is on the ground.

Karen and I drove up to Durham to watch Rachel and her mates on the University of Vermont lacrosse club play peers from UNH and the University of Massachusetts Amherst (UMass).

Nearing campus, the route took us around and over Great Bay and the Piscataqua River. These eye-catching tidal waters, with marshes, fields, woodlands and mudflats, comprise good habitat for seacoast creatures.

The lacrosse teams played on snow-cleared artificial turf beside Whittemore Center Arena.

The field is also across the street from the Durham-UNH Station Building, an attractive stone structure that serves Amtrak Downeaster travelers. At one point, a train pulled in and folks got on and off, some of the latter stopping to watch the lacrosse match.

The line also serves freight trains. During one of the games, a train rumbled by for about three minutes.

In the midst of the round-robin tournament (UVM defeated both UNH and UMass), geese skeins began to pass overhead toward the west, coming from the general direction of Great Bay and the Piscataqua River.

The geese flew relatively high in the sky. I could not hear any honking. I wasn't sure if they were locals, or migrants. But they were majestic, and there were a lot of them.

Over the course of an hour, I counted 14 skeins of geese. The largest one contained some 40-or-so individuals in its wedge.

Then, a bald eagle flew over. This was an immature bird (it takes five years to reach adult plumage), with a dark head and tail, and body and wings mottled in brown and white.

The Durham-UNH Station Building also houses the Dairy Bar Restaurant. It is a warm and inviting space on a cold day. For the ride back to Providence, Karen ordered a hot chocolate. I bought a chocolate frappe (outside New England that is called a milkshake).

Like a chickadee pecking at suet, I sipped here and there on the fatty drink. It was a tasty source of heat and energy for my cold carcass on the two-hour drive back to Providence.

On Top of the World
August 11, 2017

We were halfway up the mountain trail when thunder sent hikers already at the summit hurrying down.

The thunder sounded ominous. But the forecast contained no rain. So, the four members of our family—Karen, Rachel, Noah and I—kept climbing.

Indeed, the booms were fleeting. By the time we reached the mountaintop, the sun was out and the site empty.

This was West Rattlesnake Mountain. We climbed it via the Old Bridle Path, in Holderness, NH. It is a one-mile, not-too-strenuous hike that leads to stunning views of Squam Lake.

The trail is very popular, especially on a summer's day. The path contains several sets of stairs, but remains somewhat eroded from high use. Signs ask hikers to carry buckets of stone up the hill to help stabilize the trail.

Although species diversity generally decreases with elevation, West Rattlesnake contains a mid- to upper-level forest uncommonly rich in diversity, including large red oaks, and a well-populated understory, amid many boulders.

Even though it was August, several birds still sang. They included a wood peewee calling, "pee-a-wee," a great-crested flycatcher belting out "wheep," and a hermit thrush intoning its liquescent song.

Near the summit, we found rock ridges rimmed in fairly thick vegetation, including mosses, lichens, wildflowers and other plant growth.

On the other side of the trail, we discovered an organic-matter-laden peat land. The imprint of deer hooves marked the black-soil edge of its muck.

The bedrock on West Rattlesnake, "relatively rare" in New Hampshire, "is unusual in its structure, and in terms of its enrichment of the soil," notes the University of New Hampshire. "Weathering of this rock has created the soil conditions that support" some unique natural plant communities.

The university received this part of the mountain, called the Armstrong Natural Area, "to be left undisturbed in its natural state for scientific, educational and inspirational purposes." Meanwhile, the Squam Lakes Association manages the trails.

At the summit, ridges of pink granite were scattered among the bedrock. The ground sparkled from small squares of mica.

The summit itself was pretty rocky and exposed, with stunted trees, particularly red pine. On Squam Lake below, we saw many forested islands, large and small.

To the south and west, huge dark thunderclouds, illuminated by the sun, framed distant mountains. Somewhere out of view, a raven repeatedly called "cruck."

Here on open outcrops, which usually dripped with hikers this time of year, the four of us sat alone, sharing a box of animal crackers and sips of water. A cool, post-thunder breeze helped dry off our sweat.

Rachel is 20 and Noah is 17. That they still accompany their parents for a week together each summer in New Hampshire left Karen and me feeling as if we were truly on the top of the world.

VISITING WITH A NATIVE SPECIES
August 17, 2010

After chatting with Tom, Noah and I decided that he was as authentic a creature of northern New Hampshire as the porcupine that drilled quills into a visiting Massachusetts mutt near the cabin our family rented last week in the Granite State.

We met Tom in mountain-lipped, farmed and forested Sugar Hill, where he'd set up a table to sell hooks, carvings, canned vegetables and other items forged by his hands.

Noah called Tom someone who "logged down wood." Indeed, Tom not only felled trees but graded and milled them into exterior walls, barn stalls and more.

Tom was also a blacksmith. I bought one of his hooks as a present for a friend, who built a woodworking shed recently.

Tom crafted several sized hooks and metal racks. Plus he tended a vegetable garden. On an adjoining table were jars of pickle chips, garlic spears, pepper jelly and pickled asparagus, canned from his garden.

Various antique tack racks for sale on the table dated back to 1850.

Tom said that when his garden succumbed to rain in 2009, he switched to hammer, anvil and chisel to forge new blacksmithing items in iron and steel.

"Last year was what I call a 'depression year,' losing the garden," he said. "When they come about, you switch to something else to get by."

Tom was also a caretaker of vacation homes in Northern New Hampshire and Vermont. One of his employers was a Rhode Island couple, whose Ocean State dwelling was hit hard by flooding earlier this year.

"I could have gone down to help clean the flooded basement," Tom said.

"I didn't, but my friend worked in Rhode Island after the flooding. He said it was hot and muggy, and that's how I remember Rhode Island; don't think I've been there in 30 years."

Noah admired a football-sized carved wooden duck atop a plumper, polished, apostrophe-shaped burl covered in natural curlicue markings.

Tom found the rounded outgrowth of oak submerged in the Wisconsin River "years ago," where he stopped after visiting some of his family's land in northern Wisconsin.

Tom was tall, lean and wore glasses. He was maybe 60 years old, with only a handful of rounded, brown-tinged teeth in his mouth. A metal Marine Corp insignia pin adorned Tom's ball cap. He was interested that I also liked to collect waterlogged wood.

Some hemlock branches, I said, revealed smooth golden wood, especially if they still held their bark, which I liked to peel off to expose beetle trails.

This prompted Tom to say that sometimes he milled hemlock so that the bark stayed on. It was a way to show respect for the wood, while bringing out its best characteristics, he said.

On this trip, Noah received his first pocket knife. He showed it to Tom, who took a solid looking, four-inch, all-purpose knife from his pocket. The two of them complained about their knives' locks.

Noah's lock was difficult for him to release, while Tom said that he instinctively pressed the back of the blade against his hip to fold the blade back into the handle, but the lock kept the knife open.

Tom noted that when he used the knife to harvest the cucumbers, he pushed the locked blade against his leg. Not only did the knife not close but also his hand slid off the handle and against the sharp edge, slicing open the meat of his palm. Blood covered his pants and the cucumbers, he said.

Later on, Noah and I joked that we were glad we skipped purchasing the pickle chips. We also said that Tom, like the sweet syrup condensed from local maples, was a person distilled from the New Hampshire northern woods.

"I have not depended on just one job and wage since I was a teenager, working on my grandfather's farm," he said. "I had to work that job to eat. Look at how tall and skinny I am! You know that I took that work seriously. I had to fill up this body!"

To us, Tom came across as part of the natural heritage and raw strength of his environment. In a world of branding and impulsivity,

Tom lived every day with an element of risk unique to life in and around Sugar Hill.

As we left, Tom gave me a gripping handshake. He thanked us for the purchase and company, adding the send-off, "winter well."

Welcoming More Wildlife
August 23, 2014

Upon our arrival in the New Hampshire woods, we met a few of the property's newest residents.

Two adult wild turkeys and eight young birds, called poults, crossed the road between green corridors of new growth that shone in the late-day light like leafy green neckties.

As young turkeys grow, they band into flocks of hens and poults. While the birds walked, the flock pecked the ground continually for nuts, seeds, berries and other plant matter. This was the first time in our 10 years visiting the property that we had encountered turkeys.

Beyond the birds, we noticed two young, grazing white-tailed deer. Both animals lifted their heads every few seconds to look at us, flicking their ears and tails.

People who own woods often hire certified foresters to help plan and manage the property. Such is the case with the 36-acre New Hampshire site.

Much of the land harbors tall trees. Three years ago, several trees were selectively removed to diversify the site, creating lush sunlit habitats needed by various species of wildlife.

Plants in the clearings included ferns, grasses, sedges, shrubs, vines and tree seedlings. Some of the species that I identified were blackberry, black raspberry, Eastern hay-scented fern, American beech, Eastern hemlock and white ash.

Between the clearings and tall trees, plants included large-leaved aster, blueberry, mapleleaf viburnum, wild sarsaparilla, witch hazel, red maple and red oak.

The Eastern hay-scented fern presents a good and bad scenario. It produces a lovely hay smell, especially in August and September, as the fronds turn yellow-brown. But deer don't prefer the fern, and sometimes it colonizes clearings, keeping other plants from growing.

A gold star goes to the land managers for leaving a wolf tree. That big, old white pine once grew on what was formerly open land, as evidenced by the tree's wide spread of dead and dying branches.

The pine diversified the forest structure via its robust bare horizontal branches, peeling bark, trunk cavities, and other features sought by wildlife.

We found the rest of the property wildlife-rich in other ways such as the adult bald eagle that looked for dead or dying fish from atop the shoreline trees and the great blue heron that hunted for fish below them.

The hurrahs of fishing boat occupants suggested a good year for bass, the prized fish of the lake.

On the dock we found a petite package of poop left by a mink. The scat looked like three black curled kittens, flecked with fish scales.

There were regular loon sightings and sounds, with several birds belting out tremolo, wail and yodel calls simultaneously at night.

As usual, insects were abundant. One evening, Noah and Rachel found a grasshopper in the cabin. This was not the typical stick-legged variety but one with banded, thicker legs. Unusual.

Last year, I upset some professional foresters via a commentary (April 13, 2013, "A civil-service career in a landscape of kill or be killed"), when I called rogue colleagues "foresters." The actual title for each coworker was, in fact, "climber and pruner."

The Society of American Foresters certifies foresters for education, experience and commitment to pursuing knowledge. I can tell you that just such professionals are helping plan and manage the property in New Hampshire. It is an excellent example of forest regeneration.

FLOATING AWAY
August 16, 2014

L ast May my mom turned 80, a milestone that underscored her 40-year-old rebuke that I call home more often.

My latest call home came from a forest of mature Eastern hemlocks and Eastern white pines along Lake Winnipesaukee in New Hampshire.

As I stood with a cell phone to my ear, a brownish-green, resinous chip bounced off my bucket hat.

I looked down, discovering that similar chips surrounded me like tiny campfire stones. Shredded, resinous small sticks, missile-tipped in tight green scales, comprised a wider circle.

Somewhere in the canopy a red squirrel fed on immature white pine cones. I thought of a cartoon creature chewing at high speed, with the completion of each cone accompanied by the bell of a manual typewriter carriage return.

Mom reminded me that she would leave Sunday, with my sister and her family, for the Jersey shore. The following week, mom, my brother and his family, would head to Florida for a few days.

The loop of life at the lake encircled all sorts of family dynamics.

Several times a day for example, a set of red-eyed vireos, small olive green, sharply-eye-striped songbirds, passed by our cabin. These encounters were an opportunity to watch an adult bird stuff a caterpillar into the mouth of a wing-fluttering fledgling.

One hundred yards offshore, a small white boat showed up every morning. Usually it carried two fishermen in black slickers and Red Sox ball caps. One fellow was about 60 and the other was maybe 30. I took them for father and son.

On one occasion there were three men in the boat, plus two boys in orange life vests. When a youngster caught a fish, everyone cheered, as if celebrating a home run.

The men and boys remained silent, however, when six loons floated past. This coexistence ended sternly after a jet ski screamed through the placid water, leading the loons to dive and the boat to rock in the ski's wake.

That afternoon, while Karen, Rachel and I drifted on inner tubes (Noah was in the cabin), an adult loon popped up beside us. A handsome contrast of black and white, the loon wailed before diving, resurfacing next to three young birds.

Suddenly, the little loons began running across the water, while flapping their wings. The birds, neck and neck and neck, ran/flapped past us (the sound of splashing was prominent), before settling out of sight in the recess of a cove.

This was our 10th anniversary renting a cabin on the 36-acre property, which is owned by multiple members of an extended family.

The lake vibe feels greater and more significant than so many weeks during the year, which we rush through chores and assignments, meetings, and events.

Several mornings at the lake I watched the pale yellow light post sunrise brighten the charcoal-colored bark of the great hemlocks and pines.

Like stage spotlights, shafts of sunlight illuminated boulders scattered everywhere. Over the next few minutes, the light turned golden and warm, working its way into the deep green canopy.

At night the four of us sat on granite steps to the lake, watching the western sky glow like the coals in a fire ring. Sometimes the most meaningful activity between dawn and dusk was floating as a family on the water.

That said, we returned home to Providence from our vacation yesterday. I better call mom to let her know that we arrived safely.

Spanking-New Snow and Tales of Winter

December 10, 2011

Mats of fresh snow magnified the trunks of white birches. Boughs of fir, pine and spruce hung low under frosty blankets.

Pillow-stuffing clouds clung to the White Mountains, while bits of sky, robin's egg blue, peeked through the icy fog.

Our family entered the northern half of New Hampshire on the tail of a departing snowstorm, which left behind a brilliant landscape.

Three hours earlier we'd departed Rhode Island, headed for a couple of days of rest and relaxation somewhere "different."

Back in the Ocean State it was a 60-degree day. Now we found ourselves on what seemed like the Polar Express.

One minute we needed sunglasses. Then next, waves of gray-cloud scalloped Cannon Mountain and Franconia Notch.

Snow makes me think, Rachel said.

Indeed! Through the veil of snow, we passed Boise Rock. The massive, glacially deposited boulder is named after the man it once sheltered from severe snow and cold.

According to the State of New Hampshire, a local fellow by the name of Thomas Boise took "drastic action" here to survive winter conditions.

"He killed and skinned his horse. Crawling under the overhang of this rock, he wrapped himself in the hide and spent the night. Men sent out the next day to search for him found Tom still alive but encased in the frozen hide that had to be cut away with axes in order to release him."

I have my own gruesome snow story.

During the ages of 13-17, I delivered newspapers from 5-6 am. On some winter mornings I was the first person to leave footprints in the virgin snow.

The newest flakes of snow glittered on pre-dawn sidewalks under streetlights in the Bronx neighborhood of my childhood.

My favorite place during snow falls was a cloister-like rectangle between apartment buildings, which I reached by alleyway to watch flakes fall from an orange-tinged sky.

Sometimes I entered this cavern in the blackness of early morning, when you could actually hear snowflakes accumulating around you. The only other sounds were the occasional tea kettle whistle or a distant elevated subway train, delivering the day's first commuters to Manhattan.

In the evening, this space amassed both snow and the cooking odors of apartments on all four sides.

On one paper-route morning, when fresh snow covered the pavement, I noticed footprints into and out of the alleyway. I also noticed dark spots that led from the passage and into the apartment building.

I entered the structure to deliver papers, following the drops in the process. In the foyer, I heard a muffled sound—an almost inaudible groan. Following the trail and the echo, I peered under the steps.

There was a man covered in blood that flowed from where he once had a right ear.

I ran home, where my mother called the police. I do not know what happened to the bleeding man. But I never went back to the secret snow spot.

As we passed north out of the mountains, a hoary setting sandwiched Route 3. An orange plow, with blinking yellow lights and a hopper crammed with sand headed south past us.

I opened the window, and the countryside smelled frigid and scrubbed clean.

Sunlight slipped through the icy vapors illuminated a trillion twinkling crystals and flakes.

Look at it sparkle, Noah said.

Just as fresh snow allows animals to tell stories through their tracks left behind, the canvas of pure white provides a backdrop for our own tales.

Over the next two days, we slid on tubes down snowy hills and played touch football in our boots and winter coats.

In a room at the inn, we hung wet clothes to dry, and then headed to the library to read in front of a toasty fireplace.

Our hope for Rachel and Noah is that they come away from the snows of the Great North Woods with their own stories that are safer and less terrifying than some of the other tales we may tell during the winter-weather season.

MUSHROOM LADY
August 30, 2008

As much as we thought we knew the stretch of New Hampshire forest that we have visited the past four Augusts, we were dazed at what we found just a few days ago.

After a summer of steady rain, mushrooms, like candy buttons, festooned the forest floor. Fungi that we had never seen before in these woods had burst forth like Fourth of July fireworks, minus the booms.

Mushrooms, which flourish in cool, moist settings, particularly in summer and fall, now grew alongside familiar boulders, blossomed amidst brown leaves and pine needles, and dotted the ground beneath beech, maple, hemlock, oak and white pine.

The colors were hallucinogenic. Besides the various whites and browns, we found shades of blue, green, orange, red and yellow. The shapes were almost as wild. Mushrooms resembled backsides, brains, pancakes, tortoises, umbrellas and other recognizable forms.

Given that I am color blind, I cannot correctly determine the tint of mushroom caps, spores, secretions or bruises. Color differentiation is a critical skill to identifying fungi in the field, and I certainly wouldn't collect for consumption if I couldn't tell a hue of lavender from a shade of gray or a tinge of pink from a tint of tan.

So I was thrilled on the morning of our last day in the forest, when my 11-year-old daughter, Rachel, came running back to the cabin to take me to meet the "mushroom lady." In the woods, we caught up with Sandi; a tall elegant woman in a gray fleece vest, holding a basket of freshly picked fungi, destined for an omelet.

251

Sandi was headed back to her vacation home, but she was kind enough to spare a few minutes to introduce us to some of the local species.

The first mushroom we met was at our feet. It was a dazzling white, helmet-capped specimen that Sandi called the "avenging angel." This was a kind term, I learned, for the fungus was more commonly known as "death cap," one of the world's deadlier mushrooms. Among its identifying traits were a white sac-like wrapper around the base of the cap, white ring encircling the stem and bulbous base.

Then Sandi showed us her collection. Dominating the basket were richly gilled, orange-colored chanterelles, sometimes called "Queens of the Forest." There was also a large bolete, which featured a somewhat concave, thick, sienna-colored cap, with a bottom so spongy that it felt like foam rubber. Another mushroom was a russula. Its cap was pinkish and lushly gilled.

Neither a food-consuming animal, nor fodder-making plant, a mushroom is a fungus, usually with a fruiting body of underground strands and an above ground stalk and cap. Typically, fungi spread from spores released via the cap.

Fungi exude enzymes to digest organic matter, releasing nutrients that the fungi then absorb. Fungi serve a significant function in the environment, because they decompose dead or decaying organisms and recycle nutrients.

Mushroom identification takes real detective work. It requires patience and strict attention to detail. Sandi learned from relatives and others, and developed her skills over years of practice, often collecting and identifying specimens in tandem with other fungi enthusiasts.

Before we met Sandi, Rachel photographed many of the mushrooms, which we tried to identify, using a field guide borrowed from the local library. We did recognize a handful of species. For example, relatively small, stunning-blue specimens were heliotrope webcap mushrooms. Round warty objects at the edge of a field were pigskin poison puffballs. These thick-skinned, specimens featured hard purple-black centers.

Before we locked up the cabin, I downed my bowl of oatmeal, knowing that I didn't need to know the names of the mushrooms to enjoy their stunning presence, ecological role or value in the kitchen.

Still, on the ride out, I couldn't stop wanting a little bite of that omelet Sandi had by then, prepared and probably devoured with gusto.

TROLLING FOR TWIGS
August 18, 2012

After our week at Lake Winnipesaukee, I joked about writing a "Glimpser's Guide to Nature."

It seemed like the best wildlife sightings occurred when I turned around, looked up or glanced over my shoulder.

At the lake, my favorite activity was to search the riprap for wedged waterlogged sticks. I liked to peel the bark to reveal the wood beneath.

As I walked in knee-high water one afternoon, on a sandy, but stone-studded bottom, some sense told me to swivel. As I did, I caught sight of a mature bald eagle, flapping away steadily, with a fairly good-sized fish in its talons.

The bird, I learned later in the week, nested on an island about a mile away in tall white pines that sheltered two, massive, soon-to-fledge chicks.

Our spot on the lake was fish-rich. Each morning after dawn, small-mouth-bass fishermen showed up by boat beyond our cabin, where the lake dropped into deep-water ledges.

A man, named Joe, fished mornings from the property's stone-and-wood pier. Joe reeled in smallmouth bass, lake trout and a pickerel. A North Carolina chef, Joe said that fishing was both relaxing and kept him out of trouble.

The same was true for my stick finding and bark-peeling. The process of denuding a branch could occupy my time for more than an hour.

One afternoon, I extracted a hemlock stick, which mushroomed into an umbrella of tinier twigs, as I pulled it from the rocks.

I sat on the granite steps behind our cottage, using my fingernails to strip off the sodden bark.

The emerging wood revealed a wet, golden-orange color, which before it dried, rivaled a setting sun. The delicate little branches looked like the gilded tailings of a firework display falling through the sky.

The wood also displayed both massed, thread-thin, squiggly tunnels and pencil-line-thick channels left by different bark beetles. They reminded me of hieroglyphics.

It was during a bark stripping session that I initially missed a pitter-patter on the water. When I finally "heard" it, I looked up to see a large duck trailed by three baby birds.

They were common mergansers. The adult's silhouetted long, thin bill was both diagnostic and striking. The three young kept up with mom by scuttling atop the water like roadrunners.

Two days later, enmeshed in removing the thin bark off a branch of mountain ash, I missed a mink that slinked around the riprap.

Folks in the cottage to our northeast saw the mammal and they figured that I did too, but my head was down, as I worked on the wood.

A 2-4 pound, lithe and agile animal, an adult mink grows about 18 inches in length, plus its trailing six-inch tail. This brown predator devours most anything meaty on shore or in the water—from earthworms to fish.

Later that day, I found some of the animal's fresh scat on an adjacent stone-and-wood pier. The feces were dark, L-shaped, marked with little bits of bone, and trailing off in a matting of mouse or shrew fur.

The tail end of the scat reminded me a little of the colors and patterns of the mountain ash stick. The design of white and charcoal spots that dotted the wood looked like a concoction of Dr. Seuss.

Karen says that every twig tells a tale. In a lake the size of Winnipesaukee, 71 square miles, a fallen branch could travel miles before wedging between stones. Or, it might drop straight into the rocks, like the proverbial apple that doesn't fall far from the tree.

Some folks glimpse people, settings or something else, and treasure that memory for a lifetime. Like every fallen twig, each glimpse, I believe, tells a story.

OHIO

Taking Root and New Growth

January 15, 2011

Most times, sowing a seed is a matter of faith that new life will come to light.

In today's cynical world, it is especially hard to imagine the magnitude of faith inherent in a young Hungarian couple—my wife's grandparents—who tied the knot before a justice of the peace in Youngstown, Ohio, on a below-freezing afternoon in late 1933—the hub of the Depression.

The young man, John Wargo, was Catholic. His new wife, Ethel Czako, was Protestant. Neither of their families wanted John and Ethel to marry.

Moreover, John was looking for work at the time. He dreamed of a job in which he could make things with his own hands, and a plot of soil of his own to raise fruits and vegetables. Ethel was a domestic, who wanted a home and a family some day.

When word came of work in Paterson, New Jersey, John headed there. That job dried up, and he labored in Detroit for a while.

In 1936, John finally found steady work in a Youngstown steel mill. Right after he started the job, the mill went on strike. For a few days, John literally dodged bullets. Then, he began a career that would last more than 40 years.

The young couple had two children, and eventually settled into a modest home in Mentor, Ohio, to the east of Cleveland.

Gardening was one of their passions. Ethel and John grew and canned beans, beets, cherries, peaches and much more. Garlic and onions from the garden spiced their dishes year-round.

Every year, a bushel of cucumbers from the garden became winter pickles, while a basket of peppers was jarred in oil and garlic.

From their own apples, grapes, plums and other fruits, the couple made at least 10 different types of wine.

When I met John more than 20 years ago, he gave me a garden tour. It included the compost pile that refurbished the soil and the mulch that protected it. John also believed in rotating crops to control disease and insects and keep the soil fresh.

At the time, I asked John if it bothered him that other gardeners trumpeted chemicals over hassling with compost, mulch and rotation. No, he said, he believed in what he was doing. John had values, and he stood by them.

From John and Ethel, Karen and I learned how to garden, can our produce and make wine. But we absorbed much more.

John and Ethel built their relationship around commitment, respect and common interests. In our disposable, replaceable world, each of them were satisfied with what the other had to offer.

Their story contrasted with my own in which my parents seemed to fight with every sunrise. I grew up believing that I had nothing to say, and if I did, no one wanted to hear it. My siblings and I called ourselves, "human punching bags."

For me, John and Ethel simplified the concept of relationship. They just accepted me, and I found the courage to embrace them.

On Nov. 15, 2010, the couple celebrated their 77th wedding anniversary at an assisted-living facility in Burton, Ohio. Two days later, John collapsed. The next day, Ethel crumpled over.

John died at the age of 101 on Nov. 19. Eleven days later, 96-year-old Ethel passed away.

Karen and Noah spent a week with Ethel before her death. They sat with her in hospice, combed her hair, and shared the latest comings and goings.

When Rachel and I drove out to Ohio, we sat with Ethel, too. Rachel fed her pumpkin pie, topped with whipped cream, on Thanksgiving.

That night, Ethel struggled to speak. When I put my ear to her mouth, she said, "I love you."

If well tended, the spark of life within us, like a seed, will flourish into a life freshened with purpose and affirmation. When John and Ethel entered my life, I landed on some very good soil.

THE RICHES THAT HELP
TELL OUR STORIES

January 3, 2009

O n Christmas Day, my family crossed paths with a seemingly commonplace man who proved extraordinary. The experience reminded us that whether we're in a woodlot or a wood-paneled living room, every encounter helps us piece together the past and present, and provides insights into the future.

Like the weather, the countryside changed rapidly, as we traversed rural Northeast Ohio. Over the 10-mile trip, we drove up and down undulating hills, through vast wetlands, and finally across a flat landscape of farms, fields and forests, all blanketed by waves of sunlight, snow showers and stiff northwest winds.

My mother-in-law Jan led the way to a man who had built a two-bedroom home years ago in a rural hamlet about 40 miles east of Cleveland and 10 miles south of Lake Erie. Jan brought him a hot meal on wheels that included holiday drawings by school children and a Christmas ornament. She thought that I would enjoy meeting him, because he enjoyed the outdoors.

Wearing wire-rimmed glasses, his thick white hair parted on the side, Rudy offered a strong handshake at age 86. His home was neat, clean and spartan, suggesting the discipline of a man who had pared his life down to the essentials.

At his urging, Rudy stood, and the five of us crammed onto his couch. Rudy was hard of hearing, and we shouted out questions, as if in a news briefing.

Rudy's wife died five years ago, and his children did not visit in winter. Too much snow, he said. Two daughters lived near Philadelphia, another was in Florida, and his son lived in Virginia. This was Ohio's snow belt, averaging more than 100 inches of the white stuff per year.

Rudy told us he loved treasure hunting. In warmer months, armed with a metal detector, he searched around old homes and other "century" sites for lost or forgotten items.

Treasure hunting was a "great way to enjoy the scenery and open air," Rudy said. You walked the landscape, carting a five-pound detector, digging and filling holes, and repeating the process through the day, he said.

With his thumb and forefinger, Rudy showed how he knitted grass together to leave no sign of a hole. "You replace things exactly as you found them," he said.

Rudy also searched for gold. New owners of a favorite haunt had blown up its hillside recently to find what little gold was left. The cost of devastating the landscape was more than the few flakes of gold still in it, Rudy said, and he would not go there again.

Before a career in manufacturing, Rudy served in World War II, as a member of the 42nd Rainbow Infantry Division. One Christmas Eve, members of his Division sang carols. Later, they heard German troops singing carols across the battlefield. In the morning, the two sides fought.

"It really was kill or be killed," he said. "After a battle, we counted who was left." Rudy asked himself, "Why me?" when so many friends died, while he lived.

Rudy fought in the Battle of the Bulge and helped liberate Dachau. What he found in the concentration camp was unspeakable and unthinkable, he said.

After a few seconds of silence, we asked Rudy about his winter hobby of feeding wildlife. He took us to the kitchen window, just as a chickadee visited a feeder in a pear tree. Rudy also kept a "squirrel stump" in the backyard, where he spread chow. Daily, he put out a plate of pellets for wild rabbits.

We noticed the souvenir plates from all 50 states that snaked around the wood-paneled and pink walls. Rudy's wife had collected them on their former travels together, he said.

Before we left, Rudy showed us his military jacket, adorned with more than 20 decorations, including a Presidential Citation, Combat Infantryman Badge and Bronze Star. The garment still fit, he said.

Rudy seemed comfortable, productive and connected. I thought of Thoreau, who had built his cabin in the woods, outlined ingredients for a productive existence, and reduced his life to those essentials.

Our visit also reminded us that every day was a treasure hunt—the discoveries strengthening our relationships to our community, tradition and world.

Rudy was our holiday find. Visiting with him reaffirmed a link to what came before us and what lay ahead. It shed some light on what we knew about ourselves today and what we sought to unearth tomorrow.

PONDERING THE PROMISE OF PRIMROSE
February 10, 2017

Falling in love is one way to brighten winter.

In February 25 years ago, I was assigned to write the copy for a brochure about the nation's first international floral and garden festival, to take place in Columbus, Ohio, where I lived.

On a chilly afternoon, a team of writers, designers and others met to plan the document.

We decided to name the brochure, "Primula," which is one way to say "first" in Latin, as well as the name for first-of the-year flowering plants, called primrose.

The leader of our brochure team was a young woman, who was confident, but also playful. I noticed her bright brown eyes and shiny brown hair. Light in the darkness of winter, I thought.

At each meeting, our leader placed primrose plants on the conference-room table. Outside it was gray and cold, slushy and dreary. The primroses were inspiration. They promised of spring.

Every January and February, primroses—compact little plants topped by bright blossoms—arrive in supermarkets, garden centers and big-box stores.

Atop rosettes of attractive, furrowed green leaves, the yellow-centered flowers of primrose come in blue, magenta, orange, purple, pink, red, yellow or white.

When primroses show up in the supermarket, I smile in joy. I am amazed at their vividness.

Recently, I purchased a primrose. It featured stunning purple flowers, marked by petite yellow centers.

To thrive indoors, a primrose needs TLC. The species does best when placed in a cool spot such as a windowsill, but out of direct sunlight, which may scorch the leaves. Keep the growing medium moist and remove spent blossoms, and a plant may flower inside for a couple of weeks.

How curious that the day I bought the primrose I also heard multiple birds singing for the first time this winter. Those tunes included the "peter-peter-peter" of a tufted titmouse, "birdie, birdie, birdie" of a northern cardinal, and "ank, ank, ank of a white-breasted nuthatch.

Within a week, I discovered snowdrops blooming in a neighbor's yard, and watched a red-tailed hawk "straighten up" a nest used last year. Each of these early signs suggested that winter would once again turn to spring.

The promise of primrose also reminds me of that life-affirming woman, who led our "Primula" team 25 years ago. Her name was Karen.

Like the flowers on the conference-room table, Karen brought a warm touch of spring to each gathering. Such allure proved irresistible. Just two years after we developed that brochure, Karen and I became husband and wife.

Remembering What Is Good and Right
May 3, 2008

From 1986-93, I lived in an apartment that abutted 20-acre Clinton-Como Park in Columbus, Ohio. I defended the few acres of woods in the park, rich in flora and fauna, on the east bank of the Olentangy River, picking up trash, shooing out bikers, even urging organizers of the local Easter egg hunt to move their event from the wildflower-laden forest to an adjacent field.

Last week I made my first April visit to the park in 15 years. This was a chance to reconnect with my former environment in springtime, to consider what had changed and to compare the woodlot to a small forest in Providence's Blackstone Park that I have haunted for the last 12 years.

Upon entering the woods, I remembered that Columbus was a place of moist, high-lime, clay-rich, fine-grained, glacial drift, otherwise known as mud. It squeezed beneath our feet, lined the shore, and covered the logs and other plant debris jammed up in the river.

On seeing the Olentangy, my first thought was to look for Huck Finn and Jim on a raft. The river, maybe one-eighth of a mile wide, was a meandering muddy brown; creating bars, islands, pools, riffles and runs.

Bottomland soils usually possess above-average fertility, which explained the carpet of wildflowers in my former stomping grounds.

There were patches of Dutchman's breeches, named for the shape of the white flowers; trout lilies, both white and yellow; false rue anemone; wild ginger; and swathes of the garden escapee, lesser celandine, with its shining buttercup-like flowers.

Bottomland trees, particularly cottonwood, hackberry and American sycamore, dominated the canopy. Some trees ranged between 40 and 50 inches in diameter. Other species included black walnut, box elder, American elm, Ohio buckeye and pawpaw.

The big trees were larger than I remembered. The park had grown in other ways, too, hosting a new stretch of bikeway, a bridge and a recent planting of more than 1,400 seedlings.

Despite the bikers, hikers and egg hunters, the woods in Clinton-Como Park had survived just fine. Similar to a mature wine, it had spread out a fine bouquet for us.

My Blackstone forest sits on a waterway like Clinton-Como Park, and both are major routes for migrating birds. However Blackstone, given its location on the west bank of the much wider, brackish Seekonk River, hosts significantly more waterfowl.

In addition, the Blackstone woods sit mostly on a ridge. Much of the soil is a mix of sand, gravel and dry brown dust. It is strongly acidic. There is mud closer to the shore frontage, where birds, such as the American robin, find the muck to cement their nests in spring.

The local infertile soils are devoid of blooming wildflowers this time of year. Some plants, such as Canada mayflower and Solomon's seal, will bloom in May. Later in spring, mountain laurel shrubs will erupt into red, pink and white clusters of star-shaped flowers across the site.

The Blackstone tree canopy also consists of fewer species. It is mostly white oak and black birch, including some huge specimens. There is a smattering of pin cherry, red oak, sassafras and sugar maple.

At Clinton-Como Park, a simple, typical question told me how much I had changed. My two children, ages 7 and 10, asked, "Could we collect some wildflowers for mom?" who we would see later that day.

Life is about planting and growing. Once, I was meant to live in Columbus, where, besides defending the forest, I met the women who would become my wife. Now we were meant to live in Providence, and to raise children. "Sure, I said to the kids, "but take only what you need for a small bouquet." Acceptance and moderation were two of multiple things I had learned over the past 15 years. They came into my life, along with much more, as I had matured, just like the woods in Clinton-Como Park.

Pondering Punderson

July 31, 2010

No matter how many times some folks see a hawk or snake or salamander, they act as excited as they did the first time.

That's the impression I got from naturalist Megan Acord, who walked with me for an hour around part of Punderson State Park in Geauga County 33 miles east of Cleveland, during my family's annual summer trip to Ohio.

Acord grew up prowling the woods and streams of neighboring Ashtabula County. So, maybe it was natural that when we heard a "clump" sound in the brush, she sprang after it to glimpse a large garter snake vanish under a rotting log. Later in the walk, Acord just missed snaring a black rat snake.

We strolled up and down the lightly rolling Erie Trail around Stump Lake, one of the local kettle ponds left by Ice Age glaciers more than 10,000 years ago.

One of the first things I noticed was that trail was mowed quite high, as ticks are not a significant problem in Geauga County.

Geauga's wetlands are rich in other insects, though. Deer flies bounced off our hats like raindrops in the sunshine. Mosquitoes appeared every time we stepped into shade. That night, from our cabin in the park, my family enjoyed a lightning-bug show.

Insects, of course, support life up the food chain. On the nature walk, I heard a phoebe, pewee, red-eyed vireo and wood thrush sing from the oaks and hickories.

A male hooded warbler, with its golden mask, black neck and head covering, whistled a signature, "t-wit, t-wit, t-wit, tea-o" from a stand of sugar maples. Not far behind it, a male pileated woodpecker varied a resonating "kuk-kuk-kuk" call into what sounded like deranged laughter.

In fact, Acord said that the 1,000-acre park was home to seven breeding woodpecker species—downy, hairy, pileated, red-bellied, red-headed, northern flicker and the Ohio-endangered yellow-bellied sapsucker.

In the United States, Ohio is second to California in the percentage of wetlands lost to development, with 90 percent of original Ohio wetlands gone.

However, Geauga County still retained a significant amount of glacial-related bogs, marshes, ponds and swamps, she said.

Acord graduated from John Carroll University near Cleveland last May, with a master's degree in biology. Her thesis examined how mate choice based on color variation among red-backed salamanders might impact isolated populations of the species.

Earlier this month, Acord presented her findings at the annual Joint Meeting of Ichthyologists and Herpetologists held in Providence.

This fall, Acord will begin doctorate work in biology at Cleveland State University.

One thing I noticed about the Erie Trail was that it took a relatively slight rise in elevation for the forest composition to change from oak-hickory to beech-maple.

My favorite sighting in either woods was the fox squirrel, a species that lives in parts of the Eastern United States, but not in New England. It is bigger than the gray squirrel, with a fashionable reddish-orange belly.

The Erie Trail was home to an even larger rodent—the beaver. Like turkeys, otters and bald eagles, beavers were once extirpated in Ohio, but were released into or returned to breed in the Buckeye State in recent years.

Before we reached the shoreline beaver lodge, Acord pointed out cottonwood, aspen and other softwood saplings chewed off by the three-foot-long mammals.

Sometimes, Acord said, she walked out and sat atop the lodge, listening to the pig-like grunts of the parents and the puppy-like whimpers of their babies.

Acord studies living things and the relationships between them. From her enthusiasm and passion, and her work as naturalist, educator and scientist, I could tell that she understood that all life, including her own, changed constantly, requiring balance to sustain itself.

This reminded me that if you allowed it, vacation time could free you from daily worries, reunite you with family, and enable you to explore new places and meet new people.

The trip to Ohio provided the latest opportunity to ponder how all parts of the earth fit together around us, as well as how things come together within ourselves.

THE COLORS OF LIFE
July 26, 2014

We gathered beneath cemented sands of geologic time.

Those grains and pebbles belonged to the Black Hand Sandstone and Conglomerate that shaped the scenic cliffs and deep gorges found in Clear Creek Metro Park 50 miles southeast of Columbus, Ohio.

We flew into Central Ohio and drove deep into the 5,000-acre park to join family, celebrating my father-in-law's 80th birthday. To all of us, he is "Papa."

Along Route 33, Queen Anne's lace (wild carrot) and common chicory grew so thick that it looked like landscapers had planted it instead of Mother Nature.

Beyond, the corn grew chest high on this 19th of July. Just before the park, those fields began to undulate before a backdrop of little forested hills. For the first time on the drive, the road rose and fell in what we call "elevation."

Clear Creek valley is where geologic and climate zones overlap. As noted on hockinghills.com, "Here the prairies of the west meet the Appalachian forests of the east. Canadian hemlocks pushed south by glaciers meet southern species such as rhododendron. And it all rests on bedrock of Black Hand sandstone."

That stone is a cement of pebbles and quartz sand in gray, red, yellow, ochre, orange, tan and other shades of brown. Compared to New England granite, which formed from solidified molten material, you can break some of the sandstone in your hand. It also erodes differently, forming all sorts of curves, coves, dimples and wrinkles.

The picnic pavilion was on a summit surrounded by a wildflower field and fertile forestland. Through a cut in the greenery we saw other ridges, plus fog that dangled over the creek.

Papa sat at a picnic table, receiving gifts and greetings. Grilled chicken scented the air. Almost directly overhead, an adult Eastern bluebird fed insects to two young on the dead branch of a red oak.

At one point, several white-tailed deer bounded past. Later we saw two young bucks in the creek. Their antlers grew tawny and upright. The bucks splashed loudly through the water to escape our gazing.

Clear Creek was a bit of a misnomer. The shallow, swift water flowed through a land of clay and sand, so it looked a little muddy compared to the clearer tannic streams of New England.

We visited a haunting, looming roadside outcrop of sandstone. This was tan-colored geologic frosting of washed-out holes and ledges. In the ochre layers, rusted iron bled red and oxidized manganese imbued purplish-back lines that reminded me of exposed edges of newspaper pages.

Hemlock and ironwood grew from the sandstone. The surrounding forest featured black oak, hickories, red oak and tulip trees, some approaching 100 feet in height, plus chestnut oak and Virginia pine in spots.

So far, biologists have identified more than 800 species of plants in the park.

Across the road we found the unusual horsetail growing thickly. Horsetail often denotes a luxuriant natural setting. Each horsetail stem looked like a thin, waist-high dark-green tube divided into segments marked by lighter-green constrictions.

Horsetail reproduces by spores, and it is the only representative left of an entire class of species that was diverse and dominant in the landscape more than 100 million years ago.

Birds begin quieting down in July, yet we heard several species, such as white-eyed vireo and hooded warbler, which one finds in rich, protected sites. My favorite call came from a Carolina chickadee, because it sounded like a sped-up version of its cousin, the black-capped chickadee.

When Black Hand sandstone took shape some 350 million years ago, this area was a shallow interior sea, with bars, spits, beaches and deltas.

We do not live in such geologic ripples of time. Watching Papa (whose given name is John) and his wife, Jan, make silly faces and play with their great grandchildren, I thought of how we exist more in the here and now, of families who gather on remote ridges to rejoice. For us, time is more of the proverbial hourglass, in which each grain of sand is sacred.

Sowing a Seed in Southern Ohio
July 13, 2018

E ven during hot, sunny weather, the clayey soil of Athens, Ohio, still squished after previous days of rain.

I was with Karen and Noah, our son, who was on the campus of Ohio University (OU) in Athens to register for freshman classes. We arrived for a two-day visit on a sweltering summer morning, with a clear sky and the air temperature headed for the mid 90s, following almost a week of rainfall.

Athens is located in a swath of Southern Ohio that geologists call the "Unglaciated Allegheny Plateau," which includes some of West Virginia and Western Pennsylvania. When glaciers spread across the continent thousands of years ago, they did not cover this area. The bumpy terrain, containing significant sandstone, shale and coal, looked like smooth skin covered by mumps.

At ground level, the soil held considerable clay and organic matter, plus silty outwash from the nearby Hocking River. Where there was that much clay, water was slow to drain. So, when we crossed a campus lawn, spongy soil squirted water with each step.

Trees, in particular, grow exceptionally well in such earth. In 2017, Expedia called the deeply shaded OU campus one of the nation's 15 most-beautiful college campuses. OU has also received Tree Campus USA recognition several times from the Arbor Day Foundation.

Given that OU was established in 1804 as the first institution in the Northwest Territory, the school has had more than 200 years for some of its trees to tower toward the sky. I learned that folks at OU keep a campus-tree history, given ecological changes, such as the spread of Dutch elm disease, and a legacy of faculty, alumni and administrators playing a strong hand in planting trees, recognizing them or otherwise influencing how the campus landscape looks.

I noted all sorts of majestic specimens such as American sycamore; black walnut; pignut hickory; sugar maple; sweetgum; tulip tree; and pin, red and shingle oaks. Many of these species were what some homeowners might call "dirty" because they drop fruit or other plant material to the ground during the course of the growing season.

That said, garden neatniks would have been beside themselves at the sight of one particular campus quad, which contained fruiting horse chestnut, sycamore, sweetgum, hickory, oak and walnut. A lot of nuts and more would drop there this coming fall. Moreover, the bark was naturally peeling and sloughing off the sycamore. One man's trash was indeed another man's treasure.

Such extensive tree cover provided great relief from the searing sun. It also seemed to me that the greenery trapped some of the moisture evaporating from the soggy earth to produce a sweet-smelling scent.

Near the center of campus, I crouched to ball-up a small amount of soil. It stuck together in a black and somewhat gritty sphere that stained my fingertips dark brown. This suggested a slightly sandy clay loam. Good material for plant growth.

I also hoped that it was the right stuff to continue the cultivation of an incoming freshman from Rhode Island.

MIA AND THE MYSTERY PLANT
July 27, 2018

The plant didn't just pop up from the ground last spring, it shot up, said Karen's nephew, John, when we visited him, wife-to-be, Hannah, and their two-week-old daughter, Mia, at their brick-and-stone ranch on two fertile acres near the Chagrin River in Willoughby Hills, Ohio.

John led me to a partly shaded, loamy-soil garden plot alongside the home to show me the plant.

Was this giant hogweed, John asked? Willoughby Hills is in Northeast Ohio, a hot spot for the news-making carrot cousin of massive size; a toxic invasive perennial with sap that can cause severe burns.

Well, the plant was gigantic—over seven feet tall. Plus, it was in the carrot family, but different from any species that I knew, including angelica/wild celery, cow parsnip, poison hemlock, Queen Anne's lace/wild carrot and wild parsnip.

I looked up giant hogweed on my iPhone, and found it featured a large flat umbel of white flowers, deeply cut foliage, and stems with conspicuous white hairs and purple blotches.

In contrast, this plant displayed somewhat-serrated leaves, green stems and multiple light-yellow umbels.

I sent images of the plant, plus some notes, to a friend who works at the College of Food, Agricultural, and Environmental Sciences at The Ohio State University, and who had written about giant hogweed in Ohio. He shared the material with folks at Secrest Arboretum and in the Weed Ecology Lab, both at the Ohio Agricultural Research and Development Center (OARDC).

Two days later, I received an ID from OARDC: lovage, a perennial, giant-sunflower-sized culinary herb, usually planted for its celery-like flavor. Lovage was related to dill, carrot, parsnip and celery—and also to poison hemlock and giant hogweed.

About lovage, my friend included a line from a 2010 article in *The Washington Post*, "Imagine a celery the size of a Christmas tree."

An Eastern Mediterranean native, lovage had long-ago escaped cultivation in North America and was naturalized in many parts of the country, said a Missouri Botanical Garden fact sheet. That document also stated (and was of particular note to a young couple and their newborn) that lovage oil was once used in love potions and in charms to protect loved ones from evil spirits.

Even more striking in this tale of a mystery species was a line near the bottom of the fact sheet. It explained that the scientific name for lovage was derived, in part, from the Greek word, *lithostikon*, which was a term for (of all things), "unidentified plant." How curious.

FOOTBALL AND FRESH FOLIAGE
October 21, 2016

Every few years our family travels to Columbus, Ohio, to attend a football game.

On October 1, we joined fans in the double-decker horseshoe of Ohio Stadium on the campus of The Ohio State University (OSU). The stadium seats 105,000 people.

Part of the OSU pre-game tradition is a dramatic parade into the stadium of the school's 192-member, brass-and-percussion Marching Band.

To rhythmic applause, the band marched in and performed its complex, curving Script Ohio formation, culminated by the dotting of the "i" in the word, "Ohio."

At the end of the contest, which OSU dominated, 58-0, we walked outside and over to the adjacent Olentangy River.

In 2012, a 77-year-old dam on the river was removed south of campus. The dam once provided cooling water to a long-gone OSU power plant.

Removing that structure unshackled and shrank the lake-like waterway and allowed local environmental groups and other partners to create riffles and pools in the river and establish wetland vegetation on newly exposed ground along each shoreline.

One moment we were inside one of the nation's largest and loudest stadiums. The next we were beside what looked like a prairie in early stages of reforestation.

The shoreline wetland on the east side of the river was relatively quiet and serene. Crickets and birds chirped amidst flowering plants, rich in goldenrod and asters, plus wetland trees, such as black willow.

The native vine, Virginia creeper, which is one of the earliest plants to turn color in fall, was a mix of bright violet, red and purple in the brilliant sunshine. Among the plants, there were lots of sedges. These are low, grass-like, wet-ground native plants with triangular stems.

The blooms of the flowering plant called boneset dotted the vegetation. Boneset produces somewhat flat, fringe-like flower heads of white blossoms. There are several native bonesets, and this species looked like it was thriving in the shoreline's full sun and wet-to-moist conditions.

A turkey vulture floated past. A Cooper's hawk crossed the river. Dragonflies darted. Turtles sat on stones in the river, which ran swiftly, as if composed of multiple currents all forming little whirlpools at once.

The paved path along the foliage was a section of the Olentangy Greenways Trail, which runs north and south through the city. We walked on the trail, stepping aside for the occasional cyclist.

When people come together, there is comfort in tradition, such as at an OSU football game. There is also comfort in change for the better, as we found by the riverside.

Ohio State first played football in 1890. Its band began performing Script Ohio in 1936. Tradition has to start sometime. I expect that our ritual journeys to Columbus will now include both a football game and a ramble along a repaired and replanted riparian corridor that flows freely through campus once again.

ELSEWHERE

Drifting Forward and Cutting New Channels
September 12, 2015

An era ended Aug 28, when we delivered Rachel to Burlington for her first semester at the University of Vermont (UVM).

Our slogan on the trip was 4-1=3. Noah, 15, summed up our emotions, when he turned to me, as Karen and Rachel hugged good-bye, and whispered, "This is tougher than I thought it would be."

With our closest family in New York and Ohio, we've operated under the idea that each of us must function responsibly to the others to make moving forward together successful.

I thought of this a few days before the UVM drop-off, when the four of us floated in tubes down the Saco River in Conway, New Hampshire.

The afternoon was sunny, warm and humid. The water was cool, clear and mildly rippling.

Karen and I had roped our tubes together, as did Rachel and Noah, at least for a while.

The kids caught the current quickest, and drifted ahead. The tubes featured seat backs, so I sat back, slicked in sunscreen, hat on head and a giddy smile on my face.

Every so often, from around one of the bends ahead in the river, we could hear Rachel and Noah laughing, singing or splashing.

Sometimes the water was shin high, other times it was chest deep. The river bottom was primarily sandy. For one long stretch of wide and shallow water, the sand was rich in mica, reflecting thousands of silver specks in the sunshine.

At some of the slower-moving spots, I stood up and pulled Karen, who sat back, mimicking royalty. We loved it.

Chattering Eastern kingbirds hawked shoreline insects. A flock of 20-or-so cedar waxwings fluttered and called around a fruit-bearing hedge. We passed within 10 feet of the birds, and their whistling calls pierced our ears.

At one point, we drifted by a cigarette-dangling-from-his-lips teenager. The shirtless, sinewy young man was hooking rainbow trout in a cove.

"Float closer," he called out, "It will push in the fish."

Slowly but steadily we crept through pools, riffles and deep spots, and around fallen trees and dangling branches, when we drifted too close to shore.

If you're able to pull off your journey successfully, you'll find that a family unit is like a river. A river constantly changes, but it is still the same river.

When Rachel first spoke as a toddler, she would ask, "Are we there yet?" just a mile or two after we left home for a big trip, say to visit family in Ohio.

We would explain that the trip would take much longer—she could sleep and wake up and we would still not be there. Rachel wasn't even two years old, and what did she know? Everything Rachel experienced was for the first time.

Of course being intense and persistent, Rachel would ask over and over, "Are we there yet?" so much so that Karen would tally the inquiries in a notepad. We would explain to Rachel that repeating the question would not speed the journey, and that it was in all of our best interests for her to knock it off.

Well, Rachel, when we dropped you off at UVM, the answer to your question became "yes." Indeed, we *were there* now. We had all arrived together at a major milestone.

I am reminded of a line from the film, "Von Ryan's Express," "If only one gets out, it's a victory," as well as the opening lyrics of the song, "We'll Sing in the Sunshine."

Those words go, "We'll sing in the sunshine. We'll laugh every day. We'll sing in the sunshine. Then I'll be on my way."

Inspiring All Five Senses in Carolina
July 18, 2015

In air so saturated you could feel the hair on the back of your neck, I ran my fingers down the smooth, pinkish inner bark of a crape myrtle tree covered in clusters of small white flowers.

We were in North Carolina to attend a wedding at Mountain Island Lake, which is the water supply for Charlotte and surrounding Mecklenburg County. The Catawba River feeds the lake.

In summer, crape myrtle defines the Southern garden. Depending upon the selection or hybrid, the little tree's outer bark flakes into glossy cinnamon, rose pink and other hard-to-resist-touching shades.

The flowers, meanwhile, come in dense clusters of burgundy, lavender, pink, purple, red or white. Between landing at the airport and stopping at the hotel, we came across and caressed an assortment of crape myrtle, including one pinkish-lavender-flowering tree with a perfume of lilac.

The wedding took place at a lake house, and we parked on an access road to the property. About 75 percent of the shoreline around Mountain Island Lake is protected, with little or no development.

Cicadas pulsed from tulip and sweetgum trees growing across the road from a patch of ample and shimmering blackberries. We sampled the swelling fruit. It was supple to touch and succulent to taste.

Little beads of sweat formed above my upper lip as I sucked on a juicy blackberry, stopping to lick back a drop of liquid before it rolled down my chin.

Talk about forbidden fruit—a long black snake slithered out from beneath the blackberry patch, crossing the road into a weedy edge that included bushy specimens of the native perennial, pokeweed.

Each pokeweed held bunches of berries that would ripen into juicy, deep purple fruits. Poisonous to people, the berries would serve as important food for many birds and mammals.

The snake was large and dark; probably an adult black rat snake. As it glided, the reptile's tongue thrust steadily into the air to sense the surroundings.

People are the primary predators of black rat snakes, which are often run over by passing vehicles.

The delicate fragrance of mimosa's graceful and silky-soft pink flowers scented the air.

We spied a silver-spotted skipper butterfly working over a mimosa blossom. The skipper's brown and black wings featured lobes, transparent golden spots and a metallic silver band, which produced a neon-like glow in the evening light.

"The silver-spotted skipper almost never visits yellow flowers but favors blue, red, pink, purple, and sometimes white and cream-colored ones," notes butterfliesandmoths.org.

A motionless white-tailed deer, with prominent ears, eyed us. Later we would discover a small herd, including a brown, white-spotted fawn suckling a doe.

Southern fare was part of the weekend celebration. It included beef, chicken and pork barbeque; boiled peanuts; black-eyed peas; butter beans; collard greens; cornbread; grilled corn on the cob; grits; gumbo; hushpuppies; pecan pie; ribs; and lots of sweet tea.

I also tasted my first muscadine-grape wine. Native to the southeastern U.S., muscadine was the first native grape cultivated in North America.

The flavor was simultaneously smoky, dry and sweet. My palate sensed an aromatic aftertaste flush with the tang of grape skins, as well as a honeyed burst similar to filling your mouth with sweet tea.

This flavor mix was new and mysterious, and the musky scent of red-clay earth beneath my feet freshened my thirst for more.

While evening became night, a linen-colored full moon rose over the lake's dark waters. The powerful cadence of katydids joined the cicada song in a sub-tropical psychedelic swirl. Blinking fireflies surrounded the party.

Meanwhile, the moon morphed into a big yellow disc that appeared slightly tilted to the left. Seas and plains on the lunar surface were plainly visible. Their contrast in gray and white produced a face that seemed to wink at us, as we celebrated love deep into the moist North Carolina night.

Beautiful Moments
in Parsippany
November 17, 2017

My mother, Renee, said she could not remember seeing, or handling, a hickory nut until that afternoon.

The date was Nov. 2. The place was a worn wooden bench beside Lake Parsippany in New Jersey. The temperature was 75 degrees and a strong sun made us wish for hats, sunglasses and sunscreen.

Hundreds of shagbark hickory nuts, tan and thin shelled, as well as quartered sections of their thicker husks, obscured the turf around the bench.

The nuts were roughly the size of large grapes. The husks, which had split apart along four ribs, were in various states of decomposition from moist green to drier brown to black.

Bark on the three hickory trees beside the bench was a light charcoal in color, with long, thick, peeling scales or plates.

My mom knew walnuts and pecans, but not hickories, she said. For a city kid — now 83 years old — maybe that was not unusual.

The meat of a shagbark hickory nut is sweet. But it's not easy to dig out for several reasons. First, the thin shell is quite strong. Second, if you hammer it open, you need the skill of a dental surgeon to extract the bits of meat.

Toasting the raw nuts changes their somewhat-fetid taste and pedestrian feel to an oily, crunchy snack suggestive of tasty pecans.

My mom and I were in Parsippany to run errands, involving items that once belonged to her older brother, Jerry, of blessed memory. Shortly before the end of World War II, Jerry was killed in the Battle of Remagen in Germany.

Jerry, my mother said, was caring, fun-loving and full of life. Their father, Joe, already seriously ill from heart trouble and other ailments, never recovered from Jerry's death, she said.

Indeed in 1947, my mom, who was in eighth grade, left school to take a full-time job at age 13 to support her parents.

My mom's mobility is limited. With some free time between errands, we found the park bench, which provided her with a comfortable resting spot, and a place for us to catch up.

Our perch faced the New Jersey Highlands. The hills were colored in bronze, red and green. A turtle sunned itself on a log near the lakeshore. A cloudless sulphur butterfly fluttered around us, and four vultures teeter-tottered in the sky.

Weather-wise, this was not the early November of either of our youths. But being outside provided us with invigoration and a powerful sense of belonging to that particular place in that precise moment.

Among the definitions for nut in Merriam-Webster, is "a foolish, eccentric, or crazy person." Maybe it was a little kooky to sit outside in Parsippany, a point we were simply passing through. Nonetheless, it was definitely the best part of our afternoon together.

Nurture and Nature at a Family Fete

August 10, 2018

Where you perch matters.

Two weeks ago we attended a reunion for Karen's mother's side of the family, gathering at a woodsy North Carolina lodge at 2200-feet elevation in the western part of the state.

Besides catching up and swapping stories, we ate, swam, hiked and played games. There was BBQ night and pizza night, a white elephant gift exchange, birthday cake, singing, and more.

The event felt relaxing, welcoming and inclusive. As someone married into the family, I participated, of course, but also took the opportunity, when my attendance was not required, to wander along the bank of a pond on the lodge property.

Standing under tall tulip trees beside the shallow water I noticed a set of black-crater-like circles on the muddy pond bottom. I learned from Jim Rice, Professor of Applied Ecology & Extension Fisheries Specialist at North Carolina State University, that these were the nests of bluegill sunfish.

Fish were visible between, above and beside the nests. Rice said that bluegill sunfish males, "fan out a depression in the sand, which they guard. Females spawn with males over the nest and the male guards the eggs until they hatch. Bluegills are colonial nesters, putting their nests in groups like this, called a spawning bed. It probably helps with reducing egg predation."

293

This explanation led me to think about the reunion, which was sort of like a sleep-away camp, except surrounded by four generations of loved ones. Pods of toddlers and young children scampered about, watched by parents, aunts, uncles and others among the extended family.

As I observed the bluegills, a strident set of somewhat-manic-sounding chirps approached overhead. Those calls came from a pileated woodpecker flying over the length of the pond. The near-crow-sized bird was mostly black, except for its striking red crown crest, white face stripes and conspicuous white, oval markings on the underside of its wings.

According to the Cornell Lab of Ornithology, "Pileated woodpeckers are monogamous and hold large territories; it's rare to see more than two birds together at a time." This bit of life history reminded me of the reunion's senior couple, my in-laws, Jan and John, who are in their 56th year of marriage.

Parts of Western North Carolina harbor communities of white squirrels—color morphs of the gray squirrel. As I walked back to the lodge I saw one of these animals. It was robust in body, yet ethereal in look. To me, the squirrel was like the reunion—rich, yet otherworldly. I am 60 years old, and this was my first family reunion. My own bloodlines are too fragmented to hold such an event. Plus, most of our elders are long gone.

In North Carolina, I coalesced with kin, but also immersed myself in the natural world. Both were opportunities to celebrate the splendor that unites my life.

Finding Sanctuary at Sherwood Island
June 2, 2017

When I was a child, a handful of women in our Bronx neighborhood mustered in beach chairs each evening below our apartment windows to chit chat during the warmer months.

Last week, I remembered those street corner collectives, while listening to a commune of chattering purple martins within Sherwood Island State Park in Westport, Connecticut.

Some martins perched on metal rods alongside pole-mounted nesting gourds from which other martins poked-out their heads.

This community of dark-blue-purple-bodied males and browner females produced chirps, chortles, gurgles, rattles and twitters.

By the way, without people erecting nesting houses or gourds, purple martins would likely vanish as breeding birds east of the Rocky Mountains.

It was 7 pm, and I'd taken a break from the sluggish northbound Connecticut Turnpike, less than a half-mile from the park.

As the sun descended behind me, I walked toward Long Island Sound through sand dunes that featured beach pea plants with bright purple flowers and rosa rugosa, presenting fragrant pink blossoms.

Connecticut's first state park, Sherwood Island is roughly 235 acres of meadows, woods, saltmarshes, other water bodies and a 6,000-foot-long beach along Long Island Sound.

For a bit, I sat on the beach, the sound of lapping waves a welcome contrast to the roar of interstate traffic.

Some 150 feet offshore, a dozen common terns hovered over and plunged into the water to snare small fish.

A common tern is a medium-sized waterbird, elegant in black and white plumage, with a forked tail.

From where I sat, I could hear the terns produce a steady flow of "kip" and "kee-arr" calls.

The beach was a noticeable gradation of sand, pebbles and seashells. Shiny orange jingle shells—once the homes of a saltwater clam—were particularly common.

According to the Department of Energy and Environmental Protection in Connecticut, wave action at Sherwood Island separates sand components (based on the density and shape of those materials) into three visible layers: tan (quartz), red (garnet) and black (magnetite). I could see that pattern.

What I didn't see were any people. I looked up and down the shoreline, and as far as I could tell, I was the only person there. On the sand, the only other being was a great egret, which is an elegant tall, bright-white wading bird

Hard to believe that just .4 miles away was a clogged interstate.

Another pause for thought was that this was my first trip to Sherwood Island since 1970, when a day camp transported us Bronx kids to play in the park. That summer was spent visiting green spaces across the New York Metropolitan area.

Alas, 1970 was also a watershed year in our neighborhood. Families scattered or fell apart, neighbors passed away and the streets grew scary.

Later, I would learn that the kibitzing of the women, who had assembled on the street corner for decades, grew acidic and gossipy, before their congregation dispersed forever.

As for Sherwood Island, suddenly it was both real again, and a lovely place to come back home to.

Meeting a Committee of Vultures

August 4, 2017

Dark shadows topped tall evergreens on Long Point in Lake Chautauqua State Park in Western New York.

The previous day, Karen and I had driven to Lake Chautauqua to visit with some of our Ohio family. The trek from Providence was approximately 500 miles one way. Karen's parents came in from Northeast Ohio, a two-hour car trip from the west.

On an early morning walk in the park, we noticed hulking dusky figures in the treetops. Zeroing-in with binoculars, we spotted one of their bare gray heads. Ah-ha, a black vulture.

What we'd spied was called a "committee" of black vultures. No kidding, vultures at rest in trees are called a committee.

And these vultures were molting, as we found several dozen of their large dark feathers scattered over the ground. Black vultures molt in the second half of summer. It's fresh feathers in the fall, like new clothes for school!

The birds were in a planting of lofty conifers adjacent to deciduous woodlands. The path snaked between those habitats.

Silently, the dark creatures left the conifers one by one. We took a moment to examine the feathers. Deep black in color, they showed a somewhat bluish tint, when twisted back and forth in the low light beneath the trees.

Over the last few decades, black vultures have markedly expanded their range northward. Often, black vultures will supplant a local population of turkey vultures.

We also noticed that the shredded remains of green cones encircled the base of each evergreen. This was a sign of red squirrels. Mostly, red squirrels eat seeds found in conifer cones.

Red squirrels also claim and defend territories, and just as we squatted to look more closely at the chewed-up cones, a squirrel in the canopy grew exceptionally vocal. It barked, chattered, hissed and trilled so strongly that we left the spot.

Lake Chautauqua is 17 miles long and two miles wide at maximum width. Less than one percent of its shoreline is public property. Thus, our affinity for the state park, which sticks out into the lake like a peninsula.

The point, according to the New York State Office of Parks, Recreation and Historic Preservation, is composed of rock and silt left behind by the northward retreat of the Laurentide Glacier, which formed the lake, some 18,000 years ago.

At 1,308 feet above sea level, Lake Chautauqua is one of the highest navigable bodies of water in North America.

I found it fitting that our family activity began with a vulture encounter. Although some folks associate vultures with death, their feeding on dead carcasses helps prevent the spread of disease. I connect the vulture with cleansing and renewal, both of which I felt during a family walk well worth the 500-mile drive from home.

REDISCOVERING OUR ROOTS
June 16, 2017

When Karen and I were expecting our first child 20 years ago, we said that if our newborn were a girl we would name her after Rachel Carson, strong and fearless defender of our planet.

Last week on a brief getaway to southern Maine, Karen and I visited the Rachel Carson National Wildlife Refuge in Wells, Maine. How appropriate that the sanctuary protected a beautiful and diverse landscape, including one of Maine's most vital habitats: the salt marsh.

We walked the Refuge's one-mile loop trail around and through an upland forest of tall pine, hemlock, oak and maple. That path provided views of the salt marsh, which stretched to the sea

Looking out from the forest, we saw creeks and rivers, several types of grasses, salt pannes (shallow depressions where a marsh drains slowly), and beach and ocean in the distance.

The forest was luxurious, with shrubs, ferns and wildflowers under the trees. It looked and felt like a temperate rainforest.

Such fertile natural growth on the edge of coastal wetland both protects it and helps "produce dense meadows of grasses and other plants that support abundant wildlife," noted a Refuge brochure.

One unseen reason for this is that "clean water from the woodland seeps into the ground and then emerges in the stream. Fresh water flows into the marsh, mixes nutrients with seawater and helps keep the marsh productive."

Maybe because of the wet spring, water coursed through the marsh. In fact from one overlook we watched multiple whirlpools spin up and float away in a little river, while new whirlpools arose in their place. It looked like a kaleidoscope of eddies headed toward the sea.

White was the primary color of the forest flowers, which included blueberry, bunchberry, Canada mayflower, starflower and wild sarsaparilla. Blue violets were scattered in the woods, as were pink lady slippers.

Also coming into flower was a classic shrub of the Northeast, called hobblebush. It featured unusually large, round and slightly pointed heart-shaped leaves, as well as what would become extensive bright-white white clusters of blossoms up to eight inches across.

Many hikers identify the new foliage and fresh flowers of hobblebush as a definitive symbol of springtime in the North Woods.

Speaking of shrubs, I was tickled to learn that the wildflower, bunchberry, belonged to the dogwood family. Indeed, what we saw growing low on the forest floor, with its oval leaves and four-white-bract-surrounded flower clusters, looked like the miniaturized blooms and foliage of flowering dogwood.

Probably the most-lasting image from the trail was that of a blue jay with a beak-full of mud and white pine needles.

This relatively simple sighting was a powerful reminder of our own nesting behavior, and the inspirational and life-affirming child who entered our lives 20 years ago, named Rachel.

GREETINGS, GREEN MOUNTAIN STATE

June 13, 2015

Last weekend Karen, Rachel and I attended orientation programs for new students and families at the University of Vermont (UVM) in Burlington, Vermont.

From connecting with fellow students to signing up for classes to learning about campus life, UVM put out the welcome mat for us.

On the way home, we learned a little about Vermont nature.

We had never hiked in The Green Mountain State, and took our first steps toward learning more about its natural environment at 100-acre Red Rocks Park in South Burlington.

Red Rocks Park is probably best known for its multicolor patterned cliffs above Shelburne Bay on Lake Champlain.

But atop the park's calcium-rich rocks and limestone bluffs are plants and plant communities found in few other places in Vermont.

We took a wooded trail that was a former road from the days when the land was cleared and occupied.

From the forest floor, an ovenbird called "teacher, teacher, teacher," while from the conifer canopy, a pine warbler trilled softly. Chipmunks chirped and red squirrels chattered.

The air smelled sweet, scented by black locust tree flowers.

Even though we walked just a half-mile, the forest type changed several times.

At first, American beech, sugar maple, black cherry, red oak and white ash composed the woods. Then, the forest became more of a mix of white pine, shagbark hickory and hop hornbeam.

We admired lengthy shags of charcoal-colored bark on the hickories and long square-edged strips of upward-peeling bark on hop hornbeam.

We also strolled through woods of white pine, hemlock and red pine. I don't often see red pine in the wild, as it grows in sandy soils in the northern forest. Large red pines feature diagnostic flaky, orange-red bark in their upper crowns, and dark-green, pointy needles.

Red Rocks Park is said to contain 300 species of wildflowers, ferns and lichens. Although most woodland wildflowers come and go before trees leaf out completely, we found a good deal of false Solomon's seal, each stem tipped in clusters of tiny, star-shaped flowers.

In dappled sunshine along edges of the old road, wild strawberry bloomed, its white flowers matching nicely with the smaller and glossier yellow blossoms of cinquefoil. Among them was a compact form of blackberry covered in white blossoms.

I could not identify two species of wildflowers, so I took their pictures, which I shared with the Vermont Agency of Natural Resources the following day. Within an hour, I received a positive ID from very nice folks. Excellent service!

One wildflower was called golden Alexanders. A member of the parsley family, it featured finely toothed leaves and umbels of very small, yellow flowers. Golden Alexanders grew flower-bed-like along the road.

The second flower sprouted from a sheltered spot between boulders on a thin strip of beach along the lake. That blossom was Canada anemone, which is commonly found on the shores of lakes and rivers.

Striking white petals on each anemone flower surrounded a yellow center. The plant's abundant leaves, cut deeply and growing in clumps, made for a thick and attractive groundcover.

Native Americans used both golden Alexanders and Canada anemone as medicinal plants.

It was windy on the beach. Whipped waves lapped twice per second. Small rocks that looked like tiny red-and-tan patterned versions of the bigger stones and outcrops in the park covered the thin beach.

Behind the anemone was a stand of trembling aspen trees. Their bark was green-white, and their leaves were heart-shaped, finely toothed, and fluttered furiously in the wind.

Our walk was a chance to de-stress from a weekend of planning to send Rachel off to college. Of course, Karen and I hope that we've laid the groundwork for Rachel to launch successfully into independence.

Late August will be the next time that we visit Vermont. That's when we will drop off Rachel at UVM. After saying goodbye, a hike, like a strong tonic, will probably work wonders for our psyche.

Winds and Waves at Halibut Point
September 24, 2011

A crescent of fluorescent-yellow goldenrod rimmed the granite overlook, which was dominated by the rumbling of a swelling sea.

From this sweeping ledge, I stepped down a switchback of paths past arrowwood, red cedar and staghorn sumac toward the headlands and surf.

Stunted by thin soils and steady winds, the shoulder-sized sumac featured stout, velvety branches. Some leaves were a fall color—a shade of purple that contrasted with the scarlet red of the sumac's large seed heads. I picked a few of the deepest-red seeds to suck on their lemon-like flavor, as if they were hard candies.

The headland resembled sheets of paper. Other ridges were more rounded and polished, interrupted here and there by jagged crevices. One layer of rippled, yet spiny stone, reminded me of whipped cake batter.

Circling some of the fissures were salt rings that showed up after sunshine evaporated temporary pools of seawater.

Geologists estimate the age of the Halibut Point granite at 440 million years. Stone quarried here in Rockport has paved streets, and built bridges, tunnels and buildings.

At the foot of the sea, I met up with my family, relatives and friends.

The 11 of us had gathered in Rockport for what Karen's uncle called a toast to newfound happiness and to those no longer with us.

We sat or stood on an immense toboggan of smooth, speckled stone that looked like the bow of a great ship.

With ancient stone underfoot and the sea before us, we seemed like witnesses to the world's beginning. And no matter how different we were in our daily lives, we were all equal in the face of such creation.

Several of us stepped gingerly down to the thundering tide. For 45 minutes, surging surf slapped our feet, ankles and shins. The cold, refreshing sea washed away our troubles and transgressions.

How symbolic that we'd zipped from Providence to Rockport via the interstate fast lane, as this was life in the slow lane.

In the bright sunshine, gulls twisted and turned. Several ships passed the Point. Here and now was a chance to allow the world to go by us for a change.

We stood in awe before one of New England's most profound natural areas. No one said much. We just looked at the rolling clear waters of the Atlantic.

The bedrock, berries, flowers, leaves, sunshine, thin soils, vistas and windy slopes provided another reminder.

Sixteen years ago, Karen and I drove from our home in Central Pennsylvania to attend a family function in Boston. During a break, we visited Halibut Point.

Sitting on the same granite at the same time of day, we stared in wonder at the beautiful seascape, and said that someday we would live in New England.

The next year, we moved to Providence, where we grew close to loving family and friends.

When the sun slid behind the vast ship-shape of granite, the 11 of us turned to leave. I noticed that an aster, with drooping stems of brilliant snow-white flowers, centered the first patch of vegetation beyond the headlands.

White symbolizes purity, I thought. It was also was the color of angels, who I believe provide ministrations at the sea rocks of Halibut Point.

They Have Wings
October 17, 2015

When I first began watching birds 40 years ago, I spotted a fall-migrating scarlet tanager, a bird of the deep woods, in a small tree at the edge of a woodlot in Cape May, New Jersey.

"How did that get there?" I asked my birding mentor. "They have wings," he replied.

The question, "How did that get there?" came to Karen and me on a walk in Shelburne Bay Park by the mouth of the LaPlatte River at Lake Champlain in Vermont, when we found pitch pine trees in the off-shore-line woods.

I know pitch pine as a pine-barrens tree, growing in its own stands or mixed with oaks in central New Jersey, and on Long Island and Cape Cod.

But when I saw it so far north—an hour from the Canadian border—I was left scratching my head.

Then farther along in the forest, we discovered chestnut oak. A tree found from Maine to Mississippi, and into the Midwest, chestnut oak's best growth occurs in the mountains of the Carolinas and Tennessee.

What we eventually learned was that the lake moderated the northern climate temperatures at the mouth of the LaPlatte River, which allowed certain southern species to extend their ranges. Because it harbors species from the south, Shelburne Bay Park is referred to as a "northern refuge" by local conservationists.

At the park, we didn't have to go far to find outstanding natural features.

A few steps from the parking lot, there was a stretch of smooth red rock along the shoreline. As we walked over the stone, thin, electric-blue dragonflies rose like jets taking off from a flight deck.

Some folks exhibit tan lines; well, this red rock displayed mud and ripple cracks, lines and marks. These were evidence of a one-time flat shallow, tidal environment. Indeed, the rock, called Monkton Quartzite, formed from sediments deposited in low water on what was once the shore of an ancient ocean more than 500 million years ago.

Beyond the rock stretched extensive marshland. It had developed over the eons from organic debris deposited by northern winds. The wetland's mix of cattails, rushes and sedges were a breeding site for bass and pike.

Appropriate, then, that from our perch on the rocks, we watched several mergansers, fish-eating ducks, forage along the edge of the marsh, as well as a kingfisher fly up and down the shoreline.

As we sat on the stone before the clear water of the river's mouth, a gull on a small dock ahead of us picked at the remains of a sunfish. Although it was a mild day, no boats moved about. In fact, it was very quiet along the water.

Our stop came after visiting Rachel at The University of Vermont. For an hour or so, the park provided us with succor; a lovely spot to ponder how it was that Rachel's migration to college seemed to come so fast. After a while, the answer was obvious, "They have wings."

High-Flying Honkers
December 5, 2015

U p until the latter half of the 20th Century, Canada geese were
known as loyal-to-their-species, aloof around people, northern
breeders that migrated in great V-shaped skeins.

Today, many of us think of Canada geese as noisy, low-flying, local
nesters that foul lawns and ponds, occasionally harassing humans for
handouts.

Although such resident Canada geese now outnumber their migratory brethren in this part of the country, you can still spot populations
of northern birds in classic high-in-the-sky V-shaped skeins, migrating
from Canada, Newfoundland, Labrador and Alaska to overwintering
grounds in the continental U.S. and northern Mexico.

On the day before Thanksgiving, we spotted several such high-fly-
ers, as we drove west toward Ohio on I-90 between Albany and Buffalo
in New York.

At first glance, each skein looked like a wisp of cloud. But soon we
saw that these were the magnificent sorts of formations that once inspired wonder and wanderlust within the rest of us.

I-90 westbound parallels the Erie Canal in several places. Between
the New York State Thruway Travel Plazas, which provide food, fuel and
other traveler services to drivers and passengers, there are ponds, wetlands, flooded woods, and fields of stubbly corn and other grain for geese
and other waterfowl to rest and refuel.

Besides spying Canada geese far above the ground, we saw hundreds of the birds in wetlands and fields. Canada geese feed primarily on
submerged vegetation, grasses, sedges and agricultural crops.

308

More than 40 years ago, the Canada goose broadened my world. I was about 15-years-old and walking on the Grand Concourse in the Bronx, when a strand of sound from the sky led me to look up. Some 3-400 feet overhead and flapping fast was a skein of maybe 50 Canada geese headed south.

The sight stunned me. Here I was on a traffic- and pedestrian-busy three-roadway thoroughfare watching a phenomenon millions of years old—birds of the far north following a flyway south. I stared at the geese, until they vanished from sight, hoping to hear another honk from the wild.

What a coincidence that it was about the same time—late 60s and early 70s—that certain populations of Canada geese began to turn into resident birds.

It's hard to fathom that overhunting and habitat loss once pushed the Canada goose near extinction 100+ years ago. Today, Canada goose numbers far exceed historical population estimates due to "regulatory actions, habitat restoration, and species conservation initiatives," notes a fact sheet from Rutgers University Cooperative Extension.

According to that Extension leaflet, Canada geese have adapted spectacularly well to landscapes with large expanses of fertilized and mowed lawns adjacent to stormwater detention basins in urban and suburban settings, where fewer geese predators happen to exist than in the wild. These days, Canada goose hunting is also less popular compared to that of other waterfowl.

Nonetheless, some Canada geese remain migratory. They continue to breed in the far north, flock-up in fall and fly south in V-formation.

Since moving to Providence in 1996, we've driven to Ohio some 50 times via I-90. Thanksgiving can be an excellent time to see geese and other waterfowl near the highway, more so if there is no ice on the ponds and wetlands.

Five decades after first discovering migrant geese, I continue to find their diminished, yet ongoing high-in-the-sky V-shaped arrangements worthy of prolonged applause. Except that on I-90 I need to keep my hands on the wheel, as I prefer the honking of geese to the beeping of cars and trucks.

ROCKY NECK
May 24, 2008

As a kid growing up in a poor New York neighborhood, I was bewitched by the story of a digger who uncovered a nine-pound garnet beneath West 35th Street, near Broadway in 1885. The seven-inch-diameter gemstone was one of the largest of its kind ever found in the United States.

Several parks in my neighborhood displayed the local bedrock, mica schist, which was streaked with granite veins that contained an occasional amethyst, beryl, garnet, opal or tourmaline. My childhood search for precious stones never panned out. But I retained a fondness for shiny, geological objects. This may explain my soft spot for scouring outcrops in Rocky Neck State Park on Long Island Sound in East Lyme, CT.

It is illegal to collect rocks and minerals in Connecticut state parks. No law, however, stops you from sniffing out minerals within the park's whale-sized stone formations. The outcrops unfold like giant bodies, with subtly different colors, faults, folds and striations.

As my son scampered up a ridge to fend off imaginary pirates, my daughter counted rings on large pieces of blanched driftwood scattered over a bed of sparkling stones. My wife stretched out atop a smooth slab of pinkish rock, belonging to Potter Hill Granite Gneiss (pronounced "nice"), a now-exposed bedrock once subjected to high temperatures and pressures deep within the earth. This particular outcrop was between 543 million and 2.5 billion years old, and well polished by glacial grit more than 20,000 years ago.

311

Meanwhile, I tracked a pegmatite vein, formed long ago below the surface when molten rock solidified. The vein split toward the Sound where I spotted a great egret, three spotted sandpipers and a cormorant. Before reaching the gently lapping waves, the seams turned and came together, interweaving like railroad tracks. Orange or pinkish in color, the veins featured strips of quartz and chunks of black mica, which glittered like sharp-edged chocolate chips.

One outcrop of massive swirls of gray and white crystals reminded me of marbled halvah, the "sweetmeat" Mediterranean confection. Another formation looked like a ten-foot-tall multi-layered sandwich. The outcrop below it contained holes between two inches and two feet in diameter. These formed long ago when waves spun small rocks in place, like drill bits.

Rooting around, I found feldspar, the mineral that put a pink color in the granite. Clusters of shiny yellow buttercups grew amidst crevices of ferns, red cedars and oak.

Rocky Neck was strongly shaped by a line of glacial advance and retreat marked by miles of piles of sand, stone and clay deposits that also sculpted Fisher's Island and other offshore isles that buffer the Connecticut coastline.

The park's relatively compact beach formed a crescent between two headlands. Besides the cockle, slipper and razor clam shells that marked the tide line in the soft, white sand, there was a band of the dark, metallic mineral magnetite, settled out by the force of the waves. I read online that you could also use a magnet to separate the material from fellow quartz and feldspar grains in the sand.

While there were no gemstones to pluck at Rocky Neck, every rock still seemed precious. Camping out on the outcrops, bathed in the afternoon sun, we poked around and played together—an undertaking more valuable than any jewel in my imagination.

OLD FRIENDS SOOTHE THE SOUL
September 16, 2016

O n a late afternoon at the end of August, we drove north out of
Providence to deliver Rachel to the University of Vermont for
her sophomore year.

It's about a four-hour trip and a sad one for us parents. Four of us
go (Rachel's brother, Noah, comes along), but only three of us return.

Two hours later, outside Hooksett, N.H, we drove beneath a swirling swarm of medium-sized birds.

Their looping flights, plus white patches on slim wings told us that
they were common nighthawks. This species feeds aerially on insects at
dusk.

During fall migration, common nighthawks gather in flocks,
sometimes by the hundreds, on a long passage to wintering grounds in
southern South America.

The common nighthawk was one of the first species I identified,
when I began watching birds earnestly in 1977. Sad to say, the species has
declined precipitously over much of its breeding range.

The common nighthawk bred in our neighborhood when we first
moved to Providence in 1996. However it soon vanished not only in Providence but also across much of New England.

When we saw the nighthawks over Hooksett, I whooped it up in
the car. It felt like we had met-up with some old friends, re-starting a conversation where it had left off years earlier. And for a few minutes, the
sighting took my mind off the task at hand.

The following day, with Rachel moved in, we headed back to
Rhode Island.

Heading south on Interstate 89, we took a side trip onto Vermont Highway 100.

VT 100 stretches 217 miles from Massachusetts to Quebec. We drove it for only 10 miles. But that was enough to discover spectacular views of mountains and ranges, rivers and reservoirs.

We also stopped for coffee, cider-mill donuts, cheese and ice cream from establishments synonymous with Vermont.

Still, the most-thrilling break was beside a field of Joe-Pye weed, goldenrod and aster.

The floral mix was beautiful on its own. But one of the things that especially excited us was the Joe-Pye weed, which we don't often encounter in New England.

Actually, we associate Joe-Pye weed with late-summers in Ohio and Pennsylvania, where Karen and I once lived.

Joe-Pye weed grows primarily in sunny spots, and best in fertile soils that stay moist through the growing season. It reaches up to seven-feet in height and is topped by large clusters or somewhat-muted-in-color, softly scented, pinkish-purple flowers. Butterflies are drawn to the blossoms.

The aster was another pleasant surprise. Its flowers were sky blue with yellow centers. We must look in the wrong places, because we don't find many asters in New England, at least compared to other places we've called home.

Once again, we found comfort amidst former friends. This time, a stunning and thriving mix of flowers heartened an otherwise difficult trip.

Starting Autumn on a High Note
October 14, 2016

I t felt like the early days of parenthood.

Karen and I sat in the front seat of the car. Our children, Rachel and Noah, were asleep behind us.

Except now, the kids were teens, snoozing like infants or toddlers.

We were up in Burlington, VT to visit Rachel, who is a college sophomore. At the moment, our destination was a winery in the town of South Hero on Grand Isle, which is one of the islands in Lake Champlain north of Burlington.

When we'd left Providence it was muggy and in the low 80s. Although it was fall, the weather was an uncomfortable continuation of summer. In northern Vermont, however, the air was dry and crisp and in the low 60s.

We pulled into what called itself, "Vermont's oldest commercial vineyard." With the kids still asleep, we lowered the car windows, and Karen and I stepped out for a tasting.

The grape harvest was in progress, said our hostess. So far, about 40,000 pounds of grapes had been picked by hand, she said.

We sat down at an outdoor table across from the rows of vines. A concentrated and continuous chorus of cricket calls surrounded us.

Across the road, a marsh hawk swept over a field. Faint honks reached us from a skein of geese pushing south high overhead.

The cool air produced goosebumps on exposed skin. We rolled down the sleeves of our sweatshirts. I tugged my cap a little tighter. We did not connect to the vineyard's Wi-Fi, which meant no texts or images, just talk.

We tasted whites and reds, nibbling on slices of local pepperoni and raw-milk cheddar. Rachel and Noah remained snoozing.

Low, puffy clouds hid the sun. When sunshine emerged, the asters and goldenrod turned into luminous islands of neon blue and yellow.

We liked all of the wines. Our favorite was the award-winning ice wine. It was made from grapes left on the vine until December, our hostess said.

First Rachel, and then Noah woke up. They joined us, enjoying homemade root beer on tap.

Our hostess suggested we walk beside the rows of grapes and then up a modest hill labeled as the highest point on Grand Isle.

We did, discovering a splendid view of the lake, plus the mountains beyond.

A sign said that we stood in the best microclimate in Vermont for both growing grapes and for raising summer vegetables. I will add that this was also a spectacular place to reconnect and to enjoy what felt like the first true day of fall.

Invisible Threads, Inner Light
September 13, 2014

September sparks something within me.

Maybe it's the cooler weather, the new school year, or the lowering light levels.

Is it biological, environmental, something higher? I'm not sure. But it's an arousal of spirit, an inner flush pushing toward the surface.

The month started spectacularly, with family and cousins, as guests of Karen's uncle Scott and his wife, Karen, (yes, the same names as my wife and I) in their Rockport, MA, home.

Scott and Karen were gracious and generous, feeding us, housing us and guiding us around one of New England's most uplifting locales.

Standing on Old Garden Landing, I watched a solitary sandpiper fly stiff-winged among barnacle-covered boulders above sloshing mats of rockweed.

Beyond were sailboats, colorful floats that marked lobster pots, and at least three species of gulls. I heard the waves and smelled the sea.

Framing the landing path was thick, knee-high vegetation rich with berries that fueled songbirds on their migration south. I found the fruit of poison ivy, Virginia creeper, fox grape and juniper.

In fact, the shrubbery seemed to jiggle with songbirds, especially catbirds. Their calls surrounded me.

This was also a good year for wild cherries. Many hung from trees, while thousands covered the ground, swept by homeowners into piles that resembled mini rock walls.

Almost every cherry tree hosted cedar waxwings, whistling as they moved from fruit to fruit in near swallow-like swarms.

I had left Providence and arrived in Paradise.

The following morning we acted like lumberjacks, chopping out a maple stump rotting between granite boulders on the property. We bagged the pitted and fissured chunks for the town compost pile.

Then we visited Old Garden Beach, where the water was way colder than in Rhode Island. Stepping into it slapped every cell in my system to attention.

The water was turquoise, a living, lapping gemstone. The tidal pools looked like a bluish flavor of Kool-Aid, noted Noah.

That night, as we sat around a fire in a backyard pit, someone suggested we experiment with burning the bagged maple.

When uncle Scott went to grab some of the wood, he reported back that it was glowing.

We looked inside the bag to find rotted stump pieces giving off a whitish-green light. Here was a living example of foxfire, also called fairy fire and will-o'-the-wisp, where wood glows in the dark of night.

The radiance reminded me of plastic stars that we adhered to Rachel's bedroom ceiling 10 years ago. Witnessing foxfire was a first for all of us.

Certain living organisms, including some fungi, emit visible light, called bioluminescence, as a byproduct of complex biochemical reactions.

I dropped an email to a bioluminescent fungi specialist. He suggested that the light came from mycelium—the network of fine, hard-to-see filaments in the wood—from a type of honey mushroom, which is one of three species of light-producing fungi typically found in North America.

Honey mushrooms are common on decaying wood, and sometimes parasitic on live trees. They are often found at the base of trees, and on stumps and old wood, with their fruiting bodies showing up on the outside of the wood in late summer and early fall. Some honey mushrooms live more than 400 years.

Mycelium is the main body of a mushroom. Some mycelium spread for miles, and they are considered the world's largest organisms.

Aristotle, I learned, was the first to write about foxfire. Thoreau also described a pale forest glow, with which he enjoyed "fellowship" for "a few moments."

We took hunks of the stump home. The luminosity lasted about three days. Then I felt bad that by chopping up the stump I had helped snuff out the glow of a living organism. But who knew?

Still it seemed fitting that newfound radiance set off a soul-searching September. Talk about bringing inner glow to the surface!

The words of a popular children's song nailed it: "This little light of mine, I'm gonna let it shine."

PORTRAIT OF SALTY SEABOARD
June 22, 2018

I f you want to see a quintessential landscape of coastal New England, visit Allens Pond Wildlife Sanctuary in South Dartmouth and Westport.

The view beyond its Horseneck Road parking lot, for example, is a panorama of fields, forests, wetlands, beaches and Buzzards Bay.

A path from the lot directs you into a field dominated by waist-high grasses swaying in a sea breeze. This is grass-flowering season, and my wife, Karen, and I counted seven different types of grass seed heads, including one purple in color.

Amidst the grasses grew swathes of a little bright-white flower that was some sort of chickweed. And among the chickweed were taller buttercups, their yellow color brilliant and reflective in the afternoon light.

Also present were clumps of slender blue flag, a mostly-blue iris, with a stunning white-and-yellow vein pattern. Twisting around some of the iris was beach pea, or "sweet-pea," with lavender-pink-purple-violet blossoms.

Because it was still breeding season, birds called or sang as they crossed the sky. One sparkling refrain came from a male bobolink, which flew past us and perched on a small tree by a stonewall.

About the male bobolink, the Cornell Lab of Ornithology notes, "No other North American bird has a white back and black underparts (some have described this look as wearing a tuxedo backwards). Added to this are the male's rich, straw-colored patch on the head and his bubbling, virtuosic song."

In the past 40 years, U.S. bobolink numbers have declined more than 60 percent primarily due to "the loss of meadows and hay fields," reports Cornell Lab. Allens Pond, managed by Mass Audubon, is a haven for plants and animals of open terrain.

A "T" in the path offered two choices. On past visits, Karen and I chose the stunningly diverse and scenic Quansett Trail. This time, we selected the Beach Trail.

The trail led us past ponds and wetlands, where the blue-green heads of nesting tree swallows poked out from bird-box holes. On a twig-piled platform in the distance, an adult osprey sat with a nestling.

As we strolled past Allens Pond itself, multiple "pill-will-willet" calls sprang from its inner recesses. This was evidence of willets, relatively robust shorebirds that breed in salt marshes. A treat is to see the species' black-and-white-striped wings in flight.

We reached the beach via a dune of medium-sized oval rocks. The beach was "walk-only," given the close proximity of nesting piping plovers. The shoreline sand was some of the whitest and softest we've trod in New England.

According to Mass Audubon, Allens Pond "was created by generous families who opted to conserve their land." To these folks and to those who provide the resources and labor to maintain this archetypal landscape, an A+ for "keeping it real."

STANDING WITH SANDHILL CRANES

June 16, 2012

In these commentaries, I draw out details and emotions from everyday observations and encounters.

As such, I've struggled to give meaning to a breathtaking and extraordinary end-of-March experience in south-central Nebraska.

Figuratively, I was inserted into a video of one of nature's greatest phenomena. How could I protract words from something so magical, magnificent and mysterious?

I've seen swarms of insects and flocks of swallows, but never had I witnessed what was happening about a mile from our perch inside a long, low rectangular shack beside the Platte River.

From this "bird blind," we peered through binoculars and scopes out small openings in a clear-Plexiglas wall. Well beyond the quarter-mile-wide, one-foot deep river, what I'd taken as low, fast-moving clouds was actually throngs of circling and wheeling sandhill cranes.

An adult sandhill crane is nearly four-feet-tall. It is gray, with pale cheeks and a red crown. A crane makes croaking, gurgling and other noises on the ground and in flight.

For eons, cranes on their 4,000-mile spring migration have funneled through this region—a 75-mile stretch of the central Platte River Valley—between mid-February and mid-April. More than 500,000 cranes channel through the area annually.

When the birds arrive from southern wintering grounds, they feed on grain and invertebrates and add weight to continue their trek northward to breeding grounds in Canada.

We were clustered in the blind with about 30 other folks, some who had come from as far as Australia. This was Crane Trust property, 4,500 acres of native grassland prairie and wet meadows, and a seven-mile stretch of uninterrupted river. All around, sandbar-laden channels of the Platte braided through farmland and prairie.

This was an early year for sandhill crane migration, said Guy, our Crane Trust guide. The birds were fattening up, and some had already headed north in small groups. Nonetheless, six days before we arrived, a count suggested at least 270,000 cranes were still around.

In the sky, swirled thousands of the lanky, long-legged birds, with their open wings resembling parachutes. We could hear the cranes, but faintly. Crane calls are audible from up to 2.5 miles away.

We had flown to Nebraska to visit with former Rhode Islanders, Ted, Susan and Alex, who now lived in Lincoln. Then we all drove 100 miles west to observe the cranes roost by the tens of thousands at night in the shallow Platte.

By standing together in the river at night, cranes could hear the approaching splash of predators, including coyotes, dogs and people.

As for those crane clouds in the distance, Guy said the birds would likely head in our direction, following unseen switchbacks in the sky.

Indeed, back and forth, louder and louder, the cranes approached. They swept toward the river in fast-changing lines and shapes. Just to our left, swirling waves of cranes began to land in the water by the hundreds.

Sandhill cranes are one of the tallest birds in North America. Their wingspans reach 80 inches. In flight, their legs extend like spears behind their bodies. At roosting time, how do they not crash into one another?

Non-stop for 20 minutes, birds arrived. Calls, including bugles and horns, honks and hisses, moans and rasps, became a symphonic backdrop to their arrival. Cranes have long windpipes, coiled into their sternums, and the birds produce sounds rich in lower pitch and harmonics.

We stood hidden, silent and motionless. Guy whispered that up to 30,000 cranes were now outside the blind. One bird began walking up-river past us, and the others followed until their mass resembled a huge sliding island.

We remained huddled together, even in the dark, listening to the primal and visceral bugling grow deafening.

Days later, I found words to describe the experience: "Once in a lifetime."

Sand and Sea in the Spring
April 26, 2014

For two days last week, the four of us worked both sides of the Outer Cape.

From Race Point Beach in Provincetown, we watched humpback whales breach, surface, spout and slap their tails.

Humpbacks may reach 60 feet in length and 40 tons in weight. Their powerful tails, called flukes, help propel the big creatures. Some of the whales breached so mightily that the ocean frothed. A few tail slaps looked like giant hands waving at us before hitting the sea.

The spout of a humpback is called a blow. Humpback whales produce tall, columnar blows, which we witnessed several times.

When a whale swam on the surface, it looked like a submarine. Standing within miles of beaches and dunes of Cape Cod National Seashore, and before a great animal of the ocean made me feel insignificant, but in a good way.

Also making a splash were more than a dozen northern gannets plunging into the sea around the whales.

The northern gannet is a large white seabird with black-tipped wings. It has a long, pointed bill and tail, and long pointed wings. From up to 100 feet, some birds, wings thrust straight out over their backs, rocketed into the ocean.

At First Encounter Beach in Eastham, the tide retreated a quarter mile into Cape Cod Bay, leaving silver-mica-speckled ripples in the mud, surrounded by various pools of saltwater and lots of shells.

Amidst green strings of seaweed and hollow stems of grasses, I found shells of blue mussel, cherrystone, horseshoe crab, jingle, lady crab, littleneck, moon snail, oyster, periwinkle, quahog, razor clam, skipper and soft-shell clam. Plus there were egg cases of skate and of channeled whelk.

The most abundant shell belonged to razor clams. Brown outer skins, peeling to white, and off-white, rough inner surfaces marked these robust, two-sided, six-inch-long shells.

Two razor clams, however, showed blue-tinted insides that dried to an almost shiny, mother-of-pearl interior smooth to the touch. Lovely.

At the peak of low tide, there was hardly a wave at the water's edge. Instead, the bay seemed to roll gently in place, with schools of Atlantic silverside swimming along the perimeter.

From the water, nickel-sized snails in ornate shells wound trails into fresh mud. I followed a trail to a tidal pool in which the white roots of a vegetated hump dangled.

When I turned around the bay had changed. Now, audible, visible waves rolled in. Gone were the snails and trails. Gentle regression became active aggression. Was this what it was like when the lowest tide reawakened?

On two consecutive nights, we watched the sun go down over the bay. Each time, the orange sphere entered the horizon over fluorescent mint-green water. The colors of red and magenta, orange and green spread through wispy clouds until the sky resembled a rainbow.

From a Wellfleet cliff, we watched the sunrise. The sea seemed to give birth to an orange tip that grew into a flaming, yellow sphere, while behind us, light gray mists drifted over a kettle pond of freshwater that now reflected it's shoreline of pines in the light of a new day.

At the start of the fourth week of April, the warm afternoon sand on a bay beach defined the Outer Cape. That sand was toasty on top, but winter chilled just below the surface. After many long weeks of cold weather, the Outer Cape was just starting to warm up.

Taking Time to Observe Life
October 23, 2010

Karen and I celebrated our 17th wedding anniversary with a family hike in the Berkshires, followed by dinner in a restored 200-year-old barn.

As Woody the dog led us up the mountainside, leaves staggered down to the forest floor like wounded butterflies.

The five us stepped boulder-to-boulder through soaring single and multiple-trunk white pines, their blocky barks dripping with fragrant, exceptionally sticky sap.

White veins of quartz topped each stone, creating the illusion that we were hopping from hump to hump of a serpent.

Alongside us, racing downhill, was a rippling stream, with origins high above Route 41 in Sheffield, Mass.

The trail passed beneath towering hemlocks, thick-trunked trees at least 75 feet tall. Other trees with massive torsos included deeply furrowed sugar maples, shredding-barked yellow birches and black birches, looking like giant, charcoal-gray sentinels.

Settlers felled the ancestors of these great trees to create the posts, beams and other parts of the barn we planned to visit that night.

Beside the trail, the brook crashed through great lichen-lined boulders of granite, jumbles of fallen trees and cavern-like collections of evergreens.

The dark forest, cascading waters and steep hills were thrilling. But what stopped us cold were the tiny petals of the last flowering tree of the year.

327

Stretching ahead on both sides of the trail was witch hazel. Usually we find witch hazel blooms after the leaves have dropped. But yellowing foliage, and drooping bud clusters that looked like pawnshop coat-of-arms symbols framed each set of four wispy yellow petals of the flowers of these small native forest trees.

A few flies and one bee moved among the witch hazel flowers, which I've read contain "ample, sticky pollen," as well as nectar.

Witch hazel is best known for the astringent produced from its bark and leaves, first distilled commercially as a treatment for skin ailments more than 150 years ago.

In the United States, all plant material harvested to produce witch hazel comes from Connecticut, and parts of Massachusetts, Rhode Island and the southern Appalachians.

Stopping to examine the flowers also gave us the chance to investigate the rest of the fall understory of the great woods. This undergrowth was composed primarily of three plants: striped maple, with its large irregularly shaped leaves; the velvety foliaged mapleleaf viburnum; and deep-green, stout Christmas fern.

With the late-afternoon sun now on the other side of the mountain, we decided to head back downhill.

The dinner meal was all local foods. As we sipped creamy soup made from local turnips and onions, I scanned the old floor planks of the barn.

The worn wood reminded me of the weathered boulders of the mountain. I thought of the Native Americans and European settlers, who once stepped from rock to rock just as we did earlier in the day.

During our courtship, Karen and I hiked a lot. On our honeymoon, we trekked through Vermont and northern New York.

Our favorite courting music was the reggae album, "Toots in Memphis."

Of the tens of thousands of possible music choices in the restaurant that night, this album was played, as we ate dinner.

One of the songs was the slow, wrenching, "Love Attack," with its lyrics, "I fell for you, baby; Baby, I fell for you; just like a rock, now."

Hiking to the summit was voluntary. Getting down was obligatory. As for the trek, I offer the sappy, but fitting quote, "Life is not about how fast we can reach the top of the mountain … but how well we absorb the beauty of the path that takes us there."

GOODBYE CICADAS AND HELLO KATYDIDS
August 4, 2012

In a fifth-floor condo just north of downtown Atlanta, a four-year-old boy, named August, knows that when the katydids begin their calls at 9:30 pm, his bedtime begins.

August is the son of my wife's first cousin. Of average height, August is a bright fellow, who already reads chapter books. The brown-haired, blue-eyed boy and his family live on a leafy avenue off Peachtree Street.

In late July, we spent a couple of days with the cousins. Before the trip I whined about the heat and humidity of Rhode Island. Well, I've shut my mouth. Atlanta swelters at a level beyond anything I know up north.

To me, it seemed like a blistering sun and stickiness started at sun-up. In fact, you could see the clouds build like a time-lapse movie of the heavens.

Atlanta and environs of Buckhead and Lenox house tall modern buildings of reflective glass. These edifices reflect the golden daylong sun and rising clouds.

People—and we did experience their Southern hospitality—very polite folks—traveled from air-conditioned homes to air-conditioned stores or air-conditioned offices and back again.

Most of the relatively few people we saw on the sidewalks and in the intersections carried water bottles. Hydration was key.

Such then was my admiration for August's green, shaded street. Tall, small-leaved oaks and long-needled pines lined it. Crepe myrtle trees—slighter and smoothly slim-trunked—flowered in white, pink or salmon.

Where foliage went untended, invasive kudzu vine swallowed up ornamentals and residual bits of forests left from development that turned the former pine and oak woods into miles of buildings.

On August's block, it was from among the tree foliage in the afternoon adhesiveness that katydid precursors—cicadas—droned loudly like quacking sprinkler systems whipping 360 degrees in a rising and dueling "z-wee, z-wee, z-wee."

If you stood within this constant whirring, the sound could drown out your conversation.

At least three somewhat quieter types of cicadas, yet louder than any species I hear during the day in Southern New England, joined the refrain.

The first of these insects repeated an acute "jink," which grew noisier and faster before stopping and restarting. The second cicada sounded like the jingle bells of a horse riding through the snow, while the third reminded me of shaken tambourines.

The first evening in Atlanta, I stepped outside onto the steamy patio to listen to all of these close-at-hand, vibratory sounds. White-topped, gray-bottomed cumulus clouds—thunderheads—rumbled with what I would call "heat lightning."

On the second late afternoon, we picnicked around the outdoor pool, where August's mom, Susan, showed me a dead cicada, which she found poolside.

Long veiny wings extended well beyond the bug's brown-green body. This was a meaty creature several inches in length. In fact, it smelled of decomposition like a rotting mammal such as a mouse. I'd never smelled that stink from an insect.

At the pool, a golden setting sun peeked through the thunderheads, nipping at the top of the high-rise apartment building. The ambient sultry air contained a cacophony of "z-wee," "jink," jingle bells and tambourine sounds.

Then, as the skies and skyscrapers grew dark, the cicadas stopped calling, species by species. With nightfall, the katydids started up. They produced a sound more strident than their northern brethren. While obvious to the ear, the katydid calls were more sporadic, calmer and quieter than the chorus of cicadas.

This relative softness befitted the hour. For now, it was 9:30 p.m., and time for August to go to sleep.

Maybe We Are All
Exotic Species
May 19, 2012

On the drive in from Ft. Lauderdale airport, we visited an old-time Florida stand that sold grapefruits, oranges and alligator meat.

My younger brother, Paul, parked the SUV in front of a mango tree, drooping under the weight of its maroon, tear-shaped fruit. Paul's mission was to pick up the house specialty, key lime pie.

We were short on time, so I stayed inside the air-conditioned vehicle, with his four-year-old daughter, Hanna, and the two of us giggled about filling Paul's hat with mangoes.

Hanna has dark blue eyes and a head of thick, brown, curly hair that falls down her back. She is an energetic and quick cookie. When Hanna asked how much the SUV cost, Paul replied $25Gs. "Are you kidding me?" she replied.

In a few minutes, we would arrive at their home, and catch up with Paul's wife, Melissa, and their eight-day-old son, Jacob.

My role that afternoon was to sit with Jacob, during the Jewish covenant of circumcision, called a bris. This visit was extra important, given that major illness prevented my parents from attending.

The next morning, on the way back to the airport, we stopped briefly at Flamingo Gardens, where Hanna led me to the shade of a wide-based, soaring tree.

Flamingo Gardens harbors more than 3,000 tropical and subtropical plant species, plus a hammock of 200-year-old live oaks, one of the last remnants of original fauna.

The Everglades is the poster child for drainage and disruption. Outside of it, there is little left of the wetlands and subtropical wilderness that once defined what we call South Florida.

A regional map reflects this history—it looks like graphing paper, with lines defined by canals and roads as straight as arrows.

Flamingo Gardens sits off one such gridded thoroughfare, appearing just after a fence with a sign for land-clearing services.

We ambled—this was Jacob's first nature adventure—past wampi and star fruit trees and through an understory of lustrous green, naturally-Swiss-cheese-patterned leaves the size of baby strollers. The foliage holes, I was told, allowed sunlight and water to reach the ground.

Several locals dropped in on the walk—three white ibis descended from the skies to probe the grounds alongside us.

White ibis feature red, down-curved bills. The birds uttered subtle croaks that reminded me of the subdued growls of a dog.

I watched a wood stork land, with many flaps, atop a snag in the distance. The stork is a large, bald, white creature, with a long, thick, down-curved bill.

As the stork settled in I noticed that the tree also held four black vultures. Even from afar, I could see their bald gray heads.

Flamingo Gardens contains Everglades Wildlife Sanctuary, home to "permanently injured and non-releasable wildlife." Large cages hold a who's who of native raptors, for example, from burrowing owl to crested caracara, almost all car-collision victims.

So far, folks at the Sanctuary have bred and released almost 2,000 offspring of injured wildlife.

A breeze filtered through the sultry shade of a towering ficus, which is a Middle East native. Below it was a thicket of Philippine-native tagbak trees and a ground cover of Brazilian Finger-of God bromeliads.

Much of Flamingo Gardens may be artificial, but it is also an outpost of life. Holding on to that core is something we owe ourselves, and the next generation.

I thought about how we're all exotics in some way—mixed and matched via all sorts of circumstances. Paul, for instance, Paul grew up in the Bronx and Melissa in South Africa.

At their home, I had my first adult conversation with a cousin, Mitchell, whom I last saw in 1984. Mitchell lives in the Keys, moving there from Colorado. He was born and raised on Long Island.

Whomever you call family, it's human to find a way to honor them. And It is extra special to get outside with loved ones.

Experiencing nature also multiplied the spark of life, which we received from each other during my 22-hour trip to South Florida, as well as what we like to call "the gift of life."

Reaffirming Life in Central New York
October 11, 2014

The scent of a stream sent me over the edge.

An ozone-like odor from water bubbling out of the ground and downhill in Ithaca, New York, propelled me through upstate memories.

Once again, I was 10 years old, discovering a stony stream running through a forest of black birch, ground pine and star moss in Rockland County.

Then I was 15, stopping for the first time at the Red Apple Rest restaurant north of Harriman State Park in Tuxedo.

That acidic smell of moist New York soil reminded me of a 1980s visit to a "cookalein," or "cook alone", a kitchen-containing bungalow in the Catskills.

There, in a canoe on a weedy lake, my younger brother cast his beginner's fishing pole and immediately snared a two-foot pickerel.

The aggressive fish fled under the craft, which rocked side to side, as we fought to reel in the catch. We fumbled with that lean green-and-yellow fish, with its elongated jaw and sharp teeth. Finally, we got the hook out of its mouth, tossed the pickerel back, put the fishing pole away and rowed back to shore.

Lastly, I recalled the Ashokan Reservoir in the Catskills, where Karen and I stopped during a weeklong drive through the Northeast after our October 1993 wedding.

I thought of lost family and friends and loved ones. My eyes watered.

And why shouldn't I cry? Rachel, Karen and I were touring colleges and universities. One day in less than a year, as we planned, Rachel would leave home to begin a new phase of her education and evolution.

A trip to the Ithaca Farmers' Market helped put me back on track.

At the Steamboat Landing pavilion on Cayuga Lake, the air was warm, and the skies sunny. The market—a long T-shaped structure of stalls—swelled with growers, produce and commerce.

We found an astounding and affordable bounty of apples, pies, cider, wines, grapes, peppers, beans, mushrooms, pears, potatoes, squash, and much, much more.

There were bakers, glassblowers, jewelers and soap makers, plus chefs who cooked for you then and there.

Vendors seemed eager to engage us. With cool farm names like Oxbow, Humble Hill and Blue Heron, folks appeared happy to explain their produce, to inquire about us and to share samples.

My favorite sightings included large yellow carrots, tiny purple tomatoes and thin flaming red radishes tipped in glowing white.

We especially appreciated the woman who insisted we taste a burgundy apple. This near-black-red fruit was a white, crisp, slightly tart treat that later in the week helped us produce a lovely strudel.

Ithaca was rich in other colors, particularly blue asters, paired naturally with goldenrod, along many roadways.

Some asters were sky blue, others azure. A few appeared pale pink, while several seemed deep purple. They all displayed yellowish- or near-orange-colored centers.

This trip took place in the third week of September. It was our first 2014 encounter with fall color in trees. Many red maples, for example, were partially to entirely yellow, gold, orange and, of course, red.

I determined that the soil aroma of the Ithaca hillside was one of freshness, of richness, and of new beginnings. It was a whiff of hope. From such a scent, life emerged in a cycle much greater than the upwelling of feelings in my heart and tears in my eyes.

GIANT SHRINES TO LIFE
January 26, 2020

How fitting that it was drizzling when we arrived at the 40-acre grove of old-growth trees within Henry Cowell Redwoods State Park, located in the Santa Cruz Mountains of California, The colossal trees grow in a mossy, fern-filled terrain that looks and (especially in a rainy mist) feels like what it is—a temperate rainforest. The soaring specimens of plant life in the park are said to have inspired some of California's earliest efforts in redwood preservation.

For three of us—me, Karen and Noah—this was our first encounter with redwoods. Rachel had met these trees once before.

The park's tallest redwood rises 277 feet, sports a diameter of more than 16 feet wide, and is some 1,500 years old. The tree is 28 feet shorter than the Statue of Liberty.

Given my Eastern North America frame of reference, the redwoods were dizzyingly unfathomable. That helps explain why I spent much of our eight-tenth-of-a-mile, loop-trail stroll in stunned silence; in reverence.

Indeed, at times it was easier to concentrate on littler things in the landscape, such as the beds of wild ginger surrounding some of the giant trees, and the scattered banana slugs on the mossy fence posts and moist tree bark.

The meaty slugs looked like elongated small bananas, colored almost neon yellow. Slugs break down organic matter, such as leaves, moss and animal droppings, into soil humus.

Other plants, which had adapted to grow under the dense shade of the redwoods included the clover-like redwood sorrel, which blanketed some of the ground, as well as California bay trees, tanoaks, and hazelnut trees.

Here and there, we spotted a western gray squirrel. According to the University of California, these squirrels are "distinguished from the eastern gray and other squirrel species by their very long bushy tails that are primarily gray with white-frosted outer edges."

The copse featured a powerfully fresh, pine scent. Redwoods are evergreens, with a toolkit of survival adaptations, including long horizontal roots, thick bark, and exceptional height.

Although redwoods may grow tall, their roots are quite shallow, rarely sinking more than a dozen feet below the soil surface. On the other hand, the roots of a single tree may radiate out hundreds of feet. Noted a trail guide, "Wrapping their roots round other redwood roots, these trees help each other stay in the ground until flood and wind finally knock them over."

Redwood bark contains tannic acid, which provides defense against insects, fungus and fire. That tannic acid also gives the bark its deep-cinnamon color.

Coastal redwoods create "family circles," with young redwoods sprouting from the base of old trunks. If a tree falls, new redwoods may rise right around the former "parent" tree. Same for a logged redwood: the roots live and may give rise to a ring of new trees.

Redwood cones are only the size of olives. Each of the seeds in a cone is the size of an oatmeal flake. Given that a thick blanket of leaves covers the forest floor under redwoods, these seeds seldom find the soil surface to give rise to new trees.

It was relatively dark beneath the trees. In the Santa Cruz Mountains, the weather is said to change quickly. Sure enough, in places, where a redwood had fallen, misty silvery light sliced down through the canopy to the forest floor, giving the setting a spiritually arousing look.

For centuries, rain and fog off the coast have sustained these trees. However, climate change is decreasing the amount of rainfall and fog that have nurtured the redwoods for centuries.

Redwoods are like giant shrines to life. I still can't fathom that some trees are the size of 25-story buildings, and more than 15 centuries old! That redwood families grow off one root system and that trees across the forest intertwine their roots to hold one another up is marvelous.

On our way out of the park, we stopped to watch three black-tailed deer graze in a field. This was a moment to praise the people who preserve and protect such places, but also to sit a bit and consider that in today's warmer and drier world, nothing is sacred.

Made in the USA
Middletown, DE
10 September 2021